Troubling Questions
for Calvinists

...AND ALL THE REST OF US

F. LaGard Smith

Cotswold

PUBLISHING

TROUBLING QUESTIONS FOR CALVINISTS

Copyright © 2007 by F. LaGard Smith
Published by Cotswold Publishing
3618 Ridgecroft Drive
Lynchburg, VA 24503

Library of Congress Cataloging-in-Publication Data

Troubling Questions For Calvinists/F. LaGard Smith
Library of Congress Catalog Number _____
ISBN 978-0-9660060-5-6

Cover art: Courtauld Institute of Art Gallery, London. Used by Permission.

Printed in the United States of America

Dedicated to Barry Brewer—
My faithful friend and incomparable brother in the Lord,
whose commitment to truth has made books like this possible,
and whose unflinching courage in the face of extraordinary struggle
has been an inspiration to all.

For their unselfish contributions to this book, whether through discussions, editing, or proofing, I wish to thank my wife Ruth, Scott Self, Nathan Guy, Robert Picirilli, David Lawrence, Tony and Leslie Coffey, Ben Trotter III, Jason Charlton, Edward Fudge, Danny Hale, and Ken Keathley. I especially appreciate the participation in this process of those who count themselves to be Calvinists and returned troubling questions of their own.

My gratitude as always to Cathy Brown for typesetting, and to Amy Allison for cover design.

Cover art, *Adam and Eve*, Lucas Cranach I (1472-1553), used with permission of the Courtauld Institute of Art Gallery, London.

Contents

Preface

The fellowship in which I was born and raised was not a Calvinist fellowship. Then again, it wasn't rabidly anti-Calvinist. If there were sermons refuting Calvinism, they were not so vitriolic as to stick particularly in one's mind. Ask worshipers in the pew to tell you the five-points of Calvinism, and they'd be completely lost. Mention the word "Tulip," and spring flowers likely would come to mind. About the most anyone might tell you is that Calvinism had something to do with predestination, or perhaps "once saved, always saved."

John Calvin would certainly be recognized as one of the Reformers and a leading architect of the belief system bearing his name. But there would have been little or no appreciation of any distinctions between Calvin's personal beliefs and what has come to be known as "Calvinism." Indeed, few would have made any connection historically between Calvin and Augustine, nor between Calvinism and Reformed theology. At the mention of Pelagius or Arminius, you would get nothing but blank, questioning stares.

Of one thing you could be sure: We weren't Arminians. Arminianism was just another highfalutin theological term of which we would have been suspicious. We were simply "Christians," doing things in Bible ways–speaking where the Bible speaks and being silent where the Bible is silent.

Perhaps that is why, even to this day, I do not consider myself to be an Arminian, despite the fact that I believe in man's free will to accept or reject God's gracious offer of salvation. I certainly don't believe what Calvinists generally attribute to Arminians: that salvation occurs because of man's own work; or that man's free will somehow trumps God's sovereignty. Nor do I have any problem accepting the biblical teaching about predestination and election, properly understood.

So why write a book raising troubling questions about Calvinism? For one who has written a number of books across a wide spectrum of doctrinal issues, it's hard to ignore the fundamental concerns raised by Calvinism. Any systematic theology would be incomplete without addressing questions about God's sovereignty, the nature of man, and the eternal scheme of redemption.

More immediately, I've begun to hear increasing talk even among non-Calvinists about our being "diseased with sin," a concept which raises serious questions about the problem of sin. Whether one is a Calvinist, Arminian, or otherwise, I'm wondering if we all haven't paid far too little attention to the dynamics of how we sin and why. Have some of our most fundamental assumptions actually led us to take our sins for granted?

Interestingly enough, all this is coming at a time when there appears to be serious soul-searching among Calvinists themselves. So much so, in fact, that there has been a reactionary resurgence in some denominations to re-ignite the dying embers of Calvinism among their adherents.

Over time, of course, the language of classical, Reformed Calvinism has been transformed and softened. "Total depravity," for example, has become "total inability," or "radical corruption;" and "irresistible grace" has been toned down to a kinder, gentler "efficacious call of the Spirit." "Particular redemption" seems also to be favored over the harsher-sounding "limited atonement."

Although most Calvinists would affirm they have always believed it is necessary for the believer to *persevere* in order to be *preserved*, lately one seems to notice an increased emphasis being given to the believer's personal responsibility. Says one contemporary Calvinist author, for example, "If we do not hold out, we have no basis for assurance that God is preserving us." While those of us who are non-Calvinists find that statement to be logically problematic in view of Calvinism's bedrock premise of predestination, still, we are encouraged that there seems to be a greater articulation of that side of the coin.

Far more significant, perhaps, are the many "Calvinist" voices today openly denying the once-sacrosanct doctrine of limited atonement, not to mention the swelling ranks of those who argue–in a number of different guises–that the elect are sovereignly chosen, yet ultimately responsible for their salvation or damnation. Among them are those who urge an odd kind of *conditional* "unconditional election," as well as those who believe that the elect includes *everyone*–except those who personally reject or ignore God according to whatever light they may possess! That these novel permutations on Calvinism seem to both classical, Reformed Calvinists and non-Calvinists alike as patently inconsistent with Calvinist fundamentals does not alter the fact that much is astir in the Calvinist camp.

Perhaps no book epitomizes the softer, gentler approach better than Richard Mouw's wonderfully-titled *Calvinism in the Las Vegas Airport*. A self-proclaimed "eclectic Calvinist," Mouw presents full "five-point" Calvinism with a velvet glove so soft that virtually any personal faith experience ultimately acknowledging God's divine sovereignty is ecumenically accommodated. Mouw himself acknowledges that his Dutch Calvinist grandmother would have more than a few misgivings. Though never intended as a full defense or exposition of Calvinist doctrine, Mouw's book smoothly glosses over the many difficult, thorny issues which, in the end, cannot so easily escape closer scrutiny.

Yet another motivation prompting my pen arises out of a curious incongruity which I will share at more length toward the end of the book. I'm ever so intrigued by the observation that even five-point Calvinists aren't really all that Calvinistic in their actual faith walk; while, by contrast, those who would adamantly reject the doctrines of Calvinism are surprisingly Calvinistic in their outlook and actions. Inquiring minds want to know: What's going on here!

I confess that this book also arises, ironically, out of the common cause I passionately share with the Reformed worldview, particularly as it relates to Christian higher education which has been my calling for over thirty years. Along with Calvinists, I firmly believe that, by his sovereign will, God has given his called-out people a cultural mandate in every sphere of life–including business, science, law and politics, music and art–to do all things to the glory of God.

Having been both a professor of law for most of my working life, as well as a scholar in residence for Christian studies at an undergraduate liberal arts university, I have a keen interest in the integration of faith and learning far beyond the trendy way in which those fashionable buzzwords are being bandied about. I dream of truly Christian institutions of higher education in which there are no distinct academic divisions, nor certainly any distinction between Bible majors and all other majors. I long for the time when Christian universities can restore meaning to a fully-integrated universe of knowledge, uniquely reflecting the sovereign reign of God over the unfragmented whole of his Creation.

For me, then, the question becomes: How can I reconcile the Calvinists' biblically-based Reformed worldview with an underlying doctrinal system which seems so biblically flawed? Or, turning that around, how by any means might I raise the obvious troubling questions about the hallowed faith of those with whom I otherwise have such common cause? In the pages to come, I pray there is yet a way.

Beyond all these reasons, I find the issues surrounding Calvinism simply too personal to ignore. Along with everyone else, I too ask: Who am I? Why am I here? And where am I going? Were I to take virtually any stripe of Calvinism at face value (and there are many stripes), the answers to those crucial questions would be profoundly different from what my own biblically-informed mind and heart are telling me. So, for me, the discussion which lies ahead is far more significant than mere academic doctrinal dialogue. Considering that the issues pertain to nothing less than the plan of salvation whereby my eternal destiny (and yours) will be determined, the stakes couldn't be higher.

If there were a prize for who most believes in God's sovereignty, I dare say I wouldn't come in a distant second to any Calvinist. Even so, I simply cannot find in my Bible the picture that Calvinism paints of who I am and why I am here—nor yet, far more importantly, the image that emerges of God himself. That being the case, I cannot help but be greatly disturbed by Calvinism's vaunted theology and what I believe to be the superficially plausible, but woefully misguided, explanations we are offered.

It is often quipped that the interminable debates over Calvinism amount to little more than semantical quibbles, or tiresome, irrelevant battles over how many angels can dance on the head of a pin. To the contrary, nothing (and I do mean *nothing*) could be more important than the two critical issues involved: 1) the nature of God (Is he sovereign, loving, and just in equal measure?) and 2) the nature of man (Is he a divinely orchestrated being from start to finish, or does he possess an independent freedom and responsibility which affects his eternal destiny?).

With all that on the line, nothing less than the most thorough search of the Scriptures can give us any hope of understanding correctly the divine mind of God to the degree that he has revealed it. To the extent possible for a book of this size and intended audience, I have attempted to address, or at least reference, every passage that might have any significant bearing one way or the other on the many issues raised by this discussion.

In this regard, a word about format and style is in order. While Scripture remains the supreme arbiter of the subject under discussion, you might notice in the opening chapters that detailed analysis of the pertinent texts gives way momentarily to a methodical, logical analysis of the bundle of concepts known as Calvinism. The goal initially is to test the internal logic of Calvinism to see if it can hold together on its own terms. So if at first you get the feeling that Scripture is falling prey to human reason, rest assured that I'm only doing in reverse what apologists for Calvinism are required to do in bringing intellectual order to the widely divergent elements of this highly systematized doctrine. If it is more in-depth exegesis of the classical proof-texts you are looking for, hopefully your patience will be rewarded.

So as to keep the book well within the range of a general audience, I have chosen to limit most of my Calvinist references to four representative authors: John Calvin, from the 16th century; the 19th century British evangelist Charles Haddon Spurgeon; Loraine Boettner, whose 1932 book, *The Reformed Doctrine of Predestination* is a classic (if undoubtedly rigid) defense of Reformed theology; and the currently popular Reformed writer, R.C. Sproul.

One pitfall of which I am already aware is the potential charge of unfair, "straw man" argumentation, a charge I frequently find leveled against those who have challenged the tenets of Calvinism. All I can say is that I, for one, have done all I can to avoid that danger. Unless I have been able to verify that classical Calvinists in general teach a particular proposition, I have refused to use anything which might otherwise be to the advantage of my position.

I have tried to be particularly careful in distinguishing between the various proponents of Calvinism, knowing that "strict" or "hyper" Calvinists can be quoted for all sorts of things classical Calvinists would never accept. (In this regard, I find Norman Geisler's attempt to paint mainline Reformed Calvinists as "extreme Calvinists" unconvincing.)

That said, I fear that Calvinists oftentimes characterize as straw man arguments any challenge which holds their feet to the fire logically in view of other fundamental Calvinist premises. If a critic insists, for example, that Calvinism doesn't leave room for free will, this is said to be a straw man argument since Calvinism does hold in fact that man (or at least regenerate man) has free will.

The problem is that, since Calvinism's most bedrock premise is God's absolute sovereign will over every act, event, thought, and motive of man, the "free will" of which Calvinism speaks ends up being nothing like the free will that one would speak of in a normal conversation. But to point out this problematic feature of Calvinism is to risk the charge of making a straw man argument. (You say Calvinists don't believe in free will? Of course, we do!)

As you can see already, the task ahead for both of us is frustratingly complex and at times even perilous. Few subjects could tax our hearts and minds more demandingly, or put so high a premium on our objectivity and intellectual honesty. So whether you are a Calvinist or a non-Calvinist, we all have much to consider. Although the unsearchable mysteries of God invariably will remain, we cannot but humbly and prayerfully probe the depth and breadth of those divine precepts which he has graciously revealed. To that end, surely, we can join together in saying: To God be the glory!

–F. LaGard Smith

You are invited to correspond with the author at: Smith.LaGard@gmail.com

[Please note that the quotations at the beginning of each chapter are taken from the writings of widely-recognized Calvinists, setting forth essential Calvinist doctrine.]

Chapter 1

The Evolution of Calvinism

The counsel of the Lord is His eternal good pleasure,
according to which He willed and conceived all things
that are ever realized or occur in time.

—Herman Hoeksema

Have you ever wondered how Darwin's famous Theory of Evolution itself evolved? It's pretty simple, really. In his study of nature, Darwin observed that species tend over time to mutate in ways that pass on slightly variant traits to succeeding generations. Noting that weaker, less adaptable varieties of a species seem to be eclipsed by stronger varieties, Darwin attributed this gradual process of evolution within distinct species to what he called "survival of the fittest."

When Darwin asked himself why this process should happen, he began to theorize that fitness-driven mutation was nature's quirky way of selecting which species would survive and which would not. Hence the origin of what we now know as "natural selection." So far so good....

Flushed with success, Darwin then took what seemed to him to be the next logical step. That next step was to jump from observable micro-evolution within a particular species (say, butterflies) to macro-Evolution from one species to another (say, from butterflies to birds, or birds to ducks). In Darwin's fertile imagination, he had hit upon the origin of all species. Surely, he hypothesized, even man's origin must have come about through a relentless, if capricious, amoeba-to-man process of higher and higher life forms developing over eons of time from a single primordial source.

Unfortunately, the yawning gap between what Darwin observed in nature and what he theorized about the *origin* of nature was matched only by an equally yawning gap in the fossil record, which to this day remains the paleontologists' frustrating Holy Grail (and carefully guarded dirty secret). For all the celebrated claims to have found *the* missing link, the thousands of intermediate life-forms that should be embedded in abundance (between plants, birds, fish, and animals) are nowhere to be found.

What Darwin theorized was logical enough, but wrong. Think about it this way. If a car is caught by police radar traveling 80 m.p.h., one might reasonably conclude that the car was actually 80 miles away an hour earlier. Although that reasoning has a certain logic to it, it's probably not true. It's just as likely that the driver is a fairly local resident who simply sped up to 80 m.p.h. only a few miles back down the road.

It's a similar story for the age of the stars, generally said to be millions of years old, based on the speed of light. Assuming that the starlight we see tonight has traveled all the way from our star to the Earth, it's easy enough to calculate the age of the star in millions of light years. Yet if God in fact said, "Let there be light," it is just as reasonable to conclude that God then and there illuminated the entire gap between our distant star and the Earth, and that the light we now see has been traveling toward us at the speed of light only since the dawn of a far more recent Creation.

Have you noticed all those pesky *gaps* that keep popping up? If you've ever traveled on the London Underground, you've probably heard the recording with which arriving passengers are greeted at stations where the platform is separated from the trains at a dangerous distance. Says a droning voice over loud speakers: "Mind the gap! Mind the gap! Mind the gap!"

When it comes to the logic behind Darwin's Theory of Evolution, the scientific world would do well to *mind the gap!* In fact, the whole world would do well to mind the gap between the chance, meaningless, soulless cosmos that Darwin would offer us and the intelligent, purposeful, hope-filled Creation revealed in Scripture.

Yet, undoubtedly you've already guessed that all of this is but a parable laying a foundation for the subject nearer at hand. Since it's probably safe to assume that most Calvinists would take issue with Darwin's dubious theory, comparing the two incongruous belief systems may prove surprisingly helpful to our discussion. Along a variety of fronts, the contrasts and similarities are both fascinating and enlightening.

As suggested, then, by this brief sketch of Evolution, we begin our discussion of Calvinism, asking in a similar vein: How did the doctrine of Calvinism ever come to be? How did it *evolve*, and what are its underlying assumptions? Most crucial of all, if there are any yawning gaps, can we spot them?

Calvinism In a Nutshell

Naturally, the unabridged history behind Calvinism is a longer story than this book can tell. If you are a dyed-in-the-wool Calvinist, you probably can recite the story from memory. So what we're asking here is: How did Calvinism develop *logically*, or *conceptually*? (Because Calvinism's core doctrine of original sin was also an early tenet of Catholicism, we're not thinking so much historically as intellectually.)

As one traces Calvinism back to the French Reformer, John Calvin (under the tutelage of Martin Bucer), and further back to Augustine (the original "Calvinist"!), would it be fair to say that today's highly-evolved belief system has distinctly reactionary roots? What would you think of the proposition that (as with so many doctrines which are born out of reaction to one extreme or another) Calvinism's initial concerns were as much about what it was *against* as what it was *for*? (Merely consider how much of Calvin's *Institutes* is devoted to refuting the Scholastics and Papists.)

Have you ever considered, for instance, that Calvinism likely never would have surfaced had it not been for the single overriding concern Augustine and Calvin shared in common: the merit-based "works-righteousness" of Catholicism? Or (particularly in Augustine's case) might even have taken a less strident form had there been no felt need to rebuff what was perceived to be the view of the Pelagian school of thinking that man could pretty much achieve perfection through his own efforts?[1] Or possibly might have placed less emphasis on total depravity had there not been in Augustine's mind (echoed centuries later in Luther's own tortured self-flagellation) a profound sense of overwhelming personal guilt and total worthlessness?[2]

Whatever the underlying personal motivations, certain logical bridges do seem to be suggested by this historical background. Take a quick look at this evolution of ideas and see what you think.

The Problem Being Addressed: The fundamental concern of Calvinism, old and new, is the almost universal notion (institutionalized to a high degree in Catholicism) that, through his own effort, man must (and can) work his way to heaven by performing onerous good deeds, observing meticulous ritual, and almost masochistically denying himself all pleasures in aid of avoiding sin. To whatever extent he manages to do this, the not-so-subtle implication is that man thereby merits salvation–which is to say that God is put in his debt and obligated to reward him with eternal life.

Calvinists rightly point to Paul's repeated reminders that justification is a matter of grace–a grace that saves us through faith, not through works, so that none of us has any reason to boast. Acting on our own, there is

---

[1] Given the obscurity of primary sources and questions surrounding both the teacher and his disciples, one deals with Pelagius and Pelagianism at some peril. What does seem clear is that Pelagius was reacting against the concept of predetermined destinies by pointing to man's God-given, grace-endowed ability to make free moral choices and thereby avoid sin and its eternal consequences.

[2] For Calvin, there was also the pastoral question of why some people respond in faith to the gospel, while others remain unmoved. Convinced that it couldn't simply be a matter of individual personalities, Calvin was inclined to believe it had to involve some kind of decree from God.

nothing you or I could ever do to merit salvation. It is God who saves us, and God alone.

The Calvinist Solution: In order to insure that justification and salvation are exclusively of and from God, they must be taken completely and irretrievably out of man's hands. And how best to accomplish that...? Without Augustine, Calvin, or anybody else actually sitting down and plotting a schematic means to this end, the following logical steps gradually gave shape to the doctrinal system now known as Calvinism.

Step 1: If man is to have absolutely nothing to do with being saved, then by implication man cannot be permitted to contribute anything whatever to the process. Yet, for man to *contribute* nothing is to suggest that he *has* nothing to contribute. Which, by only a slight extension, further suggests that man has no innate ability of any kind by which he can choose good over evil in the spiritual realm. All of which sits well with the doctrine of **Total depravity**.

Step 2: With man totally depraved and incapable of contributing to his salvation, it is left to God to act according to his sovereign, secret, eternal will–predestining the limited number of those whom he will save (and, at least by implication, those whom he will not). And if before the Creation of the world God selected (elected) individuals for salvation solely according to his own prerogative, then that salvation could not possibly be based upon any condition which man himself might satisfy (not even having faith). Thus the idea of **Unconditional election**.

Step 3: If by God's sovereign decree salvation from man's sin was to be made possible by and through Jesus' blood sacrifice, no one can be saved apart from Christ's atoning work on the cross. But since salvation was decreed only for God's chosen elect, then it follows that Christ's atonement was exclusively for the benefit of the elect and for no one else. Hence, what is referred to as **Limited atonement**.

Step 4: Because it was the sovereign Lord of Creation who determined those upon whom he would bestow his grace through Christ, it is not possible for anyone included among the elect to decide otherwise or to refuse his chosen destiny. Thus, the notion of **Irresistible grace**.

Step 5: If God has already predetermined those whom he will save, it follows that none of them can ever ultimately *not* be saved. Hence the conclusion that once the elect are saved, they cannot possibly lose that salvation, a doctrine known as **Perseverance of the saints** (or, more popularly, as "once saved, always saved"[3]).

What do you make of this summary? Is it a fair representation of your own understanding? If not, how would you say it differently?

Calvinism's Flawed TULIP

You're probably already aware of the acronym, *T-U-L-I-P*, that results from the first letters of these five core doctrines of Calvinism. Wouldn't it be interesting to know what a naturalist like Darwin might observe about this variety of theological species! Upon close examination, would he find *TULIP* to be a pure biblical species, or does it exhibit signs of mutation? More on that momentarily. At the very least, he could not help but note the obvious mutations which have evolved from the seminal ideas of Calvin himself. As is widely accepted, *Calvin* and *Calvinism* are not necessarily to be equated.

In fact, were you aware of the irony that Calvinism's particular variety of *TULIP* was first developed in Holland, the land of tulips, in response to the teaching of the Dutch theologian, Jacobus [James] Arminius? Interestingly, the formulation of *TULIP* came about in a long evolutionary process beginning with Arminius' response to Calvin's teaching–or, more correctly, to the strict "high Calvinism" (some have said "hyper-Calvinism") of Calvin's student, Theodore Beza. Arminius himself had studied under Beza.

In the prolonged debate of the 16th and 17th centuries, first there was *argument* (put forward by Calvin, as more extremely interpreted by Beza),

---

[3] Whereas the Reformed view would say that all truly elect saints will remain faithful to the end (hence, "once saved, always saved"), a more extreme Calvinist view (espoused, for example, by R. T. Kendall, Charles Stanley, and the Grace Evangelical Society) holds that, once a person is saved, he can never be lost, regardless of whether he subsequently falls away either in faith or practice. (It's "once saved, always saved" with a stinger in the tail.) Adding to the confusion, the term "eternal security" is often used with reference to that latter view, but it may also be used by those who reject unconditional election altogether, yet accept that one's perseverance is due to the working of the Holy Spirit in the lives of those who are saved. In light of the many views competing for ownership of these various terms, due caution is the watchword of the day.

followed by *rebuttal* (by a cautious Arminius and later his more vociferous disciples, known as Remonstrants), then *counter- argument* (by politically powerful Calvinists against the "heretical" Remonstrants).

It was out of the fertile soil of this vehement counter-argument that *TULIP* first became its own distinct variety of the original Calvin species. In the "Canons of Dort" of 1619, the Reformed Churches officially recognized what have come to be called "the five points of Calvinism." It is these five points that give form to the flowering *TULIP* which Calvinists have found so enticingly beautiful ever since.

Don't Confuse the *TULIP* With the Bulb!

As with virtually all analogies, acronyms invariably are limited in their usefulness. Although the acronym *TULIP* accurately summarizes "five-point Calvinism" and actually flows with a kind of internal logic in the order of the letters which spell out the lovely flower, from a theological standpoint *TULIP* begins on the wrong "petal." As seen in the Canons of Dort, for example, Calvinism's starting point is not Total Depravity, but Unconditional Election.

The reason is obvious when you look more closely at the underlying "bulb" of the flower, which–first and foremost–is an affirmation of the sovereignty of God. As with Genesis, so too with Calvinism: In the beginning *God*! Examine almost any Calvinist text, and invariably what you'll find in the opening pages is a proclamation of God's sovereignty. As any worthy theology ought to be, Calvinism is a God-centered theology.

In Reformed theology, in particular, no doctrine comes anywhere close to the priority given to the doctrine of God. Indeed, Reformed theologians take great pride in the thought that they apply the doctrine of God with an exuberance found nowhere else among the various Christian communions–all of which fervently affirm the sovereignty of God. It is the very degree to which Reformed theologians take God's sovereignty that leads them ultimately to the *TULIP* of Calvinism.

In a nutshell, this is how it works. God's sovereignty is so pervasive throughout the temporal and the eternal, the physical and the spiritual, the heavenly and the earthly, that there is absolutely nothing over which he does not have total, absolute, and sovereign control. Put simply, there is not the simplest molecule, force of nature, or earthly or spiritual being that isn't moment by moment acting according to God's eternal purpose and power.

That being the case, everything that has ever happened, or ever will happen, must explicitly follow God's sovereign decrees. Does something take place? It could not have done so without God's willing it to happen. Does something *not* take place? That too is a reflection of God's sovereign control over all that is or is not. Moreover, God's absolute control must of necessity be just and right, even if at times it might seem to us quite out of character for God.

Whereas God's all-inclusive sovereignty is both knowable and known, by definition such a sovereign God himself cannot be fully known. Even given the fact that God has revealed himself through Scripture, it is axiomatic that God ultimately is incomprehensible. As God so emphatically reminded his insistent cross-examiner, Job, the distance between himself and his creatures is more vast than the remotest reaches of the cosmos. As finite beings, we simply have no capacity to fully grasp the infinite God of Creation.

Proceeding on the assumption that, whether or not we understand it, all things happen at God's behest, the conclusion is drawn that God's decrees are not always knowable. Included high on the list of those things which remain unrevealed and secret is God's eternal decree to elect who will be saved and who will be lost. The only thing of which we can be certain is that, as with the simplest molecule, your destiny and mine has been in the complete and total control of the sovereign God even from the dawn of eternity.

In such a case, how possibly could a finite human creature contribute anything to that infinite, sovereign decision? Or deserve one's salvation? Or, indeed, argue with one's eternal condemnation? From these deep theological springs, therefore, flow not just the doctrine of Unconditional Election, but the balance of the famous "five points."

For all its admirable emphasis on the sovereignty of God, the irony is that Reformed theology ends up renouncing that very sovereignty when it refuses to acknowledge that such a sovereign God has it within his sovereign power to create beings who have both the personal freedom and responsibility to choose between good and evil. And not only that, but also to hold them accountable by determining their eternal destiny according to their own moral and spiritual choices. If God is not sovereign over all possible options, whether of creation or of judgment, then he is not sovereign over all.

The wonder is not that the sovereign God of the universe would be in exclusive, ordaining control of his universe–past, present, and future. Nothing less would be expected of such a God. The wonder is that–having such absolute power–God would choose on our behalf to imbue us with something of his own freedom. "What is man that thou art mindful of him!"

Which brings us to the second major flaw in Calvinism's theology. To reduce God to all but a single facet is to miss him completely. For God is not just a sovereign being, but also a loving being. While Calvinists would never deny that God is loving, Calvinism ultimately forces God's sovereignty to trump God's love. Without denigrating either facet of God, it is well worth noting that in Scripture we don't find any single passage saying, "God is sovereign." What we do find is the compelling verse that every Sunday School child has memorized: "God is love."

So it is that Calvinism's foundational affirmation of God's exalted sovereignty is beyond all dispute. To God be the glory! But in the hands of extremist theologians, that exquisite and wondrous "bulb" is simply planted far too deep for its prized *TULIP* to survive biblical scrutiny.

Catch the Gap?

As we leave the "bulb" and return to the *TULIP* itself, it's time for a pop quiz on our earlier discussion. Did you notice any gaps in the evolutionary chain of Calvinism's *TULIP*? Any logical chasms? Any underlying assumptions that don't necessarily follow? Any biblical teaching that seems to be missing? For the moment, don't focus so much on the individual "petals." Further on, we'll scrutinize those one by one. For now, concentrate on the whole *TULIP*. Just how tight is the logic that binds this system together? Where, if at all, is this belief system vulnerable?

In order to test a theory, sometimes it's good to come through the back door, working back to front. So let's take the doctrines of Calvinism in reverse order. (You may wish to circle your answers.)

5. Is it logically possible that specific individuals whom God has foreordained and predestined to be eternally saved could ever be eternally lost? YES/NO

4. If before the beginning of time God declared that certain individuals inevitably would be saved, is there any possible way they could resist God's sovereign will in the matter? YES/NO

3. If only a predetermined number of elect are to be saved through Christ's atoning blood, does it make sense that his blood would have been shed for anyone other than that number? YES/NO

2. If even before creating the world God determined whom he was going to save, can their salvation be contingent upon *any* condition which man might satisfy (including having faith)? YES/NO

1. If man is wholly and totally depraved, would he have any *ability* to choose salvation, even if given an option? YES/NO

It would be surprising if you answered "yes" to any of those questions. Given the underlying assumptions, all the conclusions do seem logically inevitable, don't they?

Then again, conclusions are no more reliable than their underlying assumptions. It would betray your age, but you may remember the country-music classic made famous by Homer and Jethro called "I'm My Own Grandpa." Through a clever series of hilarious twists and turns in an imagined family tree, the guy actually turns out to be his own grandfather. Says the repeated punch-line: "It seems funny, I know, but it really is so: I'm my own grandpa!" Of course, "it really is so" only if you're willing to buy off on the painfully contrived assumptions which lead to the ridiculously-absurd conclusion.

Applying that principle to the subject at hand, we need to examine carefully the suppositional soil in which Calvinism's *TULIP* is firmly planted.

Think back on the doctrinal syllogism we discussed a moment ago. Did you happen to spot any gaps? If not, here's a clue. If nothing seems logically out of place in the "five points" themselves (the *conclusions*), where are we most likely to find troublesome gaps? As is obvious, it would have to be in the underlying *assumptions*.

And what, again, were those two pivotal assumptions?

1. Man could never "work his way to heaven," nor by any means merit salvation.

2. Given God's sovereign control over all things, man must not be seen to have any truly independent choice regarding his own salvation.

See any gaps there? Anything missing? Take a hard look, beginning with assumption number one.

Is There Any Merit to the "Works" Argument?

Is there a chance in the world that man could ever "work his way to heaven" or that he could merit salvation by his own good works or human effort? Surely not. Calvinists and non-Calvinist alike can agree on the first major assumption. "For *it is by grace you have been saved*, through faith," says Paul, "and this not from yourselves, *it is the gift of God*–not by works, so that no one can boast" (Ephesians 2:8-9). Could it be any clearer? To think that we could ever do enough work or sufficiently valuable service to find ourselves on the top rung of the ladder to heaven is the height of human presumption and pride.

Nor are we fooled into thinking otherwise when in the very next verse Paul continues: "For we are God's workmanship, created in Christ Jesus to do good works, which God prepared in advance for us to do" (Ephesians 2:10). The "good works" we are to do as followers of Christ are merely an extension of our faith–logically, doctrinally, and spiritually. As James reminds us, "faith by itself, if it is not accompanied by action, is dead" (James 2:17).

That line from James is notorious for having made Martin Luther squirm with apprehension that somehow James was threatening the bedrock concept of salvation by faith. This fear may partially explain why Luther famously added an extra word so as to speak of salvation by faith *alone*, or faith *only*.

Yet, even that distinction would be misleading were the juxtaposition between faith and *grace* rather than faith and *works*. As between faith and grace, no matter how much faith we might have, even that faith could not save us without God's grace making it possible for faith to save us. So faith certainly trumps works; but even faith is trumped by grace.

The concern, then, is not whether believers are to put their faith into action through doing good works. Jesus himself asked: "Why do you call me 'Lord, Lord,' and not do what I tell you?" (Luke 6:46). Yet, all the good works ever done by Christ's disciples, even if totaled together over the centuries, could never be sufficient to save even one disciple. So, is faith that *works* a faith that, in and of itself, *saves*? On that one, we can all join our voices and shout: God forbid!

On the other hand, if we are saved by our faith and not by our works, there is that intriguing dialogue to ponder. Remember when the pursuing crowd asked Jesus: "What must we do to do the works God requires?" Jesus answered, "The work of God is this: to believe in the one he has sent" (John 6:28-29).

Is there, perhaps, some sense in which even our faith is a "work"? If so, whose work is it, God's or ours? For what it's worth, the actual question was: "What must *we* do?" And what sense would it make for Jesus to say that God himself believes in the one he has sent? Wouldn't that be obvious? So who is left to do the believing, if not us? And if Jesus says that our belief is a "work," who are we to argue? (In truth, Jesus' reference to the "*work* of God" may have been spoken tongue in cheek, responding in their own terms to people who had no clue how to have a relationship with God if not through exhausting, mind-numbing human works.)

But even if our faith were said to be a "work," would this undo all that we've said about being saved by God's grace and not by our work? By no means. All it says is that any response we might make to God's grace is still a "work" that would fall far short of meriting the salvation which God alone gives us through his grace. Look as hard as you might, you'll never once find the word *merit* in Scripture, nor any such concept.

To say that you and I are required to have faith is not to denigrate the fact that ultimately we are saved by God's grace. We are saved by Christ (our Savior) *through* our faith; whereas without faith we can have no hope of salvation through Christ.[4]

If there is any single scripture that forever debunks the idea of human merit, surely it is Romans 9:16. "It does not, therefore, depend on man's desire or effort," says Paul, "but on God's mercy."[5]

Far from affirming merit-based salvation, Paul harshly chides the works-oriented Galatians for thinking that their meticulous law-keeping could ever bridge the gap between themselves and God. "After beginning with the Spirit, are you now trying to attain your goal by human effort?" (Galatians 3:4). Good question, Paul. One wonders how anyone could ever think otherwise.

Contradictory Fundamental Assumptions

Before we proceed to the next section, what do you think?

1. Do you believe that God's election was contingent upon a person's meeting *any* condition? YES/NO

---

[4] Everyone agrees that, in terms of the *source*, we are saved "by Christ." But when Calvinists and non- Calvinists speak of being saved "by faith" or even "through faith," we are talking past each other. Calvinists use those terms to mean that faith is the *instrument* of God's already-completed unconditional election to salvation. Non-Calvinists use those terms to mean that faith is a *condition precedent* to salvation. It's not just academic hairsplitting. According to Calvinism, one's faith in Christ (or lack of it) is a foregone conclusion, divinely determined by God's eternal decree. In which case, to be saved either "by faith" or "through faith" is but a mechanical, theoretical process bearing no resemblance to biblical faith, which is solely dependent upon an individual's own, unprogrammed response to God's grace.

[5] To turn this verse into a proof-text for unconditional election is to ignore the natural implication of *mercy*. Conceptually, mercy follows only in the wake of sin. Where there is no sin, there is no mercy. Only by assuming Calvinism's "secret eternal decrees" could God have bestowed mercy on his chosen elect before Adam and his descendants ever even sinned.

2. From the moment God chose the elect, is there any possibility that they would not be eternally saved? YES/NO

3. Do you believe that a person must have a personally-chosen faith in order to be saved? YES/NO

In the immortal words of Apollo 13, "Houston, we have a problem here." On one level, Calvinists are as eager as everyone else to acknowledge that we are "saved by faith" (as long as it means faith is God's unavoidable instrument for bringing his elect into the fold).[6] But as we shall see more and more clearly, the inescapable implication of Calvinism is that, for all intents and purposes, the elect were saved by God's eternal predestining decree long before the point of one's personal faith (as is most easily seen in Calvinism's insistence that we are *unconditionally* elect).

Try as it might, Calvinism can't have it both ways. Before we ever get to the Calvinist doctrine that the elect are specially and exclusively enabled by the Holy Spirit to put their faith in Jesus Christ (and thereby be saved), we are faced with an even more fundamental Calvinist doctrine: that, long before God ever created the very souls whom subsequently he would enable to have faith, God had already determined and safeguarded the ultimate salvation of his elect.

None less than Loraine Boettner, the widely-quoted apologist for Calvinism, unequivocally confirms that conclusion. "The redemption of the soul," says Boettner, is thus infallibly determined irrespective of any faith, repentance, or good works, whether actual or foreseen."[7] (Note, that's not just *election*, but *redemption*. Which is to say, *salvation*.[8])

As John Calvin himself put it in his magnum opus, *Institutes of the Christian Religion*, "We call predestination God's eternal decree, by which he

---

[6] Central to this distinction, consider Romans 1:17 (citing Habakkuk 2:4): "For in the gospel a righteousness from God is revealed, a righteousness that is *by* faith from first to last, just as it is written: 'The righteous will live by faith.'"

[7] Loraine Boettner, *The Reformed Doctrine of Predestination* (Phillipsburg, NJ: Presbyterian and Reformed Publishing Company, 1932, Reprint 1965), 144

[8] See also James White (debating Dave Hunt), *Debating Calvinism* (Sisters, Oregon, Multnomah Publishers, 2004), 93. "We see that election is personal and that it is salvific."

compacted with himself what he willed to become of each man. For all are not created in equal condition; rather, eternal life is foreordained for some, eternal damnation for others. Therefore, as any man has been created to one or the other of these ends, we speak of him as predestined to life or to death."[9]

Indeed, for all the debate surrounding the doctrine of Calvinism (including such issues as depravity, limited atonement, and perseverance of the saints), the fact is that none of those issues are of any ultimate consequence. If Calvinism's unique understanding of predestination is true, then at the point of God's predestining election somewhere in the shrouded mist of eternity past, nothing but nothing from that moment forward could possibly alter the eternal destiny of a single life that would ever come to be.

At that moment, the "plan of salvation" for any individual was law and history, not prophecy. Nor in any true sense (especially for the non-elect) was it even gospel! From that point forward, your fate and mine were forever sealed. A *fait accompli*. As far as we're concerned, "the ball game is over." End of story. Period.[10]

It must surely stand to reason, therefore, that no profession of faith secondarily resulting from this sovereign act of *unconditional* election could possibly be the basis for one's salvation. At most, God's gift of faith to the elect would be nothing more than his own vehicle of choice to implement unilaterally the salvation he has already determined for his chosen ones. (According to Boettner: "If God has ordained a man to be saved, He has also ordained that he shall hear the Gospel, and that he shall believe and

---

[9] John Calvin, *The Institutes of the Christian Religion*, (2 vols.), ed. John T. McNeill, tr. Ford Lewis Battles, (Philadelphia: The Westminster Press, 1960), 3.21.5.

[10] Calvinists take false comfort from Acts 27:24-31 where Paul is promised that none of those on board with him in the storm will be lost, followed by his warning that, unless everyone stays on board, they can't be saved. The intended analogy between Paul's shipwreck scenario and eternal salvation fails on at least three fronts. First, is the difference between a physical "salvation" from the sea and a spiritual salvation from eternal damnation. Second, is the difference between that which is explicitly revealed and that which is wholly unrevealed. Third, is the unproven assumption that God has chosen who will be saved and who will be lost in the same way as he worked providentially in the saving the passengers and crew on Paul's ship. The whole of Scripture teaches otherwise.

repent." And again: "Faith is thus referred to the counsels of eternity, the events in time being only the outworking.")[11]

Take the mask off Calvinism's version of "saved by grace *through* faith," and you'll see that it has nothing to do with grace working toward salvation through *our* faith. To speak of a person having a "personal faith in Jesus Christ" is to utter words having no real meaning. The believer is no longer the subject of faith, but the object. He who believes is not acting in faith, but being acted upon. "He who believes and is baptized shall be saved" (Mark 16:16) becomes "He who believes and is baptized *has already been saved!*"

Under this scenario, *man's "faith" is but God's decree.* Devoid of truly consensual belief and trust, the very notion of anyone "coming to faith," "having faith," or "keeping faith" loses all normal meaning.[12] It's all the difference between "Do you believe?" and "You shall believe!" Faith that is "gifted" without right of refusal is no faith at all—merely a conditioned response.

Far from championing the proposition that we are saved by faith (as opposed to works and human merit), Calvinism—practically speaking—rejects justification and salvation by faith in favor of justification and salvation by predestined election. Your faith and mine (whatever shred is left of the concept) comes too little too late to have any bearing whatsoever on our arbitrarily predetermined and thus unconsulted, uninvited, uninformed, and unconsented-to salvation.[13] How can a soul not yet even in existence "consent through faith" to his salvation?

---

[11] Boettner, 254; 303

[12] See Article XIV of the Canons of Dort (1619). "Faith is therefore to be considered as a gift of God, not on account of its being offered by God to man, to be accepted or rejected at his pleasure, but because it is in reality conferred, breathed, and infused into him; nor even because God bestows the power or ability to believe and expects that man should, by the exercise of his own free will, consent to the terms of salvation; but because he...produces both the will to believe and the act of believing also."

[13] Boettner agrees (p. 101). "A man is not saved because he believes in Christ; he believes in Christ because he is saved." (This is, of course, the exact opposite of Acts 16:31 and Romans 10:9-10.)

White also agrees (p. 96): "The divine appointment obviously precedes and brings about the act of faith. God has appointed them to eternal life, and they believe. Obviously, this statement touches upon not only unconditional election, but upon irresistible grace as well." (Compare Romans 1:16.)

Apart from the doctrine of *sola Scriptura* (by Scripture alone), nothing is more hallowed to Reformed theology than the doctrine of *sola fide* (justification by faith alone). Yet, given Reformed theology's prior commitment to unconditional election, *sola fide* ends up being put to the sword by its older brother, *sola praeordinati* (by predestination alone).[14]

When R.C. Sproul says that "Faith is a necessary condition for salvation, but not for election," he affirms the obvious, irrefutable fact that election has nothing whatsoever to do with faith.[15] Unfortunately, his follow-up attempt to distinguish between election and salvation is a difference without a distinction.

Indeed, Sproul later undermines his own case, saying: "God provides for his elect all that is necessary for their salvation, including the gift of faith."[16] Yet if God himself foreordains the very faith that is necessary for salvation, then having faith is but a foregone conclusion based on divine action. Salvation cannot factually, truly, and legitimately be conditional on a person's response to God (as Sproul contends) when how that person will respond has already been determined.

More explicit still, is Sproul's categorical insistence that "*God himself creates the faith in the believer's heart. God fulfills the necessary condition for salvation and he does so without condition.*"[17]

If in theory faith as a *means* is required to achieve the *end* of salvation, nonetheless it remains true that, from the moment of election, neither the *end* nor the *means* is ever in doubt.[18] From predestination to salvation, it is

---

[14] It's not enough to attempt a distinction between faith as the *means* of salvation and God's predestining decree as the *basis*. Any word which has been so radically redefined as to no longer have its obvious intended meaning cannot serve as a means to any end which biblically contemplates the normal, intended meaning of the un-redefined word. To contend that the means (faith) is just as predestined as the end (salvation) is to rob "faith" of its natural sense. Biblically speaking, "predestined faith" is an oxymoron.

[15] R.C. Sproul, *Grace Unknown* (Grand Rapids: Baker Books, 1997, 6th Printing, 2003), 145

[16] Sproul, 175

[17] Sproul, 156 (with my emphasis)

[18] Commenting on 1 Thessalonians 2:13, James White (p. 110) acknowledges that "the text shows that the work of the Spirit and our faith in God's truth are the *result* of that eternal choice. God ordains both the ends and the means, just as Reformed theology has taught all along."

all God, and *nothing* of man. *All* election, and *nothing* of faith—not even the "freely chosen faith" that Calvinists champion in other contexts.

Would any Calvinist deny that the eternal salvation of the elect soul is an absolute certainty before that soul is ever born? Or that, once born, that soul's *not* believing unto his or her salvation is unimaginable? The conclusion, therefore, is inescapable. Underlying the better-known Calvinist doctrine of "once saved, always saved," is the originating principle: "once predestined to salvation without faith, irreversibly saved without faith."[19]

And all the prophets cry, "Faith, faith," but there is no faith. When faith is but a foregone *eventuality*, it is stripped of any meaningful *actuality*.

If ever anyone wanted a bright-line difference between Calvinism and biblical teaching, it is this: Under Calvinism, salvation is not by (or through) faith, but by (and through) fiat.[20]

Closing In On the Suspect

By a process of elimination, we've now confirmed both the internal logic of Calvinism's *TULIP* and the obvious biblical support for the first of Calvinism's two fundamental, underlying assumptions: that we are saved by God's sovereign grace, not human merit. So it is that in our search for a tell-tale gap in the evolutionary process of Calvinism, the sole remaining suspect is the second assumption: that, because of God's absolute sovereignty and grace, you and I must not have any active role in the regeneration which leads inexorably to our salvation.

---

[19] In one breath, Calvinism insists that all of God's predestining work (including the "end" of unconditional election and the "means" of faith) takes place outside of time consistent with the very nature of an eternal God. However, in the next breath what we hear is that, for a person to have faith, it is first necessary (in linear time) that he be regenerated sometime during the span of his life in order to come to that faith. As Calvinists themselves seem to argue when discounting election being conditioned on one's faith, how can anything completed outside of time be dependent upon anything in linear time?

[20] And the same goes for our being saved by grace. For if every person was either elect or reprobate before sin entered the world, then "grace" is devoid of any practical significance. We are not saved by grace through faith, but by sovereign decree through election prior to any guilty, lost, or depraved condition which could possibly beg for an act of grace.

By Reformed teaching, one's regeneration is not a *synergistic* or cooperative process, but a *monergistic* process in which God is the sole acting party. We must wholly be acted upon rather than act. Consequently, we are absolutely unable to change the ultimate outcome, which itself depends upon whether or not God chooses to regenerate us. (Yet somehow, so we are told, the fact that we are "absolutely unable" does not prevent us from being "absolutely responsible" for our actions!)

Can this assumption withstand close biblical scrutiny? Starting from the incontrovertible biblical premise that we could never "work our way to heaven" or begin to merit our salvation, does it follow either logically or scripturally that we have no deciding role whatsoever to play in our salvation? Or is there, instead, a divinely-revealed compatibility between God's saving grace and man's own *non-predestined* decision regarding his eternal destiny which remains the illusive, stubbornly uncooperative "missing link" of Calvinism?

If Calvinists can insist against all logic that there is no incompatibility between God's absolute foreordaining predestination and the supposed free agency of the regenerate elect, then perhaps we are not that far apart after all. Maybe we just need to take a closer look at the tell-tale "fossils" in the biblical record to see what type of free agency or free will can be found. Is the type of human freedom we find in Scripture a variety which God himself created, or one that has spuriously evolved over many centuries of theological innovation?

This day I call heaven and earth as witnesses against you that I have set before you life and death, blessings and curses. Now choose life...."

Deuteronomy 30:19

Chapter Summary

- The following five points of Calvinism form a tightly-packaged, logically-cohesive belief system:

  Total depravity

  Unconditional election

  Limited atonement

  Irresistible grace

  Perseverance of the saints

- Calvinism is based upon two primary underlying assumptions:
  1. Man could never "work his way to heaven" or merit salvation.
  2. Because of God's eternal nature and sovereignty, man's eternal destiny cannot be other than what God alone has chosen.

- The first of those two assumptions is unquestionably biblical. Salvation is not based to any degree upon human effort or merit. (Discussion of the second assumption follows in Chapter 2.)

Reality Check: If in fact God determined your eternal destiny before you were ever born, then whether you have any personal faith in Christ is relevant only to the historical unfolding of what God intends to do in your life in any event. For you, the door to salvation was either open or shut before you drew your first breath, much less even heard the word *believe*.

Chapter 2

Calvinism's Elusive Missing Link

As the bird with a broken wing is "free" to fly but not able
so the natural man is free to come to God but not able.

–Loraine Boettner

We come now to the second fundamental, underlying assumption of Calvinism, and the absolutely crucial distinction that has to be made in order to make any sense of the Scriptures. Does the fact that you and I could never in a million years merit our own salvation necessarily force us to the conclusion that we must, or can, have no part whatsoever in the process of regeneration? To get the discussion started, consider for a moment two simple hypothetical scenarios.

First, suppose a man is drowning in turbulent waters and a bystander throws him a life-preserver which lands well within his reach. If the man grabs hold of the life-preserver, he will be saved. If he does not, he will drown. At this point, it's all up to him. Grab or not grab. Be saved or be lost. What will it be?

If our drowning man reaches out and grabs hold of the life-preserver and is saved, would anyone dare suggest that he *merits* being saved simply for having grasped the preserver? Or that he "worked" for his safe deliverance from peril?[21]

Here's a good test: Do you think our rescued man is going to go around boasting to all his friends about how valiantly he saved himself, or is he more likely to tell them about the person who came along and threw him the life-preserver? Is he going to take credit for his own heroism, or keep asking his rescuer, "What can I do to show my appreciation for what you've done?"

And how would you characterize the throwing of the life-preserver in the first place if not an act of grace? Just to make it more interesting, suppose the bystander recognized the man in the water as an enemy who had greatly offended him, yet threw the life-preserver anyway.

Quite incredibly there are those who ask, What's the use of the life-preserver if one can reach out and grab it by his own effort? Consider this line of questioning, for example, from none other than R.C. Sproul. "If the flesh can, by itself, incline itself to grace, where is the need of grace? If the grace of regeneration is merely offered and its efficacy depends on the sinner's response, what does grace accomplish that is not already present in the power of the flesh?"[22]

Perhaps we should let Rizal Shahputra answer those questions. As you may recall, he's the Indonesian laborer who desperately clung to a floating palm tree for eight days after being washed out into the deep by the great Indian Ocean tsunami. To follow Sproul's reasoning, because Rizal him-

---

[21] Calvinists will object that this analogy is not pertinent, contending that the only relevant analogy is of a dead man (like Lazarus) who is incapable of having any part in his regeneration from the dead. Of course, that begs the pivotal question of total depravity which will be discussed at length in the following three chapters. For the moment, the question is whether reaching out to accept God's grace in any way nullifies that grace, or somehow transforms any part of the process from being theocentric into being anthropocentric.

[22] Sproul, 188. Sproul might insist he is speaking here only of man's regeneration from depravity. But this is essentially the same argument Sproul and other Calvinists use when castigating non-Calvinists for being humanistic, anthropocentric, works-oriented, Pelagians and semi-Pelagians. Sproul gets into this trouble, of course, because he is desperately clinging to the idea of total depravity, which—as we shall discuss momentarily—is problematic both for Calvinism and orthodoxy generally.

self was able to reach out and grab hold of the tree, then the tree itself was not at all necessary! And because the "efficacy" of the tree depended on Rizal's response, then the tree could not accomplish anything more than what Rizal was able to do by his own effort!

Words fail, really. Especially when we think of that other "tree" to which so many countless millions of believers have desperately clung for salvation. Are we really to accept that reaching out in faith to grasp the cross of Christ means we are saving ourselves? That, because we are able to reach out and touch it, the cross itself thereby becomes unnecessary? And that if its efficacious effect depends in any way upon our reaching out for it, then it cannot accomplish anything more than what we are able to do by our own effort? Surely this Calvinist spin on man's response to God's divine initiatives is wildly off-axis.[23]

Far from human pride saying to God, "With just a little help, thank you, I could save myself," we desperately look to the cross knowing full well that it is the one and only source of our salvation. Augustus Toplady may have been a staunch Calvinist, but his immortal "Rock of Ages" is no less beloved by non-Calvinists for this wondrous, humbling truth...

Nothing in my hand I bring;
Simply to Thy Cross I cling....

Bringing is one thing. *Clinging*, quite another. If the former might possibly imply a degree of self-sufficient independence, the latter permits of nothing but sheer and utter, Self-denying dependence.

---

[23] In his attempt to prove that man has no free will, Martin Luther offers a similarly illogical argument regarding the relationship between free will and grace: "I allow you to enlarge the power of free will as much as you like...but once you add this doleful postscript, that it is ineffective apart from God's grace, you at once rob it of all its power. What is ineffective power, [is] plainly no power at all." [Martin Luther, *The Bondage of the Will* [636]. See *Erasmus and Luther—Discourse on Free Will, trans. and edited Ernst F. Winter* (London, New York: Continuum, Frederick Ungar Publishing Co., 1961, 1989, 2005), 97]

Does this facile insistence on "all or nothing" comport with babies reaching for cups they cannot grasp, or the blind being assisted in their movement, or—more importantly—what the Bible teaches about sinners appealing to God's grace for a strength beyond their own?

When "Work" Isn't "A Work"

The usual question everybody seems to keep asking is whether the man who reaches for the life-preserver is saved by grace or by works. That's too easy. The answer (grace) is obvious. The far more compelling question invariably seems to get lost in the fog of battle: Despite the grace of having been thrown a life-preserver, *would our man have survived had he not grabbed hold of it?* It goes without saying, really.

So what does this suggest about the possibility that those who are rescued from sin by God's amazing grace may have a role to play in their own salvation that couldn't be more greatly distanced from either "work" or merit?

Or is "work" and merit even the real concern? To the outsider, Calvinism seems absolutely obsessed about God's remaining in control. But by what twisted logic do we assume that humble acts of obedience on the part of man (such as faith, repentance, and baptism) somehow wrest control from the God who commands those very acts? How can *submitting* to God's control possibly obligate God to act, or put him in our debt?[24]

Recognizing unequivocally that no "work" on our part could ever put us in the driver's seat instead of God, still, we see Paul urging the disciples in Philippi to "work out your salvation with fear and trembling, for it is God who works in you to will and to act according to his good purpose" (Philippians 2:12-13). When it comes to our salvation, the fact that God is working within us to fulfill his own purposes does not exclude the fact that we ourselves have a vital role to play.

Calvinists undoubtedly would agree, but would insist nevertheless that our part in "working out our own salvation" is solely empowered by the Holy Spirit working within us. It's worthy of note that Paul speaks here of our being literally *energized* by God, but in other passages frequently

---

[24] When urging that the intricacies of Calvinism are unsuitable for the unconverted and newly-converted, even Boettner talks in terms which Calvinists otherwise eschew. Our work, says Boettner, "consists mainly in presenting and stressing man's part in the work of salvation—faith, repentance, moral reform, etc. These are the elementary steps so far as man's consciousness extends. At that early stage little need be said about the deeper truths which relate to God's part." (Boettner, 348.) Although "man's part" is unquestionably biblical, nothing could be more contrary to the Calvinist doctrine that salvation is wholly and solely "God's part" from start to finish.

admonishes "energized" disciples for not fulfilling their roles as they ought. If it is God alone who is responsible for "energizing" whatever *good* might manifest itself in the lives of his elect, how can we escape the conclusion that any *shortcomings* in their lives must also be attributed directly to God? Surely God must expect man to exercise initiative and bear personal responsibility in a number of ways even apart from the Holy Spirit moving in one's life.

But if man truly does have a separate role to play, does this mean that salvation is somehow a joint-enterprise? Not if that implies God's power or grace is insufficient; or that we ourselves must somehow top off the tank of grace; or that God has credited our account with 99% of what we owe and we must provide the final 1%. No!

> *Jesus paid it all;*
> *All to him I owe;*
> *Sin had left a crimson stain,*
> *He washed it white as snow.*[25]

Isn't Salvation Supposed To Be a Gift?

Time now for our second hypothetical. Suppose a generous benefactor advertises world-wide that he will give a million dollars to everyone who is willing to jump into Rome's Trevi fountain and get themselves soaking wet. To the amazement of all who take him up on the offer, the benefactor is waiting right there at the fountain to hand out towels and certified checks to the dripping throngs.[26]

How would you assess the various elements involved in that hypothetical?

---

[25] "Jesus Paid It All," Mrs. H. M. Hall.

[26] Just as analogies serve to illustrate but never prove, protesting an analogy by altering the analogy does not prove to the contrary. Such would be the case, for example, should anyone wonder how the result might change if the offer were made to a group of paraplegics or a cemetery full of the dead (reflecting Calvinism's belief that those who are totally depraved are disabled or even dead, as was Lazarus in the tomb). This tack merely serves to divert the issue from one of relative *merit* to the separate issue of *ability* (soon to be discussed).

1. Were the certified checks anything other than a free gift, pure and simple? YES/NO

2. Would anyone get a check if he read about the offer, but just laughed at what a crazy idea it was? YES/NO

3. Would anyone get a check if he sincerely believed the offer to be genuine, but made no effort to go to Rome and jump into the fountain? YES/NO

4. For those who actually went to the trouble to jump into the fountain, is "work" the first word that comes to mind? Do we normally associate the word "work" with the word "gift"? YES/NO

5. Could it properly be said that those who jumped into the fountain *earned* the million dollars? Or *merited* it? (Does getting one's self soaking wet generally *merit* a million dollars?) YES/NO

6. Is it likely that any of those who jumped into the fountain would think that the million dollars was anything other than an outrageously amazing *free gift* (even if it might have cost them air fare to get to Rome)? YES/NO

7. When a benefactor decides to offer someone a free gift, does he generally have in mind that the recipient will have to work for it? Or will have earned it? Or that there is some other reason why he is *obligated* to give it? YES/NO

8. On the other hand, does the benefactor ever expect to force his free gift on anyone who adamantly refuses to receive it? YES/NO

9. Is a free gift any less a free gift simply because there are strings attached to receiving it? YES/NO

10. Is there *ever* a free gift without at least one "string" being attached–the "string" of actually *taking* the gift? YES/NO[27]

Do we not all agree that salvation is a gift from God? A *free* gift? It's hard to see how the contrast could ever be better articulated: "For the *wages* of

---

[27] Calvinists sometimes refer us to the figure of a fireman who rescues an unconscious victim from a burning house, arguing that as depraved sinners we have no ability even to *take* a gift. But that analogy (which not only distorts the type of "gift" contemplated but also begs the question of our being "unconscious victims") does not respond in kind to the issue at hand: whether a gift is any less "free" simply because a person who *can* personally receive it must actually do so.

sin is death, but the *free gift* of God is eternal life in Christ Jesus our Lord" (Romans 6:23). By our sins we *earn* the condemnation of spiritual death; whereas our salvation from sin can never be anything but a free gift.

Even so, there are those "strings" to think about, if nothing more than the "string" of willingly receiving the free gift that is promised. Certainly, God's sublime gift of eternal salvation is far more valuable than the million dollars in our hypothetical; and he's hardly asking us to fly to Rome and jump in the Trevi fountain. But what are we to say about the extraordinary offer (together with the attached "strings") made on the day of Pentecost following Christ's ascension?

You'll recall that Peter and the apostles stood before the crowd of Pentecost celebrants and boldly proclaimed that the Jesus whom they had caused to be crucified was the promised Messiah and Lord. Hear again the crowds' conscience-stricken reaction: "Now when they heard this they were cut to the heart, and said to Peter and the rest of the apostles, 'Brethren, what shall we do?' And Peter said to them, 'Repent, and be baptized every one of you in the name of Jesus Christ for the forgiveness of your sins; and you shall receive the gift of the Holy Spirit'" (Acts 2:37-38).

The incredible offer? The free gift of God's forgiveness, together with the indwelling of the Holy Spirit! The "strings"? Repentance and getting one's self completely soaked in the watery "fountain" of Christ's cleansing blood!

The obedience? Obvious. The wages? None. The "work"? None. The merit? None.

To change the metaphor only slightly...

> *There's a fountain free, 'tis for you and me,*
> *Let us haste, O, haste to the brink;*
> *'Tis a fount of love from the Source above,*
> *And he bids us all freely drink.*[28]

Under almost any other circumstance, Calvinists would acknowledge the truth of the maxim that you can lead a horse to water, but can't make

---

[28] "Free Waters," Mrs. M. B. C. Slade.

him drink. Yet, when it comes to salvation, there seems to be great offense in suggesting that, if we drink of God's saving grace on our own accord, somehow his providing the water and leading us to it makes the water no longer free. (We mustn't forget the only alternative, that God himself must shove our heads into the trough and make us swallow—the logic of which mandates Calvinism's doctrine of "irresistible grace."[29])

If you're still not comfortable with the idea of free gifts having "strings" attached, think about it this way. What is the only alternative to the "string" of willingly receiving the free gift? Isn't it being *forced* to receive the gift? But if a gift is forced upon an unwilling recipient, how can it any longer be a *gift*? (This is a particular problem for Calvinists, who simultaneously believe that salvation is a free gift of grace, but that the gift is irresistible. More on that later.)

Maybe you remember the slick commercial advertising car-care products where the mechanic with the cynical voice threatens: "You can pay me now...or pay me later!" Almost always, *making no choice* is itself a choice. Whether we like it or not, there's always going to be some kind of strings attached to our salvation. Either it's the "strings" attached to receiving a free gift from God, which we can freely choose to accept or reject; or it's the strings by which we ourselves are attached to God—strings which we can do nothing about.

I realize this might grate, but it simply has to be said. Any scenario which leaves us without any *effective* free will or free agency (really and truly free), leaves us effectively as puppets on strings manipulated by God for his own good pleasure. If that seems harsh, I agree. Such a caricature of God's highest creation *does* seem harsh. So why would anyone wish to believe what turns out to be such a dehumanizing alternative, when Scripture paints no such picture of man?

---

[29] Naturally, Calvinists would prefer a more sympathetic illustration to reflect their belief that total depravity robs a person of the ability to accept a gift unless externally "forced" by the Holy Spirit (in the nicest possible way, of course). We are given, for example, the nurse who tenderly gives an "IV" to a comatose patient. Whether accomplished "tenderly" or "roughly," nothing about the patient's being comatose lessens in any way the fact that external force is being used to insert the "IV." Left to following chapters is the discussion of whether we are so spiritually comatose as not to be able to function without a "regenerating injection."

What we see, by contrast, is the picture of men and women who are gifted with the powers of reason and understanding and choice, yet willingly turn their backs on God. Even to those who took pride in knowing the Scriptures backwards and forwards, Jesus said rebukingly: "These are the Scriptures that testify about me, yet you refuse to come to me to have life," (John 5:39-40). Look as hard as you might...you will see no strings manipulating them to reject Jesus, only their wilful rejection of the "string" of faith.

To the same effect is Acts 13:46, where Paul and Barnabas chided the Jews, saying: "We had to speak the word of God to you first. Since you reject it and do not consider yourselves worthy of eternal life, we now turn to the Gentiles." Inherent within the rebuke is the implication that these Jews had acted freely and voluntarily on the basis of a fully informed choice. It was not God who thought them unworthy of eternal life (and thus pulled the strings of rejection), but they themselves.[30]

And the Point of All This?

In case you're wondering where all this is going, it's going back to the beginning. Back to the assumptions which underlie the "five points" of Calvinism. Back to Calvinism's evolution and the logical gap that puts the whole package of Calvinist doctrine in jeopardy.

When Calvinism asserts that man can have nothing whatever to do with obtaining salvation, it does so on the assumption that any response to God's overture of grace necessarily means man is "working his way to heaven" and meriting his own salvation. But surely by now we have dispelled this notion altogether. Surely, there is nothing of work or merit to simply reaching out and taking hold of the life-preserver which God so graciously places within our grasp. Surely, there is nothing of work or merit in freely and joyfully receiving the promised gifts of forgiveness and the Holy Spirit himself, even if God attaches "strings" to accepting his

---

[30] So-called "infralapsarian" Calvinists will agree with the foregoing two paragraphs, despite the fact that the cited texts run counter to Calvinism's most fundamental assumption that God is the determining cause of absolutely every act, event, thought, and motive. By such a view, no one possibly could have any real choice over his eternal destiny.

gracious gift, including faith, repentance, and baptism. (Are we willing to abandon even the "string" of being saved by *faith*?)[31]

Without the slightest hint of merit or works, Peter's Pentecost sermon unabashedly places the responsibility for salvation squarely in the hearts of his hearers. As Luke tells us, "With many other words he warned them; and he pleaded with them, '*Save yourselves* from this corrupt generation'" (Acts 2:40). We can almost hear Peter shouting to those in danger of being eternally lost: "Grab hold of the life-preserver! God has thrown out his grace to save you. Just grab hold!"

Does Peter anywhere here suggest that only those who are specially empowered by the Holy Spirit are able to reach out and grab hold of salvation? For that matter, does the promised gift of the Holy Spirit of which he speaks come *before* or *after* they repent and are baptized?[32]

This is not to say, of course, that there is no working of the Spirit before the drowning sinner grabs hold. Jesus himself promised that "When he [the Comforter] comes, he will convict the world of guilt in regard to sin and righteousness and judgment" (John 16:8). The man who does not realize he is drowning in sin has little reason to reach out for God's mercy. Through the Spirit-revealed gospel, therefore, man is brought face to face with both the problem of sin and its divine solution.

We see this very process in play on the Day of Pentecost. Empowered by the Holy Spirit, the gospel message delivered by Peter and the apostles

---

[31] Should Calvinists suggest that love with strings attached is not truly love, it might be worth considering that even love has its strings. As Christ admonished his disciples, "If you love me, you will obey what I command" (John 14:15). To love unconditionally (as parents do) is not to rule out the setting of conditions for what one might wish to give to those who are loved.

[32] When Calvinists cite 1 Corinthians 12:8-9 for the proposition that faith is a gift of God (irresistibly given to the elect), they put the Calvinist cart before the contextual horse. Since Paul is writing to those who were already saved regarding various spiritual gifts, it is clear that the "gift of faith," like the gifts of wisdom and knowledge, is given by the Spirit so that the saints might better serve the cause of the kingdom. (The same basic rationale also applies to Romans 12:3 and 2 Peter 1:1.)

Note also that the manifestation of the Spirit in Acts 10, which *precedes* Cornelius' baptism, is no different from the manifestation of the Spirit in Acts 2, which *preceded* the baptism of the 3000. Both being inaugural occasions, the Spirit was specially manifested in order (1) to bring about a new paradigm, in which (2) baptized believers would personally receive the Spirit as part of their conversion experience. To confuse the two manifestations or gifts of the Spirit is to misunderstand the two-fold way in which the Spirit works.

both convicts the people of their sin and brings them the good news of forgiveness through Christ. Yet clearly Peter expects his hearers to take action on their own in order to accept the gifts which God graciously wishes to bestow upon them. Why, then, should anyone be so worried on God's behalf that a conditional gift is not a gift at all, or that it somehow diminishes God's divine sovereignty? (Does it appear that God himself is concerned about that?)

A Mutual Exchange of Gifts

Central to Calvinism is the premise that any unpredestined *willing* on the part of man would make one's salvation dependent upon human will rather than on the sovereign will of God. And that, therefore, faith would be man's gift to God, not God's gift to man. Is there any logic at all to that argument?

For starters, is there something horribly wrong with man bringing gifts to God–gifts of obedience, praise, honor, and glory? What are sacrifices, tithes, and *freewill* offerings, if not reciprocal gifts from man to God, himself the consummate giver of all good gifts?

Beyond that, however, is the barely noticeable sleight of hand which begins with talk of *salvation*, but suddenly shifts to talk of *faith*, subtly suggesting that salvation and faith are one and the same and concluding that if man has any control whatsoever over his own faith he, and not God, is the moving, primal cause of his own salvation.

Suffice it to say, mixed apples and oranges belong in fruit bowls, not truth-seeking argumentation. Certainly, there are many who seem hopelessly enslaved to the notion of works-righteousness. But is there any serious student of the Word in any doctrinal camp of any stripe who believes that whenever there is faith on the part of man what results is a kind of man-ordained, self-made salvation? Need we be reminded that having faith means having faith *in God*, not faith in ourselves?

Although faith could certainly be considered a token of appreciation given to God for his having made our salvation possible, salvation itself is the gift of God alone. Man's trusting faith is but the eager reception of that matchless, unmerited gift.

It is strange indeed to think that anyone could take an act of required obedience to God—namely, faith—and turn it on its head to be a case of man's saving himself. How can doing what one is required to do in order to receive a gift possibly be considered the primary cause and ultimate basis for having received the gift? The moving force behind this matchless gift is the *Giver*, not the *recipient*.

We can argue all day about whether one's belief is in some way meritorious, but there's one thing on which we can all agree: that one's *disbelief* is blameworthy. By shifting the spotlight away from those who believe to those who don't, it's clearer than ever that when a person *does have faith* it has nothing to do with merit, only a consequent avoidance of blame.

Caution: Dangerous Intersection Ahead

While, to be sure, there are those who confuse man's *works* with man's *faith* as the means by which God imparts his grace, Paul rebukes any such notion. "For it is by grace you have been saved, *through faith*—and this not from yourselves, it is the gift of God—*not by works*, so that no one can boast" (Ephesians 2:8-9).

But we must be ever so careful here. Given the priceless valuables packed into this wonderful verse, there ought to be a label: "Handle with extreme care."

Despite the awkward word sequencing of this important passage, the two intended pairings are obvious. 1) "Salvation by grace," says Paul, "is the gift of God." (Period!) And 2) this grace comes "through faith," he insists, "not by works." Your point, Paul? It is man's trusting faith, not his works of righteousness or ritual, that is the channel through which God's free gift of salvation is both willingly bestowed and willing received.[33]

Though the precise issue of God's sovereign will versus man's individual will is not Paul's primary brief in this immediate text, the underlying truth

---

[33] Calvin agrees. On this text Calvin comments (with my emphasis): "he does not mean that *faith* is the gift of God, but that *salvation* is given to us by God, or, that we obtain it by the gift of God." [*Calvin's Commentaries*, vol. 11, 145]

about that issue could hardly be clearer. Just as man's faith triumphs over man's works, God's grace (and will) triumphs over man's faith (and will).

Even so, there is nothing here or in all of Scripture that would rob God of his sovereign right to bestow his gift of salvation on his own terms—even if he should choose to condition that gift on man's freely-exercised faith. If as a Calvinist you agree with the first part of that statement, as you surely must, why would the second part be so inconceivable or loathsome?

If it is the misguided notion of works-righteousness you're concerned about, Paul has already taken care of that foolishness for us. When Paul repeatedly and emphatically contrasts faith as against works, it begs belief that faith itself could ever be maligned as a work!

And so if God's free gift of salvation does not logically, definitively, or scripturally rule out a role for man in volitionally receiving that gift, then there's no reason for a strained, biblically-problematic belief system that explains how the plan of salvation could possibly work wholly apart from man's involvement. In the case of Calvinism's evolution, rather than being about survival of the *fittest*, I suggest it's mostly come about as a result of an underlying premise which is unquestionably well-intended but fatally *unfit*.

Word Games and Magic Tricks

In response to all of this, you may wish to protest that those who are elect are indeed involved in the process of their salvation—that they must have faith, and be obedient to God, and excel in righteousness. However, if you're saying this as a Calvinist, surely you have to acknowledge that you risk contradicting the fundamental Calvinist premise that man has no say regarding his eternal destiny which, from eternity, has been determined solely by God on the basis of an unconditional election...which alone is responsible for regenerating the elect...which alone empowers (and irresistibly compels) them to have faith, be obedient to God, and excel in righteousness.

What this striking inconsistency exposes is Calvinism's unique, two-tiered view of man's actions. On the upper tier, once those who are among the elect are regenerated, they may act "freely" to put their faith in Christ, obey God's will, and live righteously. But because of what has already happened on the lower tier, where unconditional election and irresistible grace are found, the elect on the upper tier don't have any real choice to do otherwise. Do they...?

It's not enough to contend that the regenerate elect take on a new nature having the ability to freely choose according to the "new man" which they have become. The acid test is: Could the "new man" freely choose to reject God at that point?

When Calvinism insists that all men (both the elect and the non-elect) make free choices, yet simultaneously insists that the "free choices" they make cannot possibly be contrary to the outcome which God himself has foreordained, can anyone disclaim that Calvinism is indulging in schizophrenic thinking?

Being able to "freely choose," but only according to a predetermined nature over which we have no choice, makes a sham of Calvinism's "free will." When the sum total of all our "free choices" can never add up to anything other than what has already been decided for us, then no single choice we make (whether about faith or what we eat for breakfast) can truly be free. With apologies to Janis Joplin and Kris Kristofferson, it does seem as if for Calvinists *freedom's* just another word for nothin' left to choose.[34]

In computer terms, even if the "software" appears to permit such responses as faith, repentance, and baptism, the parameters embedded within the "hardware" ultimately impose fundamental operating limitations on the capabilities of the software. Maybe, like me, you've been busted by one of those menacing pop-ups threatening to put you in some cyber-space slammer with the chilling words: "You have performed an illegal operation!" Just how free to proceed are you at that point?

Or perhaps you've encountered the frustration of having your access blocked to a particular computer program for lack of a proper password. In Calvinistic terms, God is the only one who can assign the correct password, so if he chooses not to give it to you, you're out of business. And even if, on your own, you would never have had the slightest desire to access the program, God will make certain that you end up getting the

---

[34] Words from "Me and Bobby McGee."

password...*and using it.* It's not exactly the same as when your colleague in the office says, "Feel free to use my password," is it?

In the English countryside where I have lived for a significant time over the years, one often sees signs along the road saying: "Free Range Eggs." I have to confess that the first few times I saw those signs I didn't have a clue about "free-range" chickens, and wrongly concluded that "range eggs" (whatever they might have been) were being given away for free! In a strange kind of way, Calvinism is like that: "Free" isn't really free after all! I say this kindly, but I wonder if Calvinists don't need to be far more honest about that.

Where Darwin and Calvinism Meet

It wouldn't be everyone's idea of an exciting pastime, but I confess I find the parallels and contrasts between Evolution and Calvinism absolutely fascinating. For example, *chance* is the operative word for Natural Selection. As Stephen Jay Gould put it, "Replay the tape a million times...and I doubt that anything like Homo sapiens would ever evolve again."[35] The slightest wrong turn along the path of evolution, and you and I wouldn't even exist! At least not as humans.

At the opposite extreme, strict Calvinism tells us that nothing has ever been uncertain, accidental, or subject to chance. Absolutely nothing! Consider, for example, this statement from Dutch theologian Abraham Kuyper:

> *The determination of the existence of all things to be created, or what is to be camellia or buttercup, nightingale or crow, hart or swine, and equally among men, the determination of our own persons, whether one is to be born as boy or girl, rich or poor, dull or clever, white or colored or even as Abel and Cain, is the most tremendous predestination conceivable in heaven or on earth; and still we see it taking place before our eyes every day, and we ourselves are subject to it in our entire personality; our entire existence, our very nature, our position in life being entirely dependent on it.*[36]

---

[35] Stephen Jay Gould, *Wonderful Life* (New York: W. W. Norton, 1989), 45-52.
[36] See Boettner, 17

Or as Loraine Boettner puts it in his classic defense of Calvinism: "We see from this divine view-point every event in the course of human affairs in all ages and in all nations has, no matter how insignificant it may appear to us, its exact place in the development of the eternal plan."[37]

And again (referring to Genesis 50:20): "This exalted conception of God as high and lifted up, yet personally concerned with even the smallest events, leaves no place for what men commonly call chance, or luck, or fortune."[38] (How this Calvinist tenet squares with Ecclesiastes 9:11 seems not to be addressed by Calvinist writers. There the wise teacher says plainly regarding each man's death: "...time and chance happen to them all.")[39]

Chance or no chance, Evolution and Calvinism end up with altogether similar results. Similar *deterministic* results. In each case, man's essential, fundamental, in-the-image-of-God humanity is virtually obliterated. By the Theory of Evolution, man is robbed of his soul, plus any potential for immortality, and is subject to the capricious whims of an impersonal, yet imperious Nature. In Calvinism, man is robbed of any genuine, honest-to-goodness free will (and, in the case of the non-elect, their potential for immortality), being subject to the inalterable foreordination of a destiny-dictating divine Sovereign.

In the Passionate Pursuit of Love

If you are a Calvinist, take a deep breath for a moment while I say something that might very well raise your dander. With apologies up front, it just has to be said. For reasons which I will explain further, I'm convinced that what both grand theories are missing is the very heart, soul, and essence of the gospel of Christ, which is *love*.

---

[37] Ibid., 16

[38] Ibid., 328

[39] Calvinists often cite Proverbs 16:33 and Acts 1:26 as proof that even in the casting of lots, God's hand is behind the roll of the dice. No one doubts that was true on a particular day in Jerusalem, but it is hardly likely in Las Vegas tonight.

As for the case of that "random" arrow flying from the archer's bow and into the tiniest openings of King Ahab's armor (1 Kings 22:28, 34), we all agree there was nothing random about its actually flying from God's own bow of divine providence and power.

As for Evolution, where is love to be found within globs of accidental cells bound together by complete chance in a process of capricious evolution? As for Calvinism, where is *true* love to be found in creatures who are from eternity pre-programmed in mind, soul, and body to embrace their Creator? (Do the elect have any real say in how they will respond to God? Will they not *without exception* embrace their Creator in a way that the multitudes of reprobates *without exception* will not?)

Again, forgive the directness, but do robots *love?* Despite Calvinism's understandable insistence that predestined man is *not* a robot, the fact remains that, for the elect, what love they have for God is a forgone conclusion determined by God himself, not man. Is there any difference between Calvinism's "irresistible grace" and "a person loving God because *not* loving is not allowed"? What kind of "love" are we talking about where, ultimately, there is no choice or option to do otherwise? Since when was love ever involuntary? (Don't forget that it is the sovereign God, not man, who is the moving force behind every act, event, thought, and motive.)

For that matter, what kind of "love" are we talking about even on God's part? I've just finished reading a passage in a well-respected book supporting Calvinism, and there's lots of talk about love. Those whom God foreknew and predestined, says the author, were the objects of God's love. They were not just foreknown, but "foreloved." (As when God says of Israel: "You only have I known," Amos 3:2.)

Maybe, but have you no questions in your own mind about a God who saves those he "foreloves" from a condemnation which he himself has thrust upon them for their depraved rebellion...of which he, as the all-predestining Sovereign, must necessarily be the cause? And do you not wonder what kind of "love" God supposedly has for the non-elect, when he arbitrarily chooses not to "forelove" them as he does the elect?

No one puts this irresolvable moral dilemma more crisply into perspective than Ken Keathley, who observes that "Augustinians, Calvinists, Arminians, and all other orthodox Christians agree that the lost are lost because of their own sin. But that is not the question at hand. The question is not 'Why are the lost lost?' but 'Why aren't the lost saved?' The nasty, awful, deep-dark-dirty-little-secret of Calvinism is that it teaches there is one and only one answer to the second question, and it is that God does not want them saved."[40]

If there is anything of which we can be sure, it is that God is love. Indeed, "God so loved the world that he gave his one and only Son, that whoever believes in him shall not perish but have eternal life" (John 3:16). For Calvinists to argue with equal vigor that God loves all but has no plan of salvation for all reduces this powerful, poignant passage to empty rhetoric.

To accept the obvious import of John 3:16 is to acknowledge that we are called to reciprocate in kind. In the face of so great a love, the command "Love the Lord your God with all your heart and with all your soul and with all your mind and with all your strength" (Mark 12:30) is by no means burdensome. Indeed, it is "the other side" of the universal story of love. "We love because he first loved us" (1 John 4:19).[41]

Of course, there is no dissent here from Calvinists, only the (huge) qualification that such love can only come from those who have been specially regenerated from their natural state of unloving depravity. And the further (huge) assumption that these regenerate elect will follow the precise course of loving God because that is what they have been predestined from eternity to do.

Are we to believe that this greatest of all commands–to love God–is directed only at those fortunate enough to be among the regenerate elect? (Was the Bible written only for them?) And how by any stretch of the imagination could God be said to love *us* if he gives us no real choice over our loving him in return?

What, after all, gives love its unique passion if not the ever-present potential of *not* being loved? Of being rejected, refused, and disappointed? Of being hurt so intensely by unrequited love? Is it not the painful prospect of being unloved by the object of one's affection that makes the decision to love so special?

---

[40] Ken Keathley, Associate Professor of Theology, New Orleans Baptist Theological Seminary, in his unpublished paper *"Salvation and the Sovereignty of God: The Great Commission as the Expression of the Divine Will."*

[41] Turning this elegant passage of reciprocal love into a proof-text for unconditional election and irresistible grace betrays Calvinism's vain attempts to make a distinction between wooing and compelling.

In tennis and golf, we often hear it said: "It's all in the wrist." When it comes to love, I suggest it's all in the *risk*. God himself had a choice. Either he could create us as automatons, pre-programmed to "love" him (like a child's doll which, at the pull of a string or touch of a button, says coldly: "I love you"). Or he could create us after his own image, having the real, unbiased, un-programmed, un-fudged choice either to love him or reject him. No risk would have been associated with the former. But with the latter, genuine high-stakes risk lay in store.

As with everyone who's ever taken the risk of falling in love only to end up with a broken heart, God took the risk of creating humans who were capable of not loving him in return. He took a risk, for example, that his chosen and beloved bride, the nation of Israel, might run after other lovers, which she did over and over again. And that man might worship uncaring, lifeless idols of all sorts rather than the living, loving Creator himself. For that matter, he took a risk that Charles Darwin would conclude that the universe didn't really need a God after all, thank you very much.

Closer to our immediate concern, God took the risk that man might just be foolish enough to imagine that somehow he could merit eternal life through feeble human effort. And he even took the risk that, reacting against such foolishness, others might insist that man doesn't have the capacity to love unless specially chosen and regenerated to do so. (And, given foreordained predestination, that simply has to read: *pre-programmed* to do so.)

Says Screwtape to Wormwood, "The Enemy takes this risk because He has a curious fantasy of making all these disgusting little human vermin into what He calls 'free' lovers and servants—'sons' is the word he uses, with His inveterate love of degrading the whole spiritual world by unnatural liaisons with the two-legged animals. Desiring their freedom, He therefore refuses to carry them, by their mere affections and habits, to any of the goals which he sets before them."[42]

This amazing risk of love is the very answer to Calvinism's debate-portfolio argument that God would have been foolish indeed to create creatures who, as he could foresee from eternity, would reject him. If to

---

[42] C.S. Lewis, *The Screwtape Letters* (London: Harper Collins Publishers, 1942, 2002), 7

create man with unrestrained free will portended such great potential for rejection rather than love, was it worth the risk? Considering the unsatisfying alternative of no real love at all, God must surely have thought so. Had *you* been God, which option would you have chosen?[43]

In fact, if you are a parent, which kind of offspring have you, yourself, created? Ever had a petulant child shout to you in anger, "I hate you!"? Would it have been worth creating the little darling without the ability to say such hurtful things if the alternative were knowing it is only a pre-programed response when your doting child says, "I love you"?

Lest we think for a moment that the risk to God wasn't real, we can almost feel the pain of God's broken heart when (striking a death-blow to Calvinism's unilateral version of predestination) he cries in anguish at Israel's rejection: "I thought you would call me 'Father'..." (Jeremiah 3:19).[44] There is also God's agonizing plea: "Why will you die, O house of Israel? For I take no pleasure in the death of anyone, declares the Sovereign LORD. Repent and live!" (Ezekiel 18:31-32; 33:11). And then there is God's steadfast love in the face of Israel's rejection: "All day long I have held out my hands to an obstinate people" (Isaiah 65:2).

Finally, there's that poignant lament of Jesus himself: "O Jerusalem, Jerusalem...how often I have longed to gather your children together, as a hen gathers her chicks under her wings, but you were not willing" (Matthew 23:37).[45] "Not willing"? You mean, constitutionally *unable* to

---

[43] Along with other proponents of "Open Theism," John Sanders argues in his book, *The God Who Risks*, that God cannot possibly be "risking" anything if, in fact, he has divine foreknowledge of all future outcomes. What risk is there, one might ask, if an investor exhaustively knows what the stock market will do in the future? The difference is that man is prompted to invest almost exclusively out of a desire for gain, whereas God was pleased to invest in his creatures, regardless of the outcome. As any spurned lover will testify, rational investing on Wall Street doesn't even come close to investing one's love in the heart of another long past the time when the lostness of the cause is fully known. In matters of the heart, the risk is not in the knowable outcome, but in the pain of its reality. What could be better proof than that God repeatedly predicted the unfaithfulness of his chosen bride, Israel, yet time and again risked the pain of that very rejection?

[44] See also Deuteronomy 5:29

[45] When Calvinists argue that Jesus' words were addressed to *God's people* (analogous to Christians, not the unregenerate), what does this say but that *God's people* are capable of thwarting God's intent?

will, lacking regeneration by the Spirit? Not a chance! Undoubtedly *able*, but *just not willing*.[46]

Have you ever had a broken heart from being rejected by someone you loved? I have. Maybe that's why I'm deeply suspicious of any doctrinal system which depends for its survival on a 180-degree, Alice-in-Wonderland redefinition of commonly understood words like "love," "gift," "trust," "faith," and "free will."[47]

What about you? When you think of "free will," do the words *predetermined*, *irresistible*, and *foreordained* naturally come to mind?

When you think of "love," is *predestined love* the first thing you think about?

And when you think of the word "gift," does it suggest something you cannot help but accept?

Showing the balance between divine power and human response, David best captures the essence of God's love in the lyrics of this song of Israel...

> *One thing God has spoken,*
> *two things have I heard:*
> *that you, O God, are strong,*
> *and that you, O Lord, are loving.*
> *Surely you will reward each person*
> *according to what he has done.*
>
> *(Psalm 62:11-12)*

---

[46] Along with other Calvinists, James White argues that Jesus' words are exclusively directed to the Jewish leaders, with the idea that "Jesus was not seeking to gather the leaders, but their children....The 'children' of the leaders would be Jews who were *hindered* by the Jewish leaders from hearing Christ." [See White, *The Potter's Freedom* (Amityville, NY: Calvary Press Publishing, 2000), 138.] (Are Calvinists really suggesting that the Jewish leaders were preventing Jesus from saving any and all his elect from among Jerusalem's "children"?)

What this view overlooks is that, throughout Israel's history, it was not just the leaders of the Jews who rejected and stoned the prophets, anymore than it was solely the Jewish leaders who demanded Jesus' crucifixion. Nor is it the case that *all* of the Jewish leaders, whether throughout time or at that very time, rejected God. (Witness, for example, Nicodemus and Joseph of Arimathea.) Nor, certainly, that *all* the "children" of Jerusalem in Jesus' own day rejected him. Yet clearly there was sufficient willful rejection on all sides for Jesus to lament.

Note also that references to "Jerusalem"(other than as a city itself) refer symbolically to the whole of Israel, not simply its leaders. See, for example, 1 Kings 11:13; 2 Kings 19:30-31; 21:7-15; 23:26-27; 1 Chronicles 6:15; 2 Chronicles 20:20; 24:17-21; Isaiah 4:4; 8:13-14; 40:1-9; Jeremiah 4:11-14; 8:5-6; 15:5-7; Luke 2:38.

[47] See Martin Luther, *Bondage of the Will*, 125. "Free-will is an empty term, whose reality is lost. And a lost liberty, according to my grammar, is no liberty at all." (Cited also in Boettner, 62)

Mind the Gap!

In the evolution of Calvinism's mutant *TULIP*, man's inborn, Creator-gifted but never-dictated *free will to love* will always remain the vital missing link. That you and I have the built-in, unfettered, and unmanipulated capacity to respond to God's overtures of love without either "working our way to heaven" or presuming to merit our own salvation is the carefully-guarded, top-secret fallacy of Calvinism's seductive theory. It is the yawning gap; the stubborn, uncooperative truth that won't run away; the Achilles heel of Calvinism.

For if you and I have the innate ability to freely love—with no predetermined outcomes that either force the heart to love or forbid any yearning for love—then we have the tandem ability to choose or reject the God who created us.

And because we have the inborn, unrigged, non-orchestrated, ability to freely choose, then...

We are not so totally depraved that we cannot volitionally choose to seek the lovable and shun the unlovable.

Our election is not unconditional, but wholly dependent upon whether we choose to reach out and embrace the one who woos us.

The saving effect of Christ's atoning blood, instead of being limited arbitrarily to a pre-select number, is the ultimate expression of God's universal love to any and all who would choose to accept it.

Far from being "irresistible" in the uninvited, determining sense that Calvinism uses the term, God's grace is all the more wondrously irresistible for knowing that he loved us enough to risk the possibility that we might choose to break his heart.

And, although fraught with the direst of potential consequences, nothing prevents us from turning our backs upon a love we have once declared but no longer desire—least of all the One who, having given us that freedom, would feel the pain of separation most deeply.

And we have seen and testify that the Father has sent his Son to be the Savior of the world. If anyone acknowledges that Jesus is the Son of God, God lives in him and he in God. And so we know and rely on the love God has for us. God is love. Whoever lives in love lives in God, and God in him.

1 John 4:14-16

Chapter Summary

- The second primary assumption underlying Calvinism–that man can have no part in his salvation without invalidating God's grace–is a well-intentioned but false assumption.

- A free gift is no less free simply because conditions are attached to its receipt.

- Being in control of one's faith is not the same as having control over one's own salvation.

- When it is God himself laying down the terms and conditions whereby his grace will be dispensed, his sovereignty is not even remotely threatened.

- The Achilles heel of Calvinism is man's inborn, Creator-gifted but never-dictated freedom to choose whether to love God in return.

- Since Calvinism is based directly and dependently upon a fundamentally false assumption, the whole system fails.

Reality Check: If in fact God determined your eternal destiny before the beginning of time, in the end it doesn't matter whether "free will" is given its usual meaning or permitted to be redefined by Calvinism. Since God's will alone has already decided whether you will end up in heaven or hell, you must accept that you have no choice either way.

Chapter 3

Total Depravity, Original Sin, and The Fall

There is laid in the very nature of carnal men,
a foundation for the torments of hell.
There are those corrupt principles, in reigning power in them,
and in full possession of them, that are seeds of hell fire.

—Jonathan Edwards

How many times have you watched those gripping reruns of the Kennedy assassination? With all the conspiracy theories floating around, there seems to be no end to the fascination surrounding the number of shots fired along the grassy knoll in Dallas on that tragic day, November 22, 1963. So it is that in program after program we've watched the whole awful ordeal replayed over and over, frame by frame.

Of course, the actual home-movie films shown in those programs are now technologically out of date. It's all video these days, and computerized this and digital that. Even so, today's modern video tapes are often run in stop-action slow motion, searching for the minutest clues to crimes, or perhaps seeking just the right angle on a disputed play in sports. If you don't slow down the action and take a close look frame by frame, the blur of events can be altogether misleading.

In fact, that's what so fascinating about the old-style, celluloid film itself. It was never really anything but a series of individual snapshots joined together and run at sufficient speed that a visual and mental *trompe l'oeil* filled in the gaps, making us believe we were watching movement and action.

We spoke earlier of Evolution. As long as proponents of the theory throw millions and billions of years at us, almost any hypothesis they propose seems plausible. The standard text-book answer to any pesky problem is to bedazzle us with infinite amounts of time. But suppose we had a film or video of the entire sweeping history of the cosmos. What might we see if, instead of millions and billions of years blurring by at Mach speed, we took it frame by frame in stop-action slow motion? For myself, the "grassy knoll" I would want most to scrutinize is the one where evolution supposedly moved from asexual beings to sexual beings. Even Darwin was stumped on this one, and there haven't been any satisfying explanations since.

For the Theory of Evolution to work, at some point in time asexual organisms would have to be altered dramatically so as to be constitutionally different organisms. The problem is that, in order to make such an extraordinary leap, two asexual beings, acting independently, must have developed highly complex sexual organs within a single generation. (Otherwise, how could they possibly have replicated themselves sexually, as opposed to asexually, for the next generation?) And, of course, it would have required simultaneous development of both male and female sexual organs....in two beings who just happened to be in the same spot on the planet at exactly the same time...who also just happened to be madly attracted to each other! It's not the missing link between man and apes evolutionists need to worry about most, but the missing *sex link*.

In similar fashion, there is a sense in which Calvinism is also run by us at blurring speed. At first glance, the eye hardly notices the details. It's only when you slow down this fast-moving belief system and examine it carefully, frame by frame, that you begin to see how many crucial questions typically remain unasked.

What follows in this chapter is the controversial tape of Calvinism played in stop-action slow motion. Of the scores of questions which could be asked, the first fifteen which follow are designed to take the three separate ideas of "original sin," "total depravity," and "the Fall" frame by frame, as if in stop-action slow motion.[48] Like the missing sex link, there is much to think about in the course of just one generation, moving from Adam and Eve to their immediate offspring.

What Fell in "the Fall"?

1. What do you think? Were Adam and Eve free moral beings, fully able to decide between obeying and disobeying God without any predetermined secret eternal will of God preempting their freedom to choose right from wrong?

   a) If not, is there any way that God himself is not responsible for their sin and "the Fall"?

   b) If so, were they simply exceptions to an otherwise universal rule of predestination and sovereign causation?

2. Were Adam and Eve either totally or partially depraved before "the Fall"?

3. What about immediately *after* "the Fall"?

4. By virtue of their created nature as human beings, were Adam and Eve:

   a) innately inclined more toward evil than good; or

   b) innately inclined more toward good than evil; or

   c) simply given a neutral capacity for moral choice between good and evil?

---

[48] Calvinists often speak as if *original sin* and *total depravity* are but a single, unified concept. At other times, the two terms are employed separately, with *original sin* typically referring to the judicial sentence of condemnation under which, supposedly, each of us is born; and *total depravity* referring to an ongoing state of spiritual rebellion whereby we are constitutionally unable to respond to God. Because those distinct concepts require separate consideration, for the most part you will find the two terms distinguished accordingly throughout the book.

5. Were Cain and Abel (and, more crucially, are *we ourselves*) "constitution-ally different" from Adam and Eve in respect to any innate inclination to sin? If so, in what way?[49]

6. Is there anything in the Genesis account or in the whole of Scripture specifically stating that some "constitutional change" in human nature took place between the first *created* generation and the first *procreated* generation? (We're not talking here about any imputed sin, but a fundamental difference in human nature itself.)

7. Is there any passage suggesting that Adam and Eve, themselves, were "constitutionally different" once expelled from the Garden?

8. If you believe they were inclined toward good before "the Fall," or created morally neutral, do you believe that as they left the Garden they were from then on inclined toward evil?

9. If the so-called "Fall" (replete with its assumed implications regarding original sin, depravity, and the lack of free will) is the supposed cause of *our* sins, what explains Adam and Eve's sin *prior to* "the Fall" when (presumably) they had free will unfettered by either original sin or depravity?

10. Was "the Fall" predestined by God's eternal secret will in order that mankind would be innately depraved and sinful for whatever purpose God intends? Or did "the Fall" occur without God's foreknowledge and foreordination?

11. In the "penalty clause" of Genesis 3:16-19, we are given the specific consequences of Adam and Eve's sin, including the woman's pain in childbirth and the man's having to earn his living by the sweat of his brow. Why do you suppose there is no mention in this passage that

---

[49] In Genesis 5:1-3, we are reminded that "man" (male and female) was created in the likeness of God, and then that Adam "had a son in his own likeness, in his own image," namely Seth. Unless one insinuates a change in constitutional nature which Scripture does not mention here (at the very point when it would send the clearest possible signal), the message is obvious. Seth was of the very same constitutional nature as was his father Adam, whose constitutional nature was fashioned in the image and likeness of God. And so on down the line the same constitutional nature continued from father to son for all generations, even (regarding his human nature) to Jesus of Nazareth, "the son, so it was thought, of Joseph...the son of David...the son of Noah...the son of Seth, the son of Adam, the son of God" (Luke 3:23-38). If man's nature was constitutionally changed in Seth, why in Genesis 9:6 are we told (even post-"Fall") that "in the image of God has God made man"?

everyone born from that point forward would be condemned from the moment of conception?

12. Accepting that by the "curse of Adam" mankind was reduced to struggle and pain in a way never experienced in the Garden, is there anything in Scripture necessarily implying that mankind thereafter was innately more inclined toward evil or sin?[50]

13. Even granting that ejection from the Garden put distance between God and man as compared with the close communion Adam and Eve had shared with him, is there anything in Scripture suggesting that a fundamental change in the human constitution also resulted?[51]

14. Acknowledging the obvious, that Adam's sin introduced condemnation for sin into the world for the first time, is there anything in this fact which necessarily implies that each and every person in Adam's loins would thereafter be born *innately* condemned? Is there any reason that sin's condemnation could not apply, instead, to each person's own sins, just as with Adam?

15. In Genesis 4:6-7, God says to Cain: "If you do what is right, will you not be accepted? But if you do not do what is right, sin is crouching at your door; it desires to have you, but you must master it." Was Cain's ability to do right and to master sin limited in any way either by God's eternal secret will or by some effect of "the Fall"? If you believe that Cain's ability to do right would have required a prior act of regeneration, what biblical passage indicates that?

---

[50] If there is any passage which might appear to support man's inclination toward evil, it is Genesis 8:21, where God vows: "Never again will I curse the ground because of man, even though every inclination of his heart is evil from childhood." But taking those words literally becomes problematic in the face of Noah's having been found righteous. More problematic yet is the follow-up verse in Genesis 9:6 that even post-"Fall" man is made in the image of God. Given those difficulties, the jury must await further evidence before rendering its final verdict.

[51] To reply with Jeremiah 17:9 ("The heart is deceitful above all things and beyond cure.") does not rule out Adam and Eve themselves, whose sin was a response to deceit; and further suggests what no Calvinist would affirm—that such a supposed sin nature is "beyond cure."

Not Just a Fall, But a Leap!

A quite amazing thing happens when Calvinists play that same "slow motion tape" at high speed. The result is perhaps best illustrated in a passage from Loraine Boettner, who begins with a quotation from another Calvinist author, then continues in his own words. Can you spot the giant leaps?

> *"When...[Adam] used his free will to respond to the claims of the creature in defiance of the Creator, no excuse can be found for his fall. His act, in reality, was wilful, defiant rebellion, and by it he openly transferred his allegiance from God to Satan."*[52]
>
> *And has there not been a fall—a fearful fall? The more we see of human nature as it is manifested in the world about us, the easier it is to believe in this great doctrine of original sin....Is not man now, as his progenitor Adam, fleeing from the presence of God, not wanting communion with Him, and with enmity in his heart for his Creator? Surely man's nature is radically wrong....And the only adequate explanation of all this is that the penalty of death, which was threatened on man before the fall, now rests on the human race.*[53]

What we see in the opening frame is that, as the first human prototype, Adam acted completely and totally out of free will. (Note that there appears to be no threat to God's eternal, all-purposing sovereignty, despite the fact that Adam has genuine, unfudged, undetermined free will. Nor is there any hint at all that his moral choices are already dictated by any foreordination which might preclude him from acting either way regarding the forbidden fruit.)

It is equally clear that there was no need for some special regenerative power to "switch on" Adam's ability to obey God's commands. As a free moral agent created in the image of God, Adam had that built-in ability, which (absent any evidence to the contrary) he surely retained to his dying day.

---

[52] Warburton, *Calvinism*, 34

[53] Boettner, 74. (Nothing I've edited out for brevity provides any bridges for the gaps.)

As everyone agrees, prior to Adam's sin there was no "Fall," no "original sin," and no "depravity." Then suddenly the tape starts whirring and there is talk, not simply of Adam's own personal fall, but "*the Fall*" of the entire human race.

As Calvinists (and others) tell us, the primary practical consequence of "the Fall" is that you and I were automatically doomed to have a different constitutional nature from our forefather, Adam. Unlike our totally free-willed progenitor, we no longer have the built-in ability to respond affirmatively to God's commands. Adam's sin "switched off" that ability, if not in himself, certainly in all mankind who would flow from his loins. From that point forward, it would take a special act of "flipping the switch back on again" for us to regain that ability. (No fair peeking, but we'll find out soon enough that, according to Calvinists, God does this for some folks, but not for others.)[54]

Just as quickly, we next see a leap from that supposed universal Fall to the hurriedly introduced notions of "original sin" and a "nature that is radically wrong" (read: total depravity). Unlike Adam and Eve, who came into the world with a clean slate both morally and spiritually, you and I supposedly come into the world already spiritually condemned and subject to God's wrath. Despite our having done nothing personally to commit or deserve this "original sin," judgment for sin is vicariously imputed to us at the very moment the sperm and the egg join in our conception.[55]

Also as a result of Adam's sin, so we are told, you and I cannot help but rebel against God's commands. What's more, we *love* our innate state of rebellion. It's in our nature to sin. In our genes to hate God. In our souls to despise all good unless it somehow furthers our own perverted

---

[54] Some non-Calvinists, in particular, would argue that man's nature was not changed *constitutionally* but rather *situationally or conditionally*. After "the Fall," so it is said, man still had an innate freedom of will, but it was severely limited in scope and in need of being re-enabled in order to respond in faith to God's call. Two immediate problems arise with this position: the first being that it is not consistent with our being made in the image of God (more on this to come); the second being that any "situational" or "conditional" change this drastic amounts virtually to the same thing as a "constitutional" change.

[55] I am aware that Calvinists (and many non-Calvinists) insist that, in Adam, we *all* sinned. As will be more fully discussed, however, this is possible only in theory. As a factual matter, neither you nor I (being yet unborn) could possibly have been guilty of *personal* sin at the moment Adam sinned in the garden.

self-interest. And make no mistake, this so-called "total depravity" was destined to be our nature before we were ever born. Nothing to do with us. All to do with Adam and God.

With confident assurance, we are then told that the "only adequate explanation" for man's ongoing spiritual rebellion is the death penalty which was imposed in the wake of Adam's sin–the penalty of original sin twinned with total depravity.

At least this is *one* version of the story. The other (wholly contradictory) version is that *all of mankind*, not just Adam, has joined in rebellion to God, apparently through a kind of representative democracy in which Adam–as our "Federal Head"–cast the deciding vote on our behalf. Because "we" blew our once-in-an-eternity opportunity to freely do right, all of us end up deserving God's wrath. And, for that, we have no one to blame but ourselves.

A good illustration of this particular version is provided by R.C. Sproul [with my emphasis]. "Prior to the fall," says Sproul, "*we* also had a good inclination, enabling *us* to choose the good. It is precisely this inclination to the good that was lost in the fall."[56]

We? The leap from Adam and Eve (*they*) to you and me *(we)* is one spectacular leap! Has someone forgotten a most important distinction? *They* lived prior to "the Fall," not *we*.

When there is a need to demonstrate God's absolute, foreordaining sovereignty, the tape of the first version is played for us, showing God's judicial penalty on all mankind. Yet, whenever there is a need to explain how our inborn condemnation justly can be deserved, then the second version is played, showing man's universal rebellion. (I have yet to read a Calvinist author who doesn't eventually play both tapes.)

But did you notice the most incredible part of Boettner's high-speed playback? Says Boettner (citing the usual evils chronicled in any morning newspaper): Man today has enmity toward his Creator, *just like his progenitor, Adam*! You mean, just like the prototype human being whose sin was as an act of genuine, unfudged free will? Just like the man who openly and intentionally rebelled against God *before* "the Fall," *before* original sin, and

---

[56] Sproul, 135

before anything that might remotely be called total depravity? And *prior to* any spiritual penalty whatsoever being imposed?

If that scenario is what we are talking about, then I couldn't agree more. Yet, if you and I today sin just as Adam and Eve did (and *don't we?*), of what possible relevance would be "the Fall," original sin, and total depravity...except to facilitate stripping man of genuine, Adam-like free will by radically altering the innate, constitutional nature of Adam's descendants?

But if Calvinism is right, it could hardly be said that you and I sin volitionally in anything like the same way as Adam and Eve. Encumbered with innate depravity, and thereby lacking the genuine free will of that first couple, how could we?

Then again, what would the disappearance of human free will leave as an explanation for why we sin? Calvinism's answer is as simplistic as it is simple: Adam and Eve were sinners because they sinned; they didn't sin because they were innately sinful. By contrast, you and I are not sinful because we sin; we sin because we are innately sinful.

Don't let the catchy symmetry fool you. In between those two elegant sentences lies a vast wasteland of supposition, theory, and conjecture—not solid teaching from the Word of God.

And don't forget that, in the end, the sequence of causation either way matters not in the least. By Calvinist theory, our eternal destinies were determined long before we either 1) came into the world condemned with sin, or 2) freely took it upon ourselves to sin. Neither "the Fall," nor original sin, nor total depravity has anything to do with the final outcome. Your eternal destiny and mine was a done deal before Adam was ever formed from the dust of the ground, or ever first took sight of the forbidden fruit.

Adam, Christ, and "Original Sin"

By now you may well be thinking that I must surely have more than my fair share of chutzpah to challenge, not just Calvinism, but virtually the whole of Western tradition, which accepts that all human beings born since Adam are in some way negatively affected by an inborn sinful nature.

Certainly, I am not unaware of such a daunting uphill climb. For this very reason, what I might have hoped to address in a single chapter has required no less than three. Beyond even that, I'm convinced that this complex issue is the epicenter of the entire discussion. So bear with me, if you will, while I present a perspective that may be somewhat unfamiliar (even completely wrong from your viewpoint) but will serve at the very least to raise the crucial issues all of us must think long and hard about.

If there is any single proof text that is argued by Calvinists and others as the tap root for the doctrine of "original sin," it is Romans 5:12-21, where Paul tells us that "sin entered the world through one man," and that "as the result of one trespass was condemnation for all men."[57]

It would not be overstating the case to say that this text lies at the very heart of the controversy surrounding Calvinism. For if man is born into the world with a clean slate, then he alone is personally responsible for the guilt of his sin. But if man is born into the world already burdened with the vicarious guilt of sin hanging over him, then he is patently *not* responsible for his spiritual condemnation, leaving only God–the Imputer of original sin–as the responsible party. (Which, for Calvinists, is accompanied by unconditional election, irresistible grace, and limited atonement.)

I am aware that both Calvinists and non-Calvinists who accept the doctrine of original sin generally deny that your "original sin" and mine is vicarious. (What's that famous little line–"In Adam's fall, we sinned all"?) The problem is that when Adam sinned, you and I weren't even a gleam in our parents' eyes, nor they in theirs. So, just exactly which sin or sins did *we* commit when Adam fell? (Is there such a thing as generic sin of which we are guilty through no fault of our own?)

Whether we're speaking theoretically or practically, the fact is that any sin which came in and through Adam would have to be *attributed* or *imputed*, because it is factually and logically impossible for it to have been either *actual* or *personal*. Which can only mean that we were vicariously condemned with sin at the point of Adam's fall.

---

[57] It should not go unnoticed that any number of Reformed exegetes acknowledge that this passage does not teach the doctrine of original sin *per se*. (See, for example, Douglas Moo's commentary on Romans or Henri Blocher's book, *Original Sin*.)

It's not difficult to see how one might easily conclude from what Paul says in this challenging passage that mankind's condemnation is the result of Adam's sin. Just look, for example, at those words which seem so clear on their face: "If the many died by the trespass of the one man...." Yet if Paul's reference to *the many* in this first half of the sentence means that *all men* have died spiritually in Adam, then logic likewise dictates that *all men* must actually and factually have received the gift of grace through Christ which "overflows to *the many*."[58] To say the least, the notion of universal justification does not sit comfortably with Calvinism's prized tenets of particular election and limited atonement.

The same problem arises again in verse 19: "For just as through the disobedience of the one man *the many* were made sinners, so also through the obedience of the one man *the many* will be made righteous." As before, anyone arguing from this verse that universal condemnation comes through Adam is bound by that same logic to accept universal justification through Christ. Yet, the last thing Calvinism stands for is unlimited atonement or universal justification, nor certainly universalism.[59]

In fairness, of course, Paul's parallelism is also a challenge for those of us who see it the other way around. If we claim that the grace of Christ's atonement for "the many" is universal, we are forced to explain what seems to be an equally undeniable universalism in "the many" dying of Adam's trespass.

Toward that end, I suggest, first of all, that Paul is referring to mankind's *shared sin experience* with Adam, rather than Adam's sin being the *operative cause* of mankind's universal condemnation. Take, for instance,

---

[58] In support of limited atonement, Calvinists often cite Matthew 20:28 (the Son of Man came "to give his life as a ransom for many"), arguing that in Scripture the word "many" never means "all." (See, e.g., White, *Debating,* p. 176.) Yet were that same logic applied to Romans 5:15-19, it would demolish the Calvinist argument that we are to understand Paul's use of "many" as meaning that *all mankind* was condemned by Adam's trespass.

[59] Often lost in the shadow of John 3:16 is its flip-side, John 3:18, which puts faith or no faith at the heart of one's condemnation: "Whoever believes in him is not condemned, but whoever does not believe stands condemned already because he has not believed in the name of God's one and only Son."

The suggestion by those who espouse "biblical universalism" that this verse implies a pre-Creation universal election of all except those who reject Christ ignores both the parallelism here with verse 16, and also the parallelism in Mark 16:16.

Paul's statement that "judgment followed one sin and brought condemnation." That indisputable fact says nothing about whether you and I were innately born in sin because of Adam—only that his sin paved the way for the condemnation of all subsequent sin, just as Christ's righteousness paved the way for the justification of sin.

The same goes for the penalty of spiritual death which first entered the world as a result of Adam's sin. As we shall see presently, the penalty of spiritual death for Adam's sin by no means rules out the personal penalty of spiritual death which you and I incur for our own sins.

Are We Talking About Physical or Spiritual Death?

Part of our confusion in this regard undoubtedly comes from our uncritical association between *spiritual* death (condemnation) and the *physical, biological* death of our bodies. Here in Romans 5, Paul is making an obvious comparison between *spiritual* death and *spiritual* life—the first being represented by Adam, the second by Christ. (As in Romans 6:23: "The wages of sin is death.") Adam himself died spiritually the moment he disobeyed God, long before he died physically. So there are two kinds of deaths to think about, which we confuse at our peril.

When Paul turns to the subject of the Resurrection in 1 Corinthians 15, Adam and Christ again become the representative figures, but this time Paul is comparing *physical, biological death* with the *resurrection of the dead*.

> *But Christ has indeed been raised from the dead, the firstfruits of those who have fallen asleep. For since death came through a man, the resurrection of the dead comes also through a man. For as in Adam all die, so in Christ all will be made alive. (15:20-22)*

The death of which Paul speaks here as "coming through a man" was the death which Adam experienced at the age of 930, and the same death which you and I will experience as we too are laid to rest, should the Lord tarry. But unlike in Romans 5, Paul's comparison of this *physical* death is with Christ's own bodily resurrection, and eventually our own.

Read this text with wooden literalness, and we might be tempted to think that Paul intends to prove a causal link between Adam's physical death and our own physical death ("Since death came through a man" and "For as in Adam, all die....") But even apart from the problematic detail that Adam was not the first person to die physically (since presumably the murdered Abel was long dead by then), causation is simply not Paul's point. Speaking in response to those who were denying the Resurrection, Paul argues that just as surely as all of us will die as did Adam, so too all of us shall be resurrected (made alive) as was Christ.

Exquisitely as always, Paul extends his argument even further to the nature of the resurrected body, making yet another comparison between Adam and Christ who represent radically different models—the earthly and the heavenly:

> *If there is a natural body, there is also a spiritual body. So it is written: "The first man Adam became a living being"; the last Adam, a life-giving spirit. The spiritual did not come first, but the natural, and after that the spiritual. The first man was of the dust of the earth, the second man from heaven. As was the earthly man, so are those who are of the earth; and as is the man from heaven, so also are those who are of heaven. And just as we have borne the likeness of the earthly man, so shall we bear the likeness of the man from heaven. (1 Corinthians 15:44-49)*

As is demonstrated so well here in 1 Corinthians 15, Paul makes illustrative comparisons between Adam and Christ which have nothing whatever to do with causation, only with similarity of experience. So as we turn back to Romans 5, it's important to keep in mind the critical distinction between *shared experience* and *operative cause*.

Whereas the former suggests a *solidarity of sinfulness* between Adam and all subsequent generations, the latter assumes an altogether different *heredity of sinfulness*. The divergent implications flowing from these two conflicting assumptions cannot help but have a heavy impact on one's understanding of the gospel.[60]

---

[60] When I speak of our *shared experience* with Adam, I'm suggesting far more than simply that Adam set a "bad example" for the rest of us. We do not *mimic* his groundbreaking sin, as if "monkey see, monkey do." Rather, we join in a solidarity of experience with Adam, each in our own way sinning together *with him.*

Adam and Christ As Comparative Prototypes

As we begin to work our way through this thorny passage, perhaps the first thing we need to consider is why Paul focuses on *Adam*, and not on *Adam and Eve* (or simply *Eve*). Momentarily putting aside some subtle considerations about a breach of male spiritual leadership on Adam's part, wasn't it Eve who first ate the forbidden fruit and thus, arguably, was the actual person through whom sin entered the world?[61] Does it not make sense, then, that Paul is not speaking specifically about either Adam *or* Eve, but more generally about the judgment of spiritual death which necessarily attaches to sin—a principle having its first application with Adam and Eve?[62]

An equally intriguing question brings us to our second consideration. What do you suppose would have happened if Adam (and Eve) had not sinned? Would there have been any condemnation for sin in the world? Surely not, unless, of course, someone else thereafter succumbed to sin. But to say that factually, historically, and chronologically, condemnation for sin entered the world for the first time through Adam and Eve simply doesn't get us very far. We don't seem to be any better off regarding how their inaugural condemnation relates to our own spiritual condemnation.

We come, then, to the tightly-focused interplay between Adam (without Eve) and Christ. With a straight face, Paul tells us that Adam was "a pattern of the one to come," undoubtedly referring to Christ. But how can that be? Is Paul really saying that Adam, *the sinner*, was a pattern of Christ, *the Savior*? Actually, yes, in the sense that both were prototypes: Adam being the prototype sinner while Christ was the prototype of righteousness.[63]

Think of them both as icons on a computer screen. Double-click on *Adam*, and the screen displays everything you need to know about the *problem* of sin. Double-click on *Christ*, and the screen displays everything you need to know about the *solution* for sin. In the case of Christ, moreover, there is not simply a visual display of some inanimate "solution," but The Solution himself.

---

[61] See 1 Timothy 2:13.

[62] The Calvinist idea that Adam was the "Federal Head" of all mankind, acting on behalf of every person who has ever lived, is a concept drawn from thin air. Not a single passage in all of Scripture even remotely hints at such a spurious representative role.

[63] Only by resort to the doctrine of immaculate conception could one argue that—out of all mankind—Adam (and Eve) and Jesus (and perhaps Mary) were patterned alike as having been uniquely created or born without sin.

To continue the computer analogy, clicking on *Adam* identifies the problem of sin in need of deletion, whereas clicking on *Christ* actually does the deleting. ("Are you sure you want to delete?" Yes!)

In order, therefore, to achieve a more uniform, one-to-one parallel between the principle of *sin and death* and the principle of *justification and life,* Paul side-steps Eve and presents Adam as *the man* initially embodying the first principle, and Christ as *the man* uniquely embodying the second principle.

Scrutinizing the Key Verse

We come, then, to the key verse–Romans 5:12. Though Paul's thought breaks off awkwardly at the end of the verse, importantly he begins his argument saying: *"Therefore, just as sin entered the world through one man, and death through sin, and in this way death came to all men, because all sinned–"* (Shortly, we'll pick up on what follows this abrupt ending.)

I say "key verse," because I suggest that only by understanding this verse correctly can we unlock the meaning of the larger passage. Everything which follows this opening verse builds upon the foundation it has already laid. Having said it once, Paul doesn't repeat himself. Once assumed, the underlying truth remains assumed.

And just what is Paul's cornerstone assumption? We find it in the crucial three words which conclude verse 12: "...*because all sinned....*" Apart from "In the beginning," and "God is love," and "Jesus is Lord," one would be hard-pressed to find another set of three words more important in all the Bible than "*because all sinned.*" In light of those three words, especially, it is imperative that we understand not only what Paul is saying here, but, more importantly, what he is *not* saying. It seems abundantly clear that...

<u>What Paul *says* is that</u>
>Death came to Adam because of his sin.
>And in the exact same way, death comes to all men, because all have sinned.

<u>What Paul does *not* say is that</u>
>Death came to Adam because of his sin.
>And therefore death comes to all men because of Adam's sin.

Do you agree? Just to be sure, here's the verse one more time. *"Therefore, just as sin entered the world through one man, and death through sin, and in this way death came to all men, because all sinned...."*

Is there anything here that forces us to the conclusion that subsequent generations have vicariously *inherited* Adam's sin as opposed to (each in his own way) personally *experiencing* it? Or that we are all condemned to judgment because of *Adam's* sin and not *our own*? Or that we are all totally depraved and spiritually damned from the moment we are conceived?

It could hardly be clearer. Death (which is code for spiritual condemnation) came to Adam because he himself personally sinned. Likewise death (again code for spiritual condemnation) comes to the rest of us because we ourselves have personally sinned.[64] Although condemnation for sin obviously came to Adam first in point of time, his inaugural condemnation started the ball of judgment and death rolling for all the rest of us who sin.

It is in this sense, I believe, that Paul says: "By the trespass of the one man, death reigned through that one man." And again: "Judgment followed one sin and brought condemnation." And again: "Just as the result of one trespass was condemnation for all men," and so on.

Were it not for those crucial three words—*because all sinned*—in Paul's opening sentence, each of the subsequent statements would have a completely different meaning. As it is, they are all modified and clarified by the critical assumption expressed in verse 12—the same critical assumption, importantly, which is encapsulated in Paul's better-known classic: "For all have sinned and fall short of the glory of God" (Romans 3:23).

The idea in both verses is identical. Just as Adam sinned and died spiritually, we all have died spiritually because of our sin. And crucially, our sin follows the same "clean-slate start" as Adam had. With the same free will and responsibility for choosing as he had. With the same devastating spiritual consequences as he had. And, ultimately, with the same provision for justification through Christ as he had.[65]

---

[64] If "death" is not code for spiritual condemnation but is to be taken literally as meaning physical death, then the juxtaposed reference to "life" in Christ would mean that no one who is in Christ would ever die physically. Since no one disputes that Paul is speaking of *spiritual* "life" in Christ, it follows that he is speaking of *spiritual* condemnation and death, not physical mortality.

[65] Any suggestion here of the inevitability of sin must be tempered by the biblical injunction to "master sin" and by Jesus' own challenge for his disciples to "be perfect." More on this momentarily.

A Story Within the Story of Law and Grace

Having established the fact that condemnation is universal because all have sinned, Paul then makes a practical application of his point in that section of the text which in the NIV (beginning in verse 13) follows immediately after that anticlimactic "dash" we saw earlier, and which in the KJV is placed in parentheses (inclusive of verses 13-17).[66]

Building on the foundation he's just laid about the universal nature of sin and condemnation, Paul suddenly whisks the reader back to his multi-chapter argument about the relationship between law and grace. Don't forget, says Paul (in vs. 13-14), that the principle of *sin and death* has nothing to do with the law, since that principle was in full force from Adam to Moses, even before God gave Moses the law. Consistent with the primary theme-line running throughout Paul's letter to the Romans, the contrasting principle of *justification and life* through Christ is a matter of grace, not law.[67]

---

[66] When all of the awkwardly-worded clauses of verses 12 and 13 are taken together, the natural sense seems to be that "Sin was in the world long before the law was given, having first entered through Adam and thereafter having been perpetuated in all men, casting a pall of spiritual death and condemnation over the whole of mankind."

[67] As suggested earlier, great confusion is caused by the failure to properly distinguish between physical and spiritual death. When Paul refers to "death reigning from the time of Adam to the time of Moses," what first comes to mind for many is man's physical mortality, which almost universally is presumed to have resulted from Adam's sin. From that point, all it takes is an indiscriminate melding together of physical and spiritual death, and suddenly it's not a giant leap to conclude that *spiritual* death (condemnation) is no less a part of the penalty than *physical* death.

Unfortunately, multiple problems arise from a virtually unnoticed process of circular reasoning. The often uncritical assumption that Paul is speaking about *physical* death in Romans 5:12ff is often read alongside Genesis 2:16-17 and 3:19, firming up the conclusion that universal human mortality was part of Adam's penalty. That assumption (now bearing a new aura of impregnability) is then read back into Romans 5:12ff, leading to an initial reflexive conclusion that Paul is speaking of *physical* death–generally associated by most with a universal penalty. So when the reader finally begins to understand that Paul is speaking of *spiritual* death, it is only a short step to his concluding that the same universality which applies to the temporal penalty (mortality) also applies to the eternal penalty (condemnation). [For a discussion challenging the traditional view that human mortality is a penal consequence of Adam's sin, see F. LaGard Smith, *After Life* (Nashville: Cotswold Publishing, distributed by 21st Century Christian, 2003), 15-40.]

It is possible, of course, that Paul is referring to both physical *and* spiritual death as penalties for sin, and may even intend for his readers to see the physical as symbolic of the spiritual. However, Paul's unmistakable contrast between condemnation and justification appears to militate against any reference to physical, biological death.

Whatever else one might conclude about the originating cause of man's physical mortality (and there is reason to question the widely assumed link between sin and human mortality), suffice it to say that in this particular context Paul is not comparing physical death with physical life, but spiritual death (condemnation) with spiritual life (justification). Therefore, to run headlong from any assumptions associated with physical death to conclusions associated with spiritual death risks constructing a precarious house of cards.

With this vital difference between law and grace in mind, what Paul is saying through his series of "if-then" comparisons between Adam and Christ has nothing to do with the issues which swirl around the idea of original sin. Rather, Paul's point proceeds from the operative phrase: "But the gift is not like the trespass" (vs. 15). How so, Paul?

For starters, although the gift and the trespass have something in common (the fact that man has choice both as to committing the trespass and receiving the gift), there is one profound difference between them. Whereas *all have sinned*, not all have reached out to receive the gift. "For if, by the trespass of the one man, death reigned through that one man, how much more will *those who receive God's abundant provision of grace* and of the gift of righteousness reign in life through the one man, Jesus Christ" (Romans 5:17).

The one thing we must not conclude, so it seems, is that there is an exact parallel between the two competing principles and how they work. Whereas the trespass of Adam introduced condemnation and spiritual death to all men (because, like Adam, all men sinned), the gift of Christ made justification and life possible for all men (but certainly not because all men, like Christ, were righteous).

It's the night-and-day difference, Paul insinuates, between condemnation that is *deserved* and justification that is *undeserved*. So if anyone ever dared to think that they might *deserve* justification by slavish obedience to law, they can forget it! Unlike condemnation, which is *always* deserved, justification is *never* deserved.

Woven into Paul's intricate, interlacing argument are two complementary themes. The first theme is that obedience or disobedience (generally associated with law) is always personal, whereas saving grace–by its very nature–is always vicarious. The second theme (and here is where the tables really get overturned in Calvinism's temple) is that condemnation is always deserved because it is *personal, not vicarious*; whereas justification is never deserved because it is *vicarious, not personal.*

Calvinism's insistence that we are innately born with original sin (being condemned vicariously through Adam) is completely undone by Paul's compelling argument here, which he summarizes so powerfully in the very next chapter. "For the [deserved] wages of sin [being personal] is death," says Paul, "but the [undeserved] gift of God [through the vicarious death of Christ] is eternal life in Christ Jesus our Lord" (Romans 6:23).

In a nutshell, according to Paul, this is the lesson of the *trespass* and the *gift*: Wages (representing the trespass) are *earned*, not *imputed*. And so too condemnation and death. By contrast, the gift of God is never *earned*, only *spurned*.

To superimpose what has come to be the traditional template on this great passage is to exchange a profound truth of God for an unworthy lie having devastating doctrinal consequences. The only thing original about "original sin" is that its origin is nowhere to be found in Scripture.[68]

A Far More Personal Spiritual Fall

Before we leave Romans 5, we must not overlook the fact that, even if this passage stood for the proposition that man comes into the world burdened with condemnation from Adam's sin, it speaks not a word about the quite separate issue of predisposition to sin. Whatever might be the cause and effect of any judicial penalty for sin, that alone has no bearing on whether mankind is constitutionally inclined, or bent, toward sin. The unholy, uncritical marriage between "original sin" and "total depravity" has given birth to widespread illegitimate thinking about the two distinct concepts.

That said, there is something yet screaming to leap out of this passage and into our hearts and minds. And that "something" is the ultimate truth of a spiritual fall which brings about a lostness in man that can be overcome only through the atoning, justifying blood of Jesus Christ and the regenerating power of the Holy Spirit.

---

[68] I am well aware that supporters of the traditional template include not only Calvinists but such notable non-Calvinists as James Arminius and John Wesley, particularly with regard to the idea that man is born with a fallen nature which requires divine grace to overcome. Yet even between these two lie significant differences. Arminius believed the loss of original righteousness (principally the withdrawal of the Holy Spirit) "is original sin itself"–if thereafter leading to actual sin. Wesley (somewhat following Augustine) spoke more of positive corruption–with man being constitutionally changed into a being who is depraved, corrupt, and diseased. [See Leon O. Hynson, "Original Sin As Privation–An Inquiry into a Theology of Sin and Sanctification," http://wesley.nnu.edu/wesleyan_theology/theojrnl/21-25-/22-14.htm.]

"But didn't you just say...?" No, no, not *The Fall* of man, with its supposed universal imputation of sin to every newly-conceived soul; but the *personal fall* of each and every person who, having sufficient moral maturity, knowingly and wilfully sins against God, thereby falling under the condemnation of spiritual death. (*Because all sinned!*) Having thus besmirched the pristine image of God in which we were born (which is to say, having *fallen*) our only hope is to turn to God to cleanse, restore, heal, eradicate, and regenerate–in short, to *re-create* us in his own image.

Want to believe that by virtue of being Adam's descendants we are innately diseased with sin and vicariously condemned from the moment of conception? I'm afraid Romans 5 isn't the irrefutable proof-text it's made out to be. But just in case someone were to ask you whether there was such a thing as a "fall," and "universal sin," and "death and condemnation" for every sinner accountable to God, then put Romans 5 in your pocket and never lose it. Properly understood, every one of those concepts is entirely biblical.

So what's the practical difference? Once you factor in the age of accountability (as in Deuteronomy 1:39), there isn't any. *Because all sinned!*

What, on the other hand, are the theological implications of accepting, in particular, the Calvinist view of "original sin"? Nothing short of...

- Insisting that innocent, unborn souls are spiritually condemned.
- Being compelled logically to acknowledge that God is responsible for the very sin he abhors.
- Concluding that we were born with a tarnished, distorted image of God.
- Inferring that God's majesty is dependent on man's radical wretchedness.

Ultimately, of course, there is the inescapable problem of attributing to God a dubious moral character which could preemptively condemn every soul ever born for the sins of only one man. As we are reminded in Numbers 16:22, it's not a mistake that Moses and Aaron would have dared to make. Appealing to God's notorious character for righteous justice, "Moses and Aaron fell facedown and cried out, 'O God, God of the spirits of all mankind, will you be angry with the entire assembly when only one man sins?'"

Given what *you* know of God's character (not to mention God's ratifying response to Moses), what do *you* think?

Original Sin? Easy For Calvinists To Say!

As always, of course, Calvinists must somehow reconcile their belief in original sin with their belief in particular election. For if the elect are unconditionally chosen for salvation before they ever arrive in the world, then not even emerging from the womb tainted with Adam's condemnation will change the outcome in the slightest.

If you believe you are among the elect, you have the luxury of being able to talk long and loud about original sin and depravity without having to really concern yourself with its consequences. In the end, there's no penalty for a false start. By no choice of the serendipitous elect, from eternity onwards it's *all Christ* and *no Adam*.

As always, the only ones adversely affected are the non-elect, who, by reason of an innate and irreversible depravity over which they have absolutely no control, live and die with no alternative destiny but the eternal wrath of hell–all to the glory of God. By no choice of the hapless non-elect, it's *all Adam* and *no Christ*.[69]

Surely even the original troublemaker, Adam, will come out better than that...or will he? Since presumably Adam's eternal destiny was also arbitrarily and unconditionally determined before he was ever made from the dust of the earth, his *original* sin (which supposedly engendered our "original sin") matters not in the least. No less than ourselves, Adam's eternal destiny would have been determined long before a single bite was taken from the forbidden fruit.

Which raises an interesting question. If you were to venture a guess, would you think that Adam (who single-handedly is said to be responsible

---

[69] It is interesting, to say the least, that among a number of obvious difficulties addressed openly and frankly in the pages of his softly-softly approach in *Calvinism In The Las Vegas Airport*, Richard Mouw never struggles with the most obvious difficulty of all: the horrendous inescapable fate of the non-elect. Softly-softly may be more inviting (even seductive) than hard-line doctrinal teaching, but the velvet glove of Calvinism conceals a clenched fist that must at least be seriously addressed.

for "the Fall" and man's innate, universal condemnation) is counted among the predestined elect or among the non-elect?

The Actual Transmission of "Original Sin"

Stepping back for a broader perspective, there are so many problems with the three widely-assumed theories of original sin, total depravity, and "the Fall" that it is hard to know where to begin. For example, there is the practical problem of how "inherited original sin," as it is often cast, would be passed along to each newborn baby. Can it be that we are still being asked to believe, as first postulated, that original sin is a kind of spiritual AIDS passed from mother to child; or that sin is transmitted genetically like the traits for diabetes or longevity? (If so, how is it that regenerate, justified, and saved children of God still have depraved offspring?)

Apart from Psalm 51:5 (where David's reference to "surely being conceived in sin" is arguably nothing more than an anguished exaggeration of his sense of guilt pertaining to his sin with Bathsheba), is there anywhere else in Scripture that suggests we are condemned by sin at the moment of conception?[70] Not even Psalm 58:3, which speaks of the wicked being corrupt from the moment of birth, would suggest the wicked were *conceived* in sin. ("Even from birth the wicked go astray; from the womb they are wayward and speak lies.")[71]

If we eliminate the option that Adam's sin is somehow passed along in the natural process of human procreation, the next option is that each soul born since the Garden of Eden is intrinsically imputed with sin from the moment of conception, simply by divine decree. Yet, that just raises more questions for those who believe that natural man is a child of Satan—enslaved to sin, rebellious toward God, blind to truth, and absolute-

---

[70] Not even Calvinists dare use John 9:34 where the Pharisees replied to the man born blind: "You were steeped in sin at birth…" While apparently the Jews entertained the idea that physical disability was the result of sin, and might even be a sin from the moment of birth or earlier, Jesus himself refutes such a notion in 9:3.

[71] David was no more literally "conceived in sin" in Psalm 51 than he was literally "a worm and not a man" in Psalm 22:6. Both the metaphor of the latter and the hyperbole of the former are used to emphasize the enormity of David's sense of shame and scorn.

ly corrupt. Are we to believe that all of these damning characteristics are true of each soul *at the point of conception?*

If so, such a depraved condition could hardly be the fault of the newly-conceived zygote or embryo. It would mean that God himself is responsible for man's being a child of Satan—enslaved to sin, rebellious toward God, blind to truth, and absolutely corrupt. Could that possibly make any sense?

We get the same result if we come at it from yet another direction. If, as Calvinists insist, God's unimpeachable sovereignty means that he is the proximate, effective, responsible cause of all that happens, there is no way that the spiritual condition of each new soul could be anything other than what God has ordained it to be. Therefore, if the soul is born depraved, who but God has declared it to be so? Further still, if that is true how can it be said that sinful man *deserves* God's wrath?[72]

Although not strictly Calvinistic, a third explanation of man's supposed depravity deserves at least passing mention. In line with the Eastern Church, it is believed by some that man is innately *depraved* because he is innately *deprived.* The idea is that, as we observe in the Garden, man was created to walk literally in God's presence. When God removed his unimpeded, unencumbered glory from man as a result of Adam's sin, it naturally followed that mankind was left bereft of God's goodness, and, being in darkness without God's light, became radically oriented against God.

Were that the case, however, it's the same problem as before. How do we explain *Adam's* sin, who *did* walk with God and witnessed his glory! Or both Enoch and Noah "walking" with God even after Adam's expulsion from the Garden?[73] Or—most important of all—God's incarnating in the person of Jesus who, as Immanuel (God with us!), walked among mankind, sharing his fleshly presence? Those who literally walked with the

---

[72] Even the mention of "each new soul" in the same context as "depraved from the moment of conception" raises an embarrassing historical fact for Calvinists. Have we forgotten that Augustine—who first started the Calvinism ball rolling—insisted that the human soul entered into the embryo, not at the point of conception, but only after forty days or later? (Breaking with the early Christian writers, who taught that the soul exists concurrently with conception, both Augustine and Thomas Aquinas seem to have been influenced more than a little by Aristotle, who contended that ensoulment takes place only after weeks of embryonic development.)

[73] Genesis 5:24; 6:9

incarnate God in that other "Garden" on the night in which our Savior was betrayed were not deprived of God's presence. Yet, like Adam before them, they too failed the test.

If man's depravity is but the gloom of darkness in the absence of God's light, what excuse shall we offer to the One who came into our world as "the true light that gives light to every man," whose glory "we have seen," says John, "the glory of the One and Only"?

With God having taken the initiative to come into our presence and share his glory, the deprivation theory lies in tatters. We don't sin because we are separated from God. We are separated from God because we sin.[74]

Just How "Total" is Total Depravity?

Despite Calvinism's historical reference to "total depravity" (whose "T" forms the first letter in *TULIP*), most Calvinists caution us that the word *total* doesn't literally mean that each sinner is as totally or completely corrupt in his thoughts and actions as it is possible for him to be. For most thoughtful Calvinists, total depravity describes the extent to which sin affects us, not how sinful we might be.

Yet having been given that "kinder, gentler" qualifier, we are next told by the same Calvinists that, as the result of inborn corruption, the natural man is *totally* unable to do anything good whatsoever! So which is it?

From Augustine onward, Calvinists have talked about a "general" or "common" grace to all mankind in an attempt to explain *the good* that is evident even in the unregenerate. This "common" grace supposedly restrains the full force of man's depravity so that life can proceed with sufficient orderliness to permit the implementation of God's eternal plan.

If unregenerate man does anything which externally appears to be good, say Calvinists, we're not to be fooled. Inwardly, he is acting solely from baser, fiendish motives consistent with his depraved nature.

Setting deeper motives aside (whether God-honoring or wholly selfish), crucial questions remain. Has the serial rapist or Saturday night burglar, for example, no capability whatsoever of choosing good over evil? And can

---

[74] See Isaiah 59:2

there be no genuine desire among the unconverted to be morally better than they are, or to lament the evil of which they are at times ashamed?

Inquiring minds want to know: Are we really and truly *totally* depraved, or is the term "total depravity" merely a theological buzzword meaning something quite different from what the phrase naturally would imply? Read the literature, and more often than not you'll see a softening of that term to something like "total inability." Which is to say that, unless and until God graces a person with predestined regeneration, that person is wholly unable to respond in any affirmative way to the gospel message.

Yet if one were to accept the Calvinist theory that "total depravity" robs us of every shred of ability to turn to God, it seems unlikely that we could respond even to a divine act of regeneration. To that, of course, Calvinists are quick to say, "Bingo! We can't. God does it all, or it doesn't happen at all." (Hence, the necessity for Calvinism's "irresistible grace.") But if that is the case, what is left of us as a person...?

Made In the Image of God?

If when push comes to shove we have no innate, inherent ability within our human constitution to choose the good and chase the evil, in what possible way were you and I "created in God's image?" Or does that bedrock affirmation apply only to Adam and Eve?

The implications are colossal: Can post-Fall man (you and I) legitimately claim that, no less than Adam and Eve, *we too* were created in the image of God? YES/NO?

If your answer is "Yes," and you also believe that we are born corrupt, rebellious, depraved, and condemned by original sin, how do you reconcile those conflicting assumptions? Or do you, perhaps, believe that the phrase "image of God" was never intended as meaning anything more than a unique rationality and emotional sentience which may separate us from the lower animals but has nothing whatsoever to do with reflecting God's holiness, righteousness, and love? (In such a case, what was "the Fall" all about?)

If your answer is that we *aren't* created in the image of God in the same way as Adam and Eve, is that not because you believe "the Fall" somehow emasculated the created nature of Adam's offspring? Yet how would you

explain what in a *pre-Fall* context (in Genesis 1:27) is repeated almost ver-
batim in a *post-Fall* context (in Genesis 9:6): "for in the image of God has
God made man"? [75] Surely, that phrase didn't change definition and meaning in just eight chapters! Whatever it was intended to signal in Chapter 1
must certainly be intended in Chapter 9.

One might argue, of course, that the idea of a *new creation* in Christ
would have no meaning had not the *first creation* been distorted in "the
Fall." After all, we are called "to put on the new self, created to be like
God in true righteousness and holiness" (Ephesians 4:24). But to say that
our sin-tarnished souls find restoration in Christ begs the question of
whether we were born into this world as marred images of God, or
whether subsequently we have besmirched souls created in God's image
by dragging them through the muck and mire of sin.

Particularly given the pointed repetition of the key phrase in Genesis
9:6, can it seriously be doubted that you and I were created in a pristine
moral state *in the image of God* no less than Adam was created in a pristine
moral state *in the image of God*? Surely, it is *that* spiritually innocent creation—now so disfigured by your sin and mine—that is gloriously recreated
through Christ in the image of God—not some defective, distorted, ema-
ciated image of God emerging from the womb.

Calvin himself was so perplexed by the dilemma of how man could be
born depraved yet be created in the image of God that he ended up waf-
fling in uncertainty. In his Catechism (sect. 4), for example, Calvin says
without any moderating qualification that, because of the Fall, "God's
likeness is wiped out..." as if completely. (Since for Calvin there was no
difference between God's *image* and God's *likeness*,[76] to say God's *likeness* in
man was wiped out was to say that God's *image* in man was wiped out.) But
just what did Calvin mean when he spoke of God's image and likeness?

On one hand, Calvin acknowledged that even post-Fall man retained the
natural (though corrupted) traits of understanding in "government, house-
hold management, all mechanical skills, and the liberal arts."[77] What's more,
says Calvin, "We see in all mankind that reason is proper to our nature; it dis-

---

[75] See also James 3:9.
[76] Calvin, *Institutes*, 1.15.3
[77] Calvin, *Institutes*, 2.2.13

tinguishes us from brute beasts."[78] Indeed, according to Calvin, God has even gifted certain unregenerate human beings with extraordinary traits of talent and goodness for the orderly working of his universe and the restraint of evil on behalf of his elect.

Yet, Calvin was adamant that the spiritual nature of man (inclusive of the "supernatural" gifts of faith, love, and righteousness) was not just partially corrupted but wholly effaced. "The heavenly image was obliterated in him [man]," says Calvin. "In the place of wisdom, virtue, holiness, truth, and justice...there came forth the most filthy plagues, blindness, impotence, impurity, vanity, and injustice [in which Adam] also entangled and immersed his offspring in the same miseries."[79]

Calvin's conclusion from all of that? "Even though we grant that God's image was not totally annihilated and destroyed in him [Adam], yet it was so corrupted that whatever remains is frightful deformity."[80]

So that's how our souls came into the world...as "frightful deformities"? Although a later, more thoroughly developed system of Calvinism would far eclipse Calvin himself in articulating a formal doctrine of total depravity, Calvin's own notorious pessimism supplies us with an absolutely incredible answer to our earlier question about the nature of post-Fall man. "What remains in men?" asks Calvin. "They are only vermin and rottenness."[81]

That Calvin's theology could even remotely lead him to say that post-Fall men and women (you and I) are created as "vermin," "rottenness," and "frightful deformities" is the best proof possible that Calvin's understanding of the nature of man is completely out of touch with biblical reality.[82] Indeed, alarm bells must surely go off when you consider that in

---

[78] Calvin, *Institutes*, 2.2.17

[79] Calvin, *Institutes*, 2.1.5

[80] Calvin, *Institutes*, 1.15.4

[81] Sermon 94 on Job (25:1-6); Nixon trans., 151

[82] The same must also be said of John Wesley's similar, shocking characterization. Along with other Arminians, Wesley's acceptance of original sin and depravity led him inexorably into an equally dim view of post-Fall man: "'By one man's disobedience,' as the Apostle observed...as many as were in the loins of their forefather, 'were made,' or constituted, 'sinners': Not only deprived of the favour of God, but also of this image, of all virtue, righteousness, and true holiness; and sunk, partly into the image of the devil–in pride, malice, and all other diabolical tempers; partly into the image of the brute, being fallen under the dominion of brutal passions and groveling appetites." [John Wesley, "God's Love To Fallen Man," Sermon 59 (text from the 1872 edition). See: http://gbgm-umc.org/umhistory/wesley/sermons/serm-059.stm.]

the whole of his magisterial *Institutes*, Calvin never once addresses the crucial implications of Genesis 9:6.

Ask me what it means, precisely, to be made in the image of God, and I readily will confess to knowing far less than I'd like. (Having a spiritual nature imbued with God's own Spirit, holiness, a capacity for communing with one's Maker, potential immortality toward an eternal existence, conscience, moral capacity, and liberty linked with responsibility readily come to mind.) All I know is that my Bible has nothing to say about our being created spiritually deformed, but everything to say about our being created in God's own glorious image.[83]

And if God thought it important enough to put it in those terms—even *after* "the Fall"—then I'm prepared to accept there is something sufficiently profound about my own nature as it relates to God's that it's worth holding onto at all cost. So when even the bedrock truth of *imago dei* must be sacrificed on the altar of total depravity, then count me out.

How about you?

So Many Separate Frames To Make the Picture Work

Earlier on, we noted Evolution's problem of explaining how, in one generation, there could be a transition from asexual to sexual beings, a process that would have required a number of distinct, highly complex phenomena occurring simultaneously. As you look back on our own stop-action, slow motion scrutiny of the first "petal" in Calvinism's *TULIP*—Total Depravity—is it not equally clear that separate and distinct, highly complex doctrines would be required to occur harmoniously in order for Calvinism to survive?

---

[83] In his debate with Dave Hunt, James White affirms (at p. 265) that "Human beings are made in the image of God. Our capacity to love, to adore, to worship, and even to dislike or hate, comes from the fact that we are made to have the freedom and ability to express that image in how we relate to others. The Bible commands us to love God, showing that love is not merely an emotion, but an action of the will, an attitude, a decision. Of course, the ability to love comes from our Maker, God, who is described as love (1 John 4:8)." One could be excused for thinking, therefore, that all of these traits are possible by virtue of each person's having been made in God's image. How that possibly squares with what White and other Calvinists otherwise affirm about total depravity and the need for regeneration in order to have free will and do any moral good whatsoever fairly boggles the mind.

Contrary to what might easily be assumed by the umbrella term "Total Depravity," the fact is that there are three distinct concepts involved: total depravity, original sin, and "the Fall." Each concept has its own definition, and—as we have seen—each has its own unique set of difficulties.

The truly tricky part is not just resolving the problems inherent within each concept. Even beyond that headache, the real nightmare is somehow managing to blend the three distinct notions together, both logically and scripturally. Given the dire necessity of their mutual interdependence, that's a tall order indeed.

It's not unlike the country proverb: "If we had any eggs, we could have ham and eggs...if we had any ham!" Likewise, if we had "the Fall," we could have total depravity *and* "the Fall"...if we had any total depravity!

At times, the degree of faith we are asked to have in the cobbled-together linkage between these three artificial concepts is astounding. Even if we were to assume the existence of original sin, we are still left wondering how a divine imputation of sin's condemnation on all mankind necessarily results in individuals being totally robbed of any ability to respond to God's goodness unless and until, by the selective grace of God, they are regenerated.

Nor are we any the wiser about how that regenerative process suppos-edly occurs. Calvinists themselves seem not to be agreed on whether it happens at birth, or at some later point in one's life; or whether it occurs simultaneously with conversion or otherwise. One would think that a God who gives us so many details about far lesser concerns, would have had spelled out with great specificity the process of overcoming the stifling effects of "the Fall."

Nor, significantly, can we find any express mention in Scripture of either original sin or total depravity, or how either one of them conceiv-ably might be connected to what is talked about so glibly as "the Fall." Presumably, the logic behind having a "Fall" in the first place is that *some-thing* has to explain the yawing gap between the obvious lack of depravity with which Adam was created and the "total depravity" which Calvinism makes the cornerstone of its system.

If it were just a matter of delineating between the pristine nature of Creation *Before Sin* and the spiritual consequences which followed *After*

Sin, we could simply employ B.S. and A.S., in much the same way as we refer to B.C. and A. D. (There is no denying that the disastrous, long-lasting effects of sin quickly became the order of the day throughout all of culture, leading to what Scripture often speaks of negatively as "the world" and "worldliness.") But that wouldn't provide us with a mechanism to rationalize the cataclysmic change in man's constituent nature that Calvinism demands—nor explain how the sin of the first generation supposedly tainted the next, and all subsequent, generations.

And so, without a shred of biblical evidence suggesting any fundamental, *constitutional change* in the nature of human beings following Adam and Eve's expulsion from the Garden, suddenly we have a sacred cow referred to as "the Fall," carrying on its back a burdensome bag of "original sin" along with the even heavier baggage of "total depravity."

It's all worthy of the finest conspiracy theories ever spun. The intrigues of the various Kennedy-assassination scenarios pale in comparison to how these three shadowy doctrines of Calvinism—each one biblically suspect—have gained respectability when deftly spliced together and run by us at blinding speed.

"Yet you ask, 'Why does the son not share the guilt of his father?' Since the son has done what is just and right and has been careful to keep all my decrees, he will surely live. The soul who sins is the one who will die. The son will not share the guilt of the father, nor will the father share the guilt of the son. The righteousness of the righteous man will be credited to him, and the wickedness of the wicked will be charged against him."

Ezekiel 18:19-20

Chapter Summary

- Calvinism's assumption that Adam's personal fall triggered universal consequences of original sin and total depravity suffers from a glaring lack of scriptural support. When you run the tape of Calvinism in stop-action slow motion, nothing suggests that there was a constitutional difference between the first *created* couple and their *procreated* offspring.

- It is as foolish to say that all men are condemned in Adam as it is to say that all men are saved in Christ. Paul's point in Romans 5 is that, just as *condemnation for sin* was inaugurated through Adam for all who sin, *justification for sin* has been made available through Christ for all who sin–enabling the salvation of all who would trust and obey.

- When the doctrine of total depravity forces Calvinists to insist that post-Fall man is created with a corrupted, distorted image of God, then total depravity has fallen on its own sword.

- "The Fall," original sin, and total depravity (each individually unsustainable in Scripture) are none the more true simply for being wrapped tightly together as if a cord of three strands.

Reality Check: If before the dawn of Creation God determined whether you would be saved or lost, then total depravity, original sin, and "the Fall" are all little more than superfluous window dressing. It doesn't matter in the least whether you were once totally depraved, but are now regenerate. Either you were going to heaven all along, or have always been destined to hell.

Chapter 4

When Tangled Webs Turn Tragic

This is the highest degree of faith—to believe that He is merciful,
the very One who saves so few and damns so many.
To believe that He is just, the One who according to His own will,
makes us necessarily damnable.

—Martin Luther

What the young preacher was saying was quite beyond belief. As it was not my regular fellowship, and as the preacher was a visitor himself to that particular church, I wondered whether I was simply missing something that would put his conclusions in a better light. But no, follow-up discussions after the sermon confirmed what I thought I had heard. In the midst of a bold defense of Calvinism, suddenly the preacher had startled everyone right out of their pews, stating matter-of-factly that he and his wife had experienced the death of a stillborn infant, who, because she did not have the opportunity to accept Christ in faith, would certainly and unquestionably go to hell!

While it appears from the literature that relatively few Calvinists would readily agree with the preacher's disturbing pronouncement, there was a commendable degree of intellectual honesty and consistency in what the preacher said. No matter how disturbing it might be to anyone else (and even more pitiable for that grieving couple), the preacher's shocking conclusion is certainly a logical deduction that could have emerged from his theological framework. Once you begin with the notion that total depravity pollutes the soul and brings one into eternal condemnation from the moment of conception, predictable disaster looms ahead.

Sometimes the only good thing about hard cases is that they serve to test one's beliefs in ways that otherwise might never happen. Toward that end, what if this tragic loss happened to you or someone you love? If you are a Calvinist, what would your own Calvinistic framework say about the eternal destiny of a stillborn infant? If perhaps you've never considered that question before, it might help you to see how others have thought about it, including those who are not Calvinists.

The Problem of Infant Salvation

The question is: If infants are invested with Adam's sin while still in the womb, what happens to them when they die in the process of being born or shortly thereafter?[84] It's a long story, but for Roman Catholics (at least for Augustine and the Council of Carthage in A.D. 418) the unnerving answer initially was the same as for our young preacher: that the souls of such infants would suffer the agony of hell, if perhaps only the "mildest" part.

Faced with the disturbing implications of original sin, Catholicism early on recognized infant baptism, a ritual not practiced in the primitive, apostolic church.[85] Yet this only invited another problem. If baptism (unlike Jewish circumcision) is meant to be an outward expression of an inward,

---

[84] The present discussion begs an even more fundamental question: If physical, biological death is the result of sin, why do babies die? For those who believe in original sin and depravity, it is not difficult to make a link between that innate depravity and infant death. For those of us who reject an innate depravity, the question of infant death once again invites a closer look at the generally-assumed premise that the penalty for sin was human mortality. As previously noted, a full discussion of this concern is to be found in F. LaGard Smith, *After Life* (Nashville: Cotswold Publishing, 2003), 15-40.

[85] There is some historical support for the proposition that the practice of infant baptism came first, and that original sin was only later seized upon as a welcomed rationale. Either way, the practice and the rationale go hand in hand.

active, and personal faith, infants obviously aren't mature enough to have such faith. So to deal with this second issue, Catholic doctrine came up with a creative two-part solution.

First, it declared faith to be vicarious rather than personal, calling upon the parents and the church to express a proxy faith on the infant's behalf. (Unfortunately, this also served to introduce the unbiblical notion of "baptismal regeneration" in which the rite of baptism, *in and of itself*, is effective for salvation.)

Second, Catholicism then inaugurated the rite of confirmation, at which twelve-year-olds (typically) are asked to confess the faith which obviously was lacking at the time of "baptism."[86] The resulting doctrinal mishmash mandates an initial "baptism" without faith, followed years later by an expression of faith without baptism.

Creative as these solutions were, they begged yet a further question: What happens to the infant who dies *before* "baptism"? Catholic theologians scrambled to put forward as a working hypothesis the notion of "limbo," wherein unbaptized infants rest eternally in some vaguely-defined realm which entails neither the perceived horror of hell nor the joyful bliss of heaven. Though never officially recognized by the Roman Church, limbo remains a set feature of afterlife thinking for millions of adherents.

The Protestant Dilemma

Catholics aren't the only ones to find themselves in a dilemma as a result of believing in original sin. For their part, most Protestants have simply assumed that the grace of God would take care of unbaptized infants, particularly when you factor in Christ's work on the cross. If one believes in original sin, then Christ's sacrifice provides atonement to erase the guilt of original sin, permitting infants to find their place in heaven alongside the saved.

---

[86] *"Baptism"* is in quotation marks to indicate that the sprinkling or pouring typically used for infant baptism is not the full immersion of adults practiced by the apostolic church.

But why should Protestants defy the logic of Catholics in this matter and carve out an exception for infants? Surely, if baptism is for the remission of sin, there is no salvation apart from that remission through baptism.

For most Protestants, the first answer is that baptism is not, in fact, for the remission of sin, but merely serves as an outward sign of an inward grace. Since it is held that salvation attaches at the moment of one's faith, the usual teaching is that baptism serves merely as an after-the-fact symbolic act reflecting the believer's prior redemption.

It is another discussion altogether, but if that is the case, passages such as Mark 16:16, Acts 2:38, Galatians 3:26-27, 1 Peter 3:21, and even Luke 3:3, become problematic. Though one could wish for more consistency of analysis in his commentary on the subject, John Calvin could not have been clearer when he wrote: "For [the Lord] wills that all who believe be baptized for the remission of sins [Matt. 28:19; Acts 2:38]. Accordingly, they who regarded baptism as nothing but a token and mark by which we confess our religion before men...have not weighed what was the chief point of baptism. It is to receive baptism with this promise: 'He who believes and is baptized will be saved.' [Mark 16:16]."[87]

Yet, even today's sweeping relegation of baptism's crucial role does nothing more than beg a further question of those Protestants who believe that personal faith is necessary for salvation. If by virtue of infancy the newborn baby is not mature enough to place his faith in Christ through anything like the commonly-accepted (if biblically unknown) "sinners prayer," where does that leave the infant's condemned soul before the point of faith? Was our young preacher right, after all, about his child being in hell?

If the answer is simply that God makes an exception for infants, upon what basis would that exception be made other than the quite proper realization that in infancy the child is incapable of either accepting or rejecting God's gracious offer of forgiveness and salvation? (If you are tempted to suggest that an exception is made on the basis that children of the

---

[87] Calvin, *Institutes*, 4.15.1.

elect are "covenant children," a surprising conundrum lurks just around the corner....)

Confusion in the Calvinist Camp

For Calvinists, making an "exception" for children opens up a can of worms. Even if faith is seen by Calvinists as a gift of grace given to God's regenerated elect to bring about justification, what is the eternal destiny of infants who die before they are regenerated, or perhaps before the moment they respond in faith to that regeneration (if there is a time gap between the two)? Will they be counted among the predestined saved (since, being elect, they *would have* responded in faith); or are they simply consigned to hell if not among the elect in the first place?

As a starting point, there is the Westminster Confession which holds that "*Elect infants*, dying in infancy are regenerated and saved by Christ through the Spirit, who worketh when, and where, and how he pleaseth."[88] But is this to say that *only infants who are elect* (or only those who are "covenant children") will be saved?

Although there appears to be no hard-and-fast consensus, the literature seems to indicate that many (most?) Calvinists actually believe that *all* who die in infancy will be saved. There is, for example, the 1903 Declaratory Statement of the Presbyterian Church U.S.A. which reads: "We believe that all dying in infancy are included in the election of grace, and are regenerated and saved by Christ through the Spirit, who works when and where and how He pleases."

Consider also Charles Spurgeon's confident conclusion: "I rejoice to know that the souls of all infants, as soon as they die, speed their way to paradise."[89]

How that conclusion could follow from the crucial Calvinist premise that infants are born depraved must surely raise more than an eyebrow or two. And one could be excused for wondering how God's election of *some but not all adults* among the general population suddenly becomes the elec-

---

[88] Westminster Confession of Faith, Chapter 10, "Of Effectual Calling," Articles 1 and 3.

[89] From *C.H. Spurgeon, Autobiography*, Vol. 1, *The Early Years: 1834-1859* (Edinburgh: Banner of Truth, 1962), 163-75.

tion of *all infants*–a certain percentage of whom, had they lived to adulthood, would *not* have been elected to salvation!

How, exactly, does that work? Are we to understand that in one moment at conception these infants were condemned and depraved, but in the very next moment (or possibly at the point of death) were made regenerate and suddenly saved? (And would that not be *without faith*, as we pointed out earlier?) At least one widely-accepted Calvinist explanation, provided here by B. B. Warfield, is that "their salvation is wrought by an unconditional application of the grace of Christ to their souls, through the immediate and irresistible operation of the Holy Spirit...."[90]

Are we to take it, then, that *all* infants who die are regenerated and saved? If so, it must also mean that all infants who die are counted among the predestined elect; and, further, that no person predestined for damnation could ever possibly die as an infant! Is that what Calvinists believe? Is that what *you* believe?

For Calvinists, complication times complication equals complication squared. How, for instance, does Calvinism's vaunted "covenant theology" figure into all of this? Woefully misunderstanding the intent of 1 Corinthians 7: 12-14, Calvinists believe that the children of the elect are automatically holy.[91] But if that were the case, then how can Calvinists simultaneously believe that *all* children who die in infancy are holy? (And how does one explain the obvious inconsistency when some of those same children of the elect grow up to exhibit every characteristic of a reprobate?)

Commenting on John Calvin's thinking about all this, Calvinist R. A. Webb argues that Calvin's own reasoning "compels him to hold (to be consistent with himself), that no reprobate child can die in infancy, but all such live to the age of moral accountability, and translate original sin into actual sin."[92]

---

[90] B. B. Warfield, *Two Studies in the History of Doctrine*, 230. (Cited by Boettner, 144)

[91] If the same reasoning used to sanctify the children of the elect were applied to the unbelieving spouses of the elect, it would mean that those unbelieving spouses were equally as "holy" as the children. Because it is marriage which brings legitimacy to procreation, Paul says that, for the sake of the children as well as for the sanctity of the marriage relationship itself, the believing spouse should do everything possible to hold the marriage together. Paul is not addressing the spiritual advantage children of an elect couple have over children of a non-elect couple, particularly given the fact that here we have only *one* of the two who is elect.

[92] R. A. Webb, in *Calvin Memorial Addresses*, 112. (Cited by Boettner, 147-148)

So there we have it. If a child dies in infancy, then he or she was one of God's elect all along—which must be at least some comfort to the bereaved parents. Or is it? Just how comforting would it be to stand over a tiny open grave and think that God himself was directly responsible for robbing you of the life of the precious child being lowered down into the earth? How comforted should any of us be at the thought that, by that same token, God is also responsible for the death of every baby who dies as a result of a miscarriage or abortion; or who is stillborn, or dies in adolescence—whether in each instance by natural causes or by the hand of violence? In such a case, all these deaths would be "acts of God" in the strictest sense. How that thought is supposed to give comfort to grieving parents, one is hard-pressed to say.[93]

Never does the water get more muddied than when John Calvin wades into the stream. Addressing the controversial subject of infant baptism, Calvin maintained that "infants are not barred from the Kingdom of Heaven just because they happen to depart the present life before they have been immersed in water."[94] But he ends up in a wasteland of inconsistency when, in an attempt to defend the practice of infant baptism, he declares that "the children of Christians are considered holy."[95] Holy? Not *wholly depraved*? Well, yes, Calvin equivocates: "Although those who are born of believers may by nature be lost, they are holy by supernatural grace"![96]

Given the obvious inconsistency of that logic, even Calvin undoubtedly knew he was skating on thin theological ice. "Though I admit," says Calvin," that all the offspring of Adam begotten of flesh bear their condemnation from the very womb itself, I still deny that this prevents God from providing an immediate remedy."[97]

---

[93] The larger implications are even more disturbing. If the time and manner of each soul's death is not just foreknown but foreordained by God, it must mean God is directly responsible for every adult death as well, including those who die from war, starvation, and disease, not to mention from brutal rapes and torture. How, also, could God not be directly responsible for the deaths of six million Jews in the Holocaust and millions more lost to genocide in Stalin's Russia, Armenia, India, Ruanda, and all the other atrocities the world has known?

[94] Calvin, *Institutes*, 4.15.22

[95] Calvin, *Institutes*, 4.16.6

[96] Calvin, *Institutes*, 4.16.31.4

[97] Calvin, *Institutes*, 4.16.31.4

Of course, "remedy" only has meaning given the lostness of one tainted by original sin at birth. But that pivotal Calvinist assumption runs counter to Calvin's own primary argument in support of infant baptism–drawn from the incident where Jesus blessed the children who were brought to him. "Anyone Christ blesses," Calvin insists, "is freed from the curse of Adam and the wrath of God. Since, therefore, it is known that infants were blessed by him [Matt. 19:13-14; Mark 10:13-16], it follows that they were freed from death."[98]

Amen and amen! What more compelling argument do we need? Who, possibly, could have said it better–unless, perhaps, someone who was willing to follow that clarion truth through to its logical end, which admits of no conclusion but that children do not emerge from the womb depraved, condemned, and lost.

When children are properly seen as not being spiritually accountable until they are mature enough to accept or reject Christ's lordship in their life (a quite separate question from whether they know fundamental right from wrong), then they are not spiritually "lost." If they are not lost in the first place, then God need make no exception to welcome them into heaven along with lost sinners who have been saved by grace through faith. The aborted fetus, the stillborn child, the newborn baby, and the immature youngster all have one thing in common: not total depravity, but total impeccability.[99] Which is to say that, what to the more mature would be accounted as sin in need of redemption, is not reckoned as sin in the immature.

So tell us again why our grieving preacher felt compelled to believe that God consigns to hell even newborn babies (who under any other circumstances we would refer to as "innocents")? His problem, as it turns out, was reasoning from the fundamental Calvinist doctrine of total depravity with a consistency that eluded Calvin himself. Makes you wonder, really. If

---

[98] Calvin, *Institutes*, 4.16.31.3

[99] Addressing the issue of infant mortality, A.A. Hodge unwittingly assumes an important truth when he says, "Remember that all who die before complete moral agency have been given to Christ." [Archibald Alexander Hodge, *Evangelical Theology: A Course of Popular Lectures* (Edinburgh: Banner of Truth, 1976), 401.] The words *before complete moral agency* assume a state of innocence incompatible with infant depravity.

one so gifted as John Calvin had to engage in theological gymnastics in a frantic attempt to avoid the unthinkable implications for dying infants, is it too much to ask of Calvinists today to have a serious re-think about this first petal of the *TULIP*?

The Nature of Infants

In support of inherited sin and depravity, Calvinists sometimes cite Exodus 20:5, where God tells the Israelites that he is a jealous God "punishing the children for the sin of the fathers to the third and fourth generation of those who hate me...."

Yet an immediate problem would arise from the concluding words of that same sentence: "...but showing love to a thousand [generations] of those who love me and keep my commandments." If this passage stands for the proposition that *sin* (as opposed to the temporal *consequences* of sin) is passed along to the offspring of the wicked, would it not follow that the offspring of the righteous would *not* be imputed with sin?

As any parent who has had to deal with the trepidations of "the terrible twos" can testify, children in the infant stage are notoriously self-centered. Yet, there is nothing in that alone which necessarily implies infants are spiritually depraved, or more inclined toward evil than good.[100] (Otherwise, what accounts for their expressions of unconditional love and their capacity for extraordinary trust?) That youngsters have an undeveloped sense of morality is not to be equated with either innate moral depravity or an inbred proclivity to sin.

In fact, that self-same moral immaturity militates against the idea of innate depravity. Consider, for example, this line from Deuteronomy 1:39:

---

[100] As noted previously, Genesis 8:21 ("every inclination of his heart is evil from childhood") does not prove to the contrary. First, because one would get a different idea than "inclination" from the KJV's "imagination," which seems to be the truer rendering of the original. Second, because in the context of God's smelling the sweet aroma of Noah's sacrifice we are reminded that even in the NIV the phrase could not be taken literally, otherwise Noah and his family could not have been inclined to righteousness. Third, because the inclination is *from childhood*, not from conception or birth, as would be necessary according to the notion of original sin and depravity. As with Genesis 6:5 and Psalm 51:5, surely this is yet another example of the Bible's frequent use of hyperbole.

"And the little ones that you said would be taken captive, your children *who do not yet know good from bad*—they will enter the land." Of course, it's not that little children don't understand early on about what is "good" and what is "bad." But because they cannot fully appreciate the moral consequences of good and bad, they are not held responsible for doing "bad." Which explains both biblical and universal recognition of the moral innocence of youngsters well outside the womb. If God didn't attribute moral or spiritual guilt to children, what warrant is there for us to impute innate, guilt-laden depravity?

Certainly, innate depravity is the last thing one would conclude from Jesus' words: "the kingdom of heaven belongs to such as these" (Matthew 19:14).[101] Consider, too, his admonition that "unless you change and become like little children, you will never enter the kingdom of heaven" (Matthew 18:3). Few indeed would interpret that as a call to sin and depravity!

Even a thoughtful Calvinist must surely ask what possible purpose God would have to impute sin to developing embryos in the womb, long before they have any choice between right and wrong, good and evil, obedience and disobedience. Though Calvinists generally say that the imputation of original sin makes it possible for God to bring glory to himself (since only sinful man could appreciate God's grace to the elect), it begs belief that the only way for God to be glorified is through wholesale condemnation of his creatures.

Since Calvinists agree that, on our own, "all have sinned and fall short of the glory of God" (Romans 3:23), is *original sin* actually necessary for us to have an appreciation of God's redeeming grace? Indeed, would it not be just cause for our *refusing* to appreciate any "act of grace" offered by one who had already condemned us before we were ever born?

---

[101] For Calvinists to suggest that the "these" referred to are "covenant children" is baseless speculation. Even if there were such a thing as "covenant children," are Calvinists prepared to defend the proposition that these "covenant children" were therefore born "clean"? Would that not run counter to the assertion that, because of original sin and depravity, *everyone* is born "unclean"? More telling still, in the very next verse cited (Matthew 18:3) Jesus is not even remotely talking about some special category of children, but of children generally.

The Character of God, Christ, and Man

Wholly apart from God's obvious sovereign power to do as he pleases,[102] are you at all bothered by the thought of a God who would thrust damnable sin upon otherwise innocent infants as they come into the world? Would that be consistent with the loving, just, and righteous character of God as revealed in Scripture? (For the moment, we're not talking about ultimate salvation or damnation, only the starting point for each newborn soul.)

Then again, if ever you wanted to put God's character and justice to the test, it would have to be in the Flood. In light of the anguish we felt at the deaths of scores of thousands in a tsunami, what are we to think of a God who not only permits wholesale death by drowning but specifically decrees it for the entire then-known world of men, women, and children?

Some would say that Noah's generation would have deserved it, not only because of their exceeding wickedness but also (in the case of infants) because of their innate depravity.[103] In that regard, is there a case to be made for man's depravity from the fact that "the Lord saw how great man's wickedness on the earth had become, and that every inclination of the thoughts of his heart was only evil all the time" (Genesis 6:5)?

Central to that sentence, of course, are those two key words–"had become"–which would hardly suggest either imputed sin or inborn depravity. We see those same words again in Genesis 6:11, followed by the observation that "all the people on earth had corrupted their ways."

Doesn't exactly sound like the result of a divinely-imposed penalty of universal condemnation, does it? If it were, how could Noah have escaped the penalty and turned out to be righteous? It must not be overlooked that God said to Noah: "Go into the ark...because I have *found you righteous* in this generation" (Genesis 7:1)–not, "I have *specially foreordained you to be righteous*."[104]

---

[102] See Psalm 135:6; Proverbs 19:21; 20:24; 21:1; Isaiah 43:12-13; 46:9-11; 55:10-11; Lamentations 3:37-38; Daniel 4:17.

[103] The thorny problems which Calvinists (and Arminians) face regarding the deaths of infants is put in bold relief in the Flood. Haphazard deaths of innocents is one thing; wholesale consignment to death another.

[104] Why did Noah find favor in the eyes of the Lord (in Genesis 6:8)? Not because of a special predestined election, but as the very next verse tells us: "Noah was a righteous man, blameless among the people of his time, and he walked with God."

What's more, if the foreordaining sovereign God himself had imposed the twin penalties of original sin and total depravity in the wake of Adam's sin, it would be strange indeed for him to lament mankind's universal wickedness, saying: "I am grieved that I have made them" (Genesis 6:8). Why should God grieve about a state of human existence over which he had, not just foreknowledge, but total predestining control from before the dawn of Creation?

Of one thing we can be sure: The notion that God arbitrarily assigns condemnation for sin is not even remotely harmonious with the theme-line running throughout the entire Bible, in which God demands, pleads, begs, and implores man *not* to sin!

If, as appears to be the case, Psalm 8 is describing not just Adam and Eve but all of mankind, it seems hardly likely that the pen of inspiration would say of depraved, inherently-sinful man: "You made him a little lower than the heavenly beings and crowned him with glory and honor." (The same is true of Ecclesiastes 7:29, where the wise man tells us: "God *made mankind upright*, but men have gone in search of many schemes."[105])

More serious yet, Psalm 8 is quoted in Hebrews 2:5-18 where, speaking of Jesus, the writer says: "Since the children have flesh and blood, he too shared in their humanity..." And as if to underscore the point, Paul refers to the "Son, who as to his human nature was a descendant of David" (Romans 1:3). So if Jesus really and truly did share in our humanity, how possibly could Jesus have escaped the pollution of original sin and human depravity?

If the answer is "his virgin birth," it can only mean that Jesus was fully God, but not fully human. The divine conundrum can't be played both ways–that Jesus was sufficiently human as to be tempted in all points like ourselves, but–unlike his fellow man–not sufficiently human as to be born depraved.

Recognizing this mammoth problem, many Calvinists and non-Calvinists alike have attempted to remedy it through the doctrine of

---

[105] Although it is possible to translate the NIV's "mankind" as "Adam," the KJV best captures the contextual meaning: "God hath made man upright; but *they* have sought out many inventions." The obvious parallelism between the two clauses rules out a singular reference to Adam alone.

immaculate conception, by which Jesus was miraculously born without imputed sin or depravity. (Roman Catholics go one step further, holding that Mary, too, was born of immaculate conception.) But, of course, there is not a shred of scriptural warrant for this doctrinal escape hatch.

As it happens, the doctrine of immaculate conception unwittingly expresses a great unintended truth: that both Jesus and Mary *were* born without sin. Rather than being exceptions to the rule, however, they not only exemplify but highlight the rule of nature by which each newborn soul comes into the world completely unshackled by sin.[106]

Can a Leopard Change His Spots?

Anyone familiar with the ongoing debate will know that Calvinists place a lot of stock in the now-proverbial leopard that can't change his spots (unless and until the Holy Spirit chooses that particular "depraved leopard" and regenerates him.) But have you ever checked out the context of this highly-touted passage (in Jeremiah 13:22-27)? It's not at all about some unalterable, inborn sinful nature that you and I might have, but about specific sins in which we persist—acting for all the world *as if* we couldn't change.

> *And if you ask yourself,*
>   *"Why has this happened to me?"—*
> *it is because of your many sins*
>   *that your skirts have been torn off*
>   *and your body mistreated.*
> *Can the Ethiopian change his skin*
>   *or the leopard its spots?*
> *Neither can you do good*
>   *who are accustomed to doing evil....*
> *because you have forgotten me*
>   *and trusted in false gods.*

---

[106] Even Aquinas gets caught out when Jesus comes into the picture. Having contended that ensoulment takes place long after conception, Aquinas apparently felt forced to make an exception for our Lord, insisting that Jesus had a soul from the very first moment.

Far from affirming that we have an inherent sin nature which we *can't* change, this oft-cited passage closes with a "woe" and a "plea"–both of which necessarily assume the ability (and attendant responsibility) to change one's "spots."

> *Woe to you Jerusalem!*
> *How long will you be unclean?*

If God is talking to those who are in such a spiritually depraved state that they couldn't possibly change their wicked ways without his own selective act of divine regeneration, why would he plead with them to change? (And if one insists that God was speaking only of his chosen elect, what does it say of the elect that they could–and did–irredeemably fall away?)

A similar question can be asked regarding Calvinism's use of John 8:42-47, where Jesus is confronting those Jews who take pride in their being the sons of Abraham...and thus, by that fact alone, sons of God. "The reason you do not hear," Jesus concludes, "is that you do not belong to God."

Subjected to Calvinist exegesis, Jesus' words are changed from "do not hear" to "cannot hear." By virtue of their unregenerate depravity, so it is said, these Jews have no ability to hear. (Lurking in the shadows, of course, is also the implication that they will forever remain unregenerate because they are not among the elect who "belong to God.")

Yet if that were the case, why should Jesus upbraid these Jews for their unregenerate disbelief–something over which they would have had no control (and doubly so should they happen to be among the non-elect)? If Jesus knew they lacked the fundamental ability to "hear the words of God" and respond to them, why exert any effort at all trying to convince them?

Virtually the same logic applies to God's condemnation of the Gentiles. Were not the Gentiles "without excuse," who, "although they knew God, they neither glorified him as God nor gave thanks to him" (Romans 1:18-23)? The text does not say they were without excuse because, being unregenerate, they were constitutionally unable to incline their minds and hearts to God. Indeed, had that been the case, they would have had the *perfect excuse!*[107]

Where Is the Smoking Gun?

If only there were a scripture text that could provide a "smoking gun," proving beyond all doubt that man is helplessly bound by depravity unless and until divinely regenerated. One of the texts which Calvinists frequently cite as a "smoking gun" (Romans 3:9-12) is, as argued, merely smoke and mirrors. In the context of reminding his Jewish brethren that the Jews were just as sinful as the reprobate Gentiles, Paul says:

> *As it is written: "There is no one righteous, not even one; there is no one who understands, no one who seeks God. All have turned away, they have together become worthless; there is no one who does good, not even one."*

Naturally, Calvinists seize on that last line in particular as proof of man's universal, pre-regenerative depravity. Suffice it to say that two aspects of Paul's statement instantly alert us that this passage is not the "smoking gun" Calvinists would hope.

When Paul says, first of all, "there is no one righteous," he obviously doesn't intend for us to take him literally. Otherwise, we'd be at a loss to explain the scores of references in Scripture to those who *were* righteous, including Jesus' comment to his disciples: "Many prophets *and righteous men* longed to see what you see..." (Matthew 13:17). And then there's Paul's own words: "The righteous will live by faith" (Galatians 3:11).

Second, when Paul says "there is no one who seeks God," surely he does not intend to contradict the many passages which refer to various ones seeking God, including, for example, the young king Josiah. "In the eighth year of his reign," says the text, "he began to seek the God of his father David" (2 Chronicles 34:3).[108] What's more, the same David who

---

[107] In support, Ephesians 4:17-18 reminds us that the ignorance and darkness of the Gentiles arose from the futility of their thinking which led to a hardening of their hearts.

[108] See also Deuteronomy 4:29; 2 Chronicles 15:2, 4, 15; 19:3; Psalm 34:4; and Jeremiah 29:13.

penned the psalms quoted by Paul in the full text of Romans 3 turns right around and says of himself: "O God, you are my God, earnestly I seek you" (Psalm 63:1).

So when we hear Paul saying, "there is no one who does good, not even one," we have no reason to believe he expects us to take that with wooden literalness, nor yet to extract from it a novel doctrine of universal, inherited, inescapable depravity. Paul here is simply repeating the point of Ecclesiastes 7:20, which tells us: "There is not a righteous man on earth who does what is right *and never sins*." Or, as Paul himself puts it only a few verses later (in Romans 3:23), "All have sinned and fall short of the glory of God."

Universal sin? Absolutely. *All have sinned!* Universal depravity of a type which condemns even unborn children before they have ever thought about sinning? Not by this text, or by any other.

The Arminian Problem

Calvinists are not alone in spinning tangled webs. Despite taking issue with all other major Calvinists doctrines, many Arminians agree completely with Calvinists on the doctrine of depravity. From his own writings, we have Arminius himself saying:

> In his lapsed and sinful state, man is not capable, of and by himself, either to think, to will, or to do that which is really good; but it is necessary for him to be regenerated and renewed in his intellect, affections, or will, and in all his powers, by God in Christ through the Holy Spirit, that he may be qualified rightly to understand, esteem, conceive, will, and perform whatever is truly good.[109]

For openers, wouldn't it be great if we had a single passage anywhere in Scripture that came right out and said that?

---

[109] James Arminius, *The Writings of James Arminius* (three vols.), tr. James Nichols and W.R. Bagnall (Grand Rapids: Baker, 1956), I:252

Beyond that, having denied that the elect are chosen unconditionally apart from faith freely exercised by the believer, Arminians who espouse original sin and depravity are forced to explain how a person who is depraved can possibly respond to the gospel.

Recognizing the problem, Arminius resorted, as did others before him, to the fire-exit notion of "prevenient grace." Probably better understood in current word usage as something like *pre-regenerating grace* or *enabling grace*, the idea is that God takes the initiative to open the door which inevitably leads to regeneration unless the recipient of that grace refuses the gift and slams the door shut.

Along with Calvinists, "Reformation Arminians" (as Robert Picirilli has coined the term[110]) believe that, were it not for God's enabling grace through the work of the Holy Spirit in the proclamation of the gospel, depraved man–though imbued with free will in God's own image–would be unable to respond to God's overture of love, forgiveness, and salvation. (It's like a man in prison whose will and freedom of decision is severely limited.) Unlike Calvinists, Reformation Arminians believe that this enabling grace (not to be confused with Calvinism's selective regeneration) is extended to all who hear the gospel, to the end that all who respond to the truth may receive salvation and regeneration through Christ.

The Case of Lydia's Open Heart

As evidence of an enabling grace, Reformation (or "classical") Arminians join with Calvinists in citing, among many others, the following three key passages. The first is taken from the account of Lydia's conversion, where Luke tells us: "The Lord opened her heart to respond to Paul's message" (Acts 16:14). But are we to believe that this was a special and particular "opening of the heart" which enabled Lydia to escape the depravity which otherwise would have rendered her incapable of freely responding to the gospel?

---

[110] Robert E. Picirilli, *Grace, Faith, Free Will* (Nashville: Randall House, 2002)

If so, is this to say that God opened Lydia's heart in some way unique to her? Or that God opens some hearts but not others? Surely, Arminians can't be thinking what their Calvinist adversaries are actually saying!

Since Arminians forcefully deny *selective, unconditional, and irresistible* "open heart surgery" (their chief point of disagreement with Calvinists), what more can they be saying but that God's grace is implemented through the proclamation of the Word to stir the hearts of any and all who will receive it?

If that is all we're talking about, who could argue otherwise?[111] "For since in the wisdom of God the world through its wisdom did not know him, God was pleased through the foolishness of what was preached to save those who believe" (1 Corinthians 1:21). "Consequently, faith comes from hearing the message, and the message is heard through the word of Christ" (Romans 10:17). It is only by God's grace in providing the gospel of salvation that anyone can be drawn to God!

The expansive rendering of Romans 10:17 in *The New English Bible* wonderfully captures the idea that "faith is awakened by the message, and the message that awakens it comes through the words of Christ."

Even Calvinists (with their own unique understanding of those passages) undoubtedly would agree that the preaching of the gospel is the immediate *means* whereby God seeks out his elect that they may turn to him in faith. But for Calvinists, the gospel not only *doesn't* play a part in regeneration, it *can't*. Unless and until the Holy Spirit regenerates a person, there is no capacity to receive the gospel. And because that regeneration is wholly unconditional, it cannot have anything to do with whether or not one is receptive to the gospel.

From a non-Calvinist perspective, by contrast, God had it in mind from eternity to choose all those whose free, non-predestined response to the gospel would exhibit an unwavering love for the truth.[112]

The point of diversion between Calvinists and those who accept Arminius' view is how, and to what extent, God regenerates depraved men

---

[111] Boettner seems to agree, saying: "He who reads and meditates upon the word of God is ordinarily regenerated by the Holy Spirit, perhaps in the very act of reading. 'While Peter yet spake these words, the Holy Spirit fell on all them that heard the word,' Acts 10:44." (Boettner, 257)

[112] See 2 Thessalonians 2:9-14.

and women. Since classical Arminians vehemently reject the Calvinist doctrine of special election (believing instead that the preaching of the gospel empowers everyone who hears it with the ability to respond freely to the good news), their citing the case of Lydia's heart being opened is somewhat mystifying. As presumably there were other women that day who spurned the same gospel message, Arminians must somehow respond to Calvin's argument that the Spirit opened Lydia's heart, but not the hearts of the others. The answer given by Arminians—that the Spirit's enabling through the gospel does not invariably lead to regeneration and salvation—is certainly closer to the truth, but is made unnecessarily difficult by their resort to Lydia's conversion.

A separate but crucial question, of course, is how we are to understand the various Scriptures that refer to the "hardening" and "opening" of hearts—an important subject which will bear closer scrutiny as we go along. Suffice it to say for the moment that the case of Lydia's conversion does little to promote the Arminian doctrine of enabling grace. Indeed, having to grab for such counter-intuitive straws raises a suspicion that the case for enabling grace totters precariously on a shaky underlying premise.

Is There a Problem With the Receiver?

This brings us to a second proof-text we are offered, John 16:8. "When he [the Holy Spirit] comes, he will convict the world of guilt in regard to sin and righteousness and judgment." With perhaps a difference in nuance here and there, virtually everyone agrees that the power of the Spirit is inherent within the preaching of the gospel, inwardly convincing men of the truth and persuading the human will to accept that truth. Even so, is there anything in this passage hinting that some switch has to be flipped in *the hearer* before the power of the gospel can take effect? Or that the Spirit must overcome some innate depravity in individual hearers in order for them to have the capability of responding to the gospel call?

All sides readily acknowledge the mega-watt power of the "transmitter," which is to say the gospel itself. For, along with Paul, we too can exult: "I am not ashamed of the gospel, because it is the power of God for the salvation of everyone who believes" (Romans 1:16). But are we really to believe that every single "receiver" ever produced has a design flaw which first must be repaired in order for it to receive signals from the transmitter? If so, it seems odd that Arminius would have gone to so much trouble to flip the switch of enablement off (in affirming man's depravity), only to flip it back on again, affirming that the Spirit's enabling grace has patched the problem in each and every "receiver" who hears the Word.

For Sinners All, What's the Draw?

A third passage offered by classical Arminians to explain "prevenient" or enabling grace brings us to these words from Jesus' own mouth: "No one can come to me unless the Father who sent me *draws* him...." (John 6:44).

Are Calvinists right, then, to conclude that only those elect who have been specially *drawn* even before Creation can come to faith? Those who follow Arminius' view, certainly, would never hold to special, unconditional election. They would be right to point Calvinists to John 6:40, where Jesus says: "My Father's will is that everyone who looks to the Son and believes in him shall have eternal life." That certainly *sounds* more like a universal offer of salvation than some limited edition of specially-chosen saints.

Have you ever considered that this same universal offer comes complete with the word *draw* in John 12:32? Says Jesus of his crucifixion: "But I, when I am lifted up from the earth, will *draw all men* to myself." If *draw* (*helkuo*) in John 6:44 refers to an irresistible drawing toward regeneration, then the same word *draw* (*helkuo*) in John 12:32 must mean that *all men* are irresistibly drawn toward regeneration. For Calvinists, certainly, this must surely put the logical cat among the theological pigeons!

Of course, the question remains: What, in fact, did Jesus mean when he talked about believers being *drawn*? Are we talking about targeted individuals being *dragged* kicking and screaming? Or might one instead be "irresistibly drawn," as to a person, idea, or mission? To begin with, Jesus tells us straight out precisely *how* God draws men to himself. "It is written in the Prophets: 'They will all be taught by God.' Everyone who listens to the Father and learns from him comes to me" (John 6:45).

As all Arminians would agree, *teaching* is God's principal method of drawing men unto himself, not simply drawing names out of a hat before the dawn of creation. However, this doesn't get us very far, since Calvinists will insist that it is only the foreordained elect—those who have been specially and particularly regenerated by the Spirit—who will *listen, learn,* and *come.*

In the crucial pursuit of context, context, context, perhaps we all need to hit the Pause button while we go back and re-read the whole of John 6:24-71 which records Jesus' intriguing discourse on the Bread of Life.

When the discussion moves from Jesus' recent "miracle of the loaves" to the manna miraculously provided to the Jews in the desert, Jesus declares himself to be the bread of life (the spiritual manna) sent by God down out of heaven to feed the world with his life-giving words.

While the Jews had loved the bread and circuses aspect of the "miracle of the loaves," what jolts them to attention is Jesus' claim to have come down out of heaven. How possibly could he have descended from heaven, they query, knowing that he was the local hometown boy who had grown up right there in their midst—whose father was *Joseph!*

Jesus' reply—replete with seemingly macabre calls for them to eat his flesh and drink his blood—offends many in his audience who fail to appreciate Jesus' mystical reference to his body and blood which would be given as an atonement for sin. Yet what offends them most is not the repugnant thought of some bizarre, ritual cannibalism, but his audacious claim to have come down out of heaven. Which explains why Jesus concludes his discourse by asking: "Does this offend you? What if you see the Son of Man ascending to where he was before!"

Instinctively, the crowd senses that, unlike any prophet before him, Jesus is claiming a special relationship with God, which for them approaches blasphemy. Far from dispelling their suspicions, Jesus repeatedly affirms his divinity.

Crucial to our own discussion, it is those very affirmations, woven seamlessly into the dialogue about his being the bread of life, that talk about *drawing, enabling,* and *receiving.* As for those specific words of empowerment, of course, it is beyond dispute that had not God (Father, Son, and Holy Spirit) planned, provided, and implemented a divine process whereby we are called into a saving relationship, we would be without hope. If God did not initiate, we could not reciprocate.

It is important to note here, however, that the drawing, the enabling, and the receiving are not the central subject of Jesus' discourse. Rather, Jesus is pointing his skeptical audience to the unified, indistinguishable aims and purposes between Father and Son. Those who seek the Father must do so through the Son, says Jesus in effect, for we are one in being, and thus one in will and one in purpose. Those who come to me, come to the Father.[113] (Or as Jesus puts it in John 16:6- 7, "No one comes to the Father except through me. If you really knew me, you would know my Father as well.")

Conversely, "All that the Father gives me will come to me" (for we are but the right hand and left hand clasped together). "Everyone who listens to the Father and learns from him comes to me," (for we proclaim the same truth). "No one can come to me unless the Father who sent me draws him," (for if you are drawn to one, you must also be drawn to the other). "This is why I told you that no one can come to me unless the Father has enabled him"...(or come to the Father, unless I myself have enabled him).[114]

Far from being a treatise on *how* the Holy Spirit regenerates (less yet, *whom*), Jesus' discourse here is intended to underscore the fact that he is the bread of life for the very reason that his "Father" was not *Joseph*, as they supposed, but *the God of heaven*! That he was *God himself in flesh and blood*! That, as Peter confesses so powerfully in the closing punch line to the entire discussion, "We believe and know that you are the Holy One of God."[115]

---

[113] This same analysis applies to Matthew 11:27, often cited by Calvinists in support of particular election. "All things have been committed to me by my Father," says Jesus. "No one knows the Son except the Father, and no one knows the Father except the Son and those to whom the Son chooses to reveal him." However, Calvinists typically fail to mention what Jesus says in his very next breath: "Come to me, all you who are weary and burdened, and I will give you rest." The universality of that invitation is hardly supportive of particular election.

[114] As for the "enabling" itself, it is no mystery that we of ourselves could never approach God had he not already made that possible by his grace. When John the Baptist was asked about the multitudes who were flocking to Jesus to be baptized, John observed that "A man can receive only what is given him from heaven" (John 3:27). Far from addressing anything like (limited) irresistible grace, John underscores just the opposite, saying: "For the one whom God has sent [Jesus] speaks the words of God, for God gives the Spirit without limit" (John 3:34).

This verse is not addressing freedom of will, rather the fact that we alone could not accomplish anything whatsoever were it not for the blessing of God's (heaven's) grace taking what we do and imbuing it with significance. Which, on the other hand, does not negate the value of what we do. Consider Psalm 127:1–"Unless the LORD builds the house, its builders labor in vain. Unless the LORD watches over the city, the watchmen stand guard in vain." That whatever we receive ultimately comes from heaven does not negate our freely receiving it.

[115] See also John 5:16-29, a parallel passage making all the same points.

To miss the context is to miss the whole point. What's more, are we meant to understand that Jesus is saying he can't get a foot through the door unless either the Father or the Holy Spirit has already unlocked it and pushed it slightly ajar?

How, then, should we understand Jesus' words to the teeming crowd listening to his sermon on the mount: "Ask and it will be given to you; seek and you will find; knock and the door will be opened to you" (Matthew 7:7)? Or his plea to the lukewarm believers in Laodicea: "Here I am! I stand at the door and knock. If anyone hears my voice and opens the door, I will come in and eat with him, and he with me" (Revelation 3:20). Whether speaking to the unsaved or the saved, is there any hint from Jesus about enabling grace...or the *need* for it?

The truly amazing thing is this: *Christ himself*, standing wistfully at our door and knocking even before we do, *is our enabling grace!* Is that not a picture worth a thousand words?

But that is hardly the theological double-speak we hear from classical Arminians. Seizing on verses talking about *drawing* and *enabling* to explain how man's supposed depravity is overcome by "prevenient" or enabling grace, they end up back where they started. Just as Calvinists are forced to have an artificial, two-tiered system in order for the elect to have any semblance of "free will" to accept Christ, classical Arminians must likewise come up with an equally inventive, two-tiered explanation of their own to explain how a person whose innate free will, temporarily disabled by depravity, is enabled through the gospel to respond to Christ.

For Arminians who believe in man's innate depravity, the curious anticlimax turns out to be that everyone who's ever heard the gospel proclaimed is automatically and invariably a recipient of "prevenient," enabling grace. The end result is that what is taken away with one hand through depravity is suddenly given back with the hand of enabling grace. Like magic, now you see man's depravity, now you don't!

Why not simply acknowledge that, if God had not extended his grace to call us unto himself, we on our own would have no means whatsoever to bridge the yawning gap between our sinning self and a holy God?[116] Isn't that

---

[116] See, for example, Ephesians 2:1-3; 4:17-19; and 2 Corinthians 4:3-4, all of which would be cited eagerly by Reformed Arminians.

the underlying concern leading to the idea of total depravity in the first place? Must we resort to, not one but two, unbiblical notions (total depravity *and* "prevenient grace") in order to bolster a truth that already stands firmly on its own–the truth that without God's grace we would all be, not totally depraved, but totally lost?

That Arminius went to such excruciating lengths to create an elaborately embroidered theory which, in the end, merely brought him back to square one suggests he took a wrong turn to begin with.

Despite rumors of a debilitating "Fall" which lowered man into the depths of depravity and effectively imprisoned his free will, the truth is that man was never put in any situation where (as Arminius believed) his free will was limited, impaired, or disabled; or (as Calvin believed) was wholly non-existent apart from selective regeneration. Whenever and wherever God's Word is preached, sinners are drawn to the good news of God's forgiveness. And it is here–at the point when John 3:16 is boldly proclaimed–that classical Arminians are clearly right to remind Calvinists that God *calls*, but never *stacks the deck*.

For God so loved the world that he gave his one and only Son, that whoever believes in him shall not perish but have eternal life.

John 3:16

Chapter Summary

- The doctrines of original sin and total depravity have spinoff consequences which, at best, are problematic. At worst, they are unthinkable.

- The biblically-unknown Catholic concept of limbo was made necessary only because of the biblically-unknown concept of original sin.

- Protestants who accept original sin and total depravity, yet believe that God makes exceptions in cases of infant deaths, unwittingly confirm the incongruity between infant damnation and the obvious innocence of the young.

- John Calvin tied himself up in knots mixing inconsistent positions on the various subjects related to infant baptism, original sin, and the eternal destiny of unbaptized infants.

- Far from arriving in this world tainted with the condemnation of sin, infants are Jesus' own "poster kids" for the Kingdom.

- Reformation Arminians who accept original sin and total depravity are forced unnecessarily to contrive the doctrine of "prevenient grace" in order to ensure that every person has the free will to accept God's grace.

- We are neither damned from conception nor totally or partially depraved so as to lack the ability to respond to the gospel without either some special regeneration for the elect or "pre-regenerating grace" for all.

Reality Check: If in fact God decided your spiritual destiny before you were ever conceived, then it doesn't matter whether you might have died in the womb, or perhaps before you were old enough to read this book, or might yet live to be 110. At any stage of life, no matter how unconscious, immature, or well-informed, your designated place in heaven or hell is irreversible.

Chapter 5

The Persistent Problem of Sin

*We have all sinned...because we are imbued with natural corruption,
and for this reason we are wicked and perverse.*

–John Calvin

On the same day in November, 1963, on which Lee Harvey Oswald shot and killed John F. Kennedy in cold blood, every other man and woman on the face of the planet also sinned in the eyes of God. Whether Hindu, Buddhist, Muslim, atheist, agnostic, or "Christian," not a single soul was free from sin that day.

Certainly that would include John F. Kennedy himself (whose sins were many, despite the esteem with which he is remembered), and even the widely-acclaimed Christian author, C. S. Lewis, who by some quirk of circumstance also died on that most memorable of days. Despite the esteem with which he, too, is remembered, Lewis would be the first to tell us that his sins, if perhaps different from John Kennedy's, were none the less grievous for being less notorious.

Naturally, it also included myself, who first heard the news of Kennedy's assassination during a choral practice at college. Along with millions around the world, I sat transfixed for hours listening to radio and television accounts of the assassination. While I can remember many details of the day in vivid technicolor, I have to confess that I don't remember in what specific ways I might have affronted God that particular day. But, given my consistent track record, I have no doubt but that I was as guilty of sin that day as was Oswald, Kennedy, Lewis, and everybody else.

I could never prove it, of course, but I can well imagine that there were thousands of resolute reprobates in Dallas who were lying, cheating, and stealing that very day. They were sinners all, but what else would one expect of unbelievers? Yet I can also well imagine that in Dallas that day there were thousands of committed believers who were also lying, cheating, and maybe even stealing. You can bet they were coveting, gossiping, cursing, and undoubtedly lusting in forbidden ways. Like the city's many reprobates, the believers, too, were sinners all.

Included among them might possibly have been a Baptist deacon having an illicit affair that day. Or perhaps an Episcopalian housewife maliciously backstabbing her neighbor. With complete certainty, the list of sinners would also include (for a variety of sins too numerous to mention) every Methodist, Pentecostal, and Presbyterian within the city limits...whether Calvinist or non-Calvinist.

Is "Total Depravity" Responsible For *All* Sin?

Why this rehearsal of the obvious? One of the most interesting aspects of Calvinism is that it begins by employing the concept of total depravity as a means of explaining (insuring?) that man has no ability to contribute anything whatsoever to his salvation, but ends up in a far more interesting place.

First to the opening volley. Because man is totally depraved, so goes the argument, he can only respond to God if God himself brings a person from death to life by a divine act of regeneration. All of which arguably might explain the actions of Lee Harvey Oswald (and later Jack Ruby) and the multitudes of those whom we might assume (in Calvinist terms) to be unregenerate reprobates.

Yet even after Calvinism's regeneration has done its work (selectively) in overcoming man's innate depravity, that self-same depravity is cited by Calvinists as the continuing cause of the sin committed by C. S. Lewis, our hypothetical Baptist deacon and Episcopalian housewife, and all the conscientious, Bible-believing, church-going, prayer-offering Methodists, Pentecostals, and Presbyterians within the Dallas city limits. Even regarding those who might be considered "saved," there is more than a hint that Calvinists believe in the doctrine of "once predisposed to sin, always predisposed to sin."

The most curious aspect of Calvinism's treatment of ongoing sin is that virtually all of the many scripture texts which are clearly addressed to baptized believers about the problem of persistent sin are commandeered, instead, in aid of proving pre-regenerate sin and depravity. By the time those passages have been thoroughly exhausted in that misdirected effort, hardly anything remains to raise the obvious problem being dealt with in those texts. Little wonder. To face head-on the issue of persistent sin in regenerate, saved believers is to seriously jeopardize the very notion of total depravity, since at least part of that depravity is fully and completely "switched off" at the point of regeneration.

When Calvinist authors address the issue of persistent sin, the same depravity which was "switched off" to allow for free will, faith, and justification, remains "switched on" as the cause of continuing sin. The fact that the unregenerate person is now regenerate does not nullify altogether the bundle of depravity for which regeneration was made necessary.

As Loraine Boettner puts it, "So long as people remain in this world they are subject to temptations and they still have the remnants of the old nature clinging to them. Hence they are often deluded, and commit sin; yet these sins are only the death struggles and frenzied writhing of the old nature which has already received the death blow."[117]

R.C. Sproul agrees, insisting that "Love for God is not natural to us. *Even in the redeemed state* our souls grow cold and we experience feelings of indifference toward him."[118] Even when fully redeemed, so it is argued, we are tainted by what we might call the "bathtub rings" of original sin.

---

[117] Boettner, 171
[118] Sproul, 127 (with my emphasis)

Not unlike unsightly scum, depravity has a way of clinging forever to the sides of our redeemed souls.

While there is no disputing the sad fact that sin persists in the lives of the redeemed, the question is one of cause and effect. Is original sin and depravity the continuing root cause of persistent sin?

Intending to include even the saved, Sproul's answer is that "Just as a corrupt tree yields corrupt fruit, so sin flows out of a corrupt human nature. We are not sinners because we sin; we sin because we are sinners. Since the fall human nature has been corrupt. We are born with a sin nature. Our acts of sin flow out of this corrupted nature."[119]

Yet, if we sin *because we are sinners*, is this not to say that, somewhere along the line, we *cannot help but sin*? By contrast, if we *can* refuse to sin (as the Scriptures implore us to do), surely we must conclude that we have no innate corruption which makes sin necessary. (And merely consider this sobering thought: If we sin because it is our inborn nature to sin, who but God is responsible for that nature, and ultimately for our sin?)

It's important to remember that it's not *the lost* we're talking about here, but *the saved*, whose sins are said to be caused by man's inherited depravity. This sinister echo of original sin's effect on unregenerate reprobates may be even more pernicious than the first, suggesting as it does that, even after regeneration, we may claim some valiant victories, but ultimately we are powerless against sin.

Again we turn to Sproul, who asserts that "We simply are unable to live without sinning. We sin out of a kind of moral necessity because we act according to our fallen nature."[120] Wow! Sin, *a moral necessity*?[121] Can that possibly be what God had in mind when he said to Cain, "Sin desires to have you, but *you must master it*" (Genesis 4:6-7)?

---

[119] Sproul, 118-119

[120] Sproul, 123

[121] Even when trying to avoid Sproul's "extreme Calvinism" on this point, Norman Geisler appears to end up in a similar boat. "Sin in general is inevitable," says Geisler, "but each sin in particular is avoidable–by the grace of God." I don't mean to nitpick, but if each and every sin is in fact "avoidable" (as the Scriptures teach), then there is nothing strictly "inevitable" about sin. To acknowledge that "all *have* sinned" is not to say prospectively that sin is inevitable. (Giving Geisler the benefit of the doubt, perhaps his use of "inevitable" is intended merely to reflect this factual reality.) [See Norman L. Geisler, *Chosen But Free*, 2nd Ed. (Minneapolis: Bethany House Publishers, 1999, 2001), 65.]

Is Our "Sinful Nature" Made Necessary By "Depravity"?

In order to clear up some of the confusion about man's sinful nature and the nature of sin, we briefly need to address a number of passages which typically are offered as proof-texts by Calvinists in support of *pre-regenerate* depravity. In each case, as we shall see, Paul is addressing the problem of sin in the life of the baptized believer, not the unregenerate reprobate.

Yet the very presence of ongoing sin in the life of baptized believers raises serious questions about Calvinism's assumption that the taint of original sin overstays its welcome long past the point of regeneration. Do even unquestionably regenerate believers have a sin nature that continues in some way to prompt their sin? Even after being brought from death to life, do we sin out of some moral or constitutional necessity because we are sinners?

In light of Paul's discussion in Romans 7-8 and 13 regarding the "desires of the sinful nature" (as the NIV puts it) or "the lusts of the flesh" (as the KJV renders it), one might conclude that, because of "the Fall," there is something so innately sinful about us that, even after our redemption, we remain constitutionally predisposed to sin.

To test that theory, we should begin by asking whether the "pre-Fall," *in-the-image-of-God* nature of Adam and Eve was somehow spared having a "sinful nature" or "the lusts of the flesh." Given what we are told about their having yielded to temptation because the fruit "looked good to eat," it's clear that Adam and Eve shared the same lust of the eyes, or desires of the "sinful nature," as do we. So, whatever our "sinful nature" might be, it didn't result from any supposed "fall of man" in the Garden.

Which brings us to the crucial question: What, exactly, does Paul mean when he refers in Romans and Galatians to the "sinful nature" or the "flesh"? Does it have anything to do with any innate sinfulness over which, in the end, we are powerless? At the very least, Paul assures us in Galatians 5:24 that "Those who belong to Christ Jesus *have crucified* the sinful nature [flesh] with its passions and desires." Even if Paul is speaking more from aspiration than hard reality, from this passage we can be certain of at least this: We aren't helpless victims at the hands of our sinful nature.

And how did this "crucifixion" of the sinful nature happen, Paul? "In him you were also circumcised, in the putting off of the sinful nature [flesh], not with a circumcision done by the hands of men but with the circumcision done by Christ, having been buried with him in baptism and raised with him through your faith in the power of God, who raised him from the dead" (Colossians 2:11-12).

Just as flesh is cut away in the process of circumcision, says Paul, our sinful nature is taken away by God as he powerfully regenerates us through faith and baptism. (At least this is objectively true, in the same way that we are both *already* and *not yet fully* sanctified. Paul would not disagree with the proposition that our sinful nature will not be finally and fully taken away until the Resurrection, anymore than our sanctification will be finally and fully complete in this life.)

This act of conversion-related regeneration, of course, couldn't be further from the pre-conversion regeneration contemplated by Calvinists, which not only *precedes* a person's faith and might, but also might not, even be "sensed" at the moment it happens. That the two explanations of regeneration are so radically different speaks volumes about why we disagree regarding Paul's use of the phrase "sinful nature."

Listen closely when Paul speaks about our "sinful nature" [flesh], and you'll appreciate that he isn't talking about an inherited, innate state of depravity out of which we are constrained to sin even after being regenerated and redeemed. Rather, he is highlighting the fact that—even after being saved—we freely, knowingly, wilfully, and rebelliously continue to engage in sin.

Mind you, that's not just "engage in *sin*" in some generic sense, but, more specifically, engage in *sins*. (As in, name them one by one.) Look closely at Galatians 5:19, for instance, where Paul writes: "*The acts of the sinful nature [flesh] are obvious*: sexual immorality, impurity and debauchery; idolatry and witchcraft; hatred, discord, jealousy, fits of rage, selfish ambition, dissensions, factions and envy; drunkenness, orgies, and the like." Whatever the "sinful nature" is, it is notably and identifiably active, not passive.

As always, context is the key to our understanding of the Word. To whom was Paul addressing his warnings about the "sinful nature" [flesh]? It's clearly not to the unregenerate reprobate, but to "sons of God" who had been "baptized into Christ" (Galatians 3:26-27). And what is Paul's message to these sons of God? "You, my brothers, were called to be free. But do not use your freedom to indulge the sinful nature [flesh]" (Galatians 5:13).

You mean, Paul, that children of God do not sin out of necessity? That they are really and truly free not to indulge in the sinful nature? That there are no lingering side-effects of original sin which make even the children of God sin because it remains their built-in nature to sin? If Paul had understood the problem of sin as Calvinists understand it, one might think he (indeed, the Holy Spirit) would have been far more explicit to say so.

Yet, the crucial question remains: Just how are we to understand the phrase "sinful nature" (or "flesh")? R.C. Sproul would have us believe that "To be in the state of original sin is to be in the state Scripture calls the 'flesh.'"[122] Turning that sentence around so we can get a better view of it, Sproul is saying that, to be in the state Scripture calls the "flesh," is to be in the state of original sin.

But if Sproul is right about that, then by virtue of what Paul tells us about the "flesh" in Galatians 5:13-26, regenerate baptized believers would be lapsing back into, not simply "the flesh" (of the unconverted) as opposed to "the Spirit" (of the converted), but actually back into *original sin*. Are we so depraved by original sin that regeneration, conversion, and being in the Spirit count for so little?

So what exactly are we to learn from this passage? First, that Paul never uses either the "sinful nature" or the "flesh" in the same sense as "depravity" or "original sin." Nowhere does Paul suggest that we *must* sin because we are sinners by nature (whether before or after we are saved).

The second lesson to be learned is that, for Paul, the "sinful nature" or the "flesh" has to do with *conduct, habit, and a developed character*, not some inbuilt *proclivity to sin*. The former is a condition for which you and I are personally responsible, and over which (with varying degrees of difficulty) we can exercise control. The latter is a condition for which you and I are not responsible, and over which ultimately we have no control.

As everyone surely agrees, while only God can change our lost *status*, we ourselves can (and continually must) change our *conduct*. So when we

---

live by the flesh, as opposed to the Spirit, it is certainly true that *the nature of what we do is sinful*. But the natural sense of that conclusion couldn't be further removed from some predisposing, sin-necessitating *sin nature*.

Paul's Own Struggle With Sin

Perhaps you have heard Romans 7:14-20 cited in support of Calvinism's claim that man is a slave to his sin nature. It's that famous passage where Paul says he *wants* to do good, but finds himself doing what is evil. (We can all relate to that!) The Calvinist argument is taken particularly from verse 18, where Paul laments: "I know that *nothing good lives in me*, that is, in my sinful nature. For I have the desire to do what is good, but I cannot carry it out. For what I do is not the good I want to do; no, the evil I do not want to do–this I keep on doing."

"*Nothing good* lives in me"? What a remarkable statement from this remarkably good man of God–which immediately raises a huge problem whenever this passage is offered as proof of man's *unregenerate* depravity. Whether by Calvinism's definition or by any other, Paul just might be the most regenerate man we could possibly point to! So whatever else we are to understand from Paul's frank self-assessment, it cannot have anything to do with a pre-regenerate state of depravity. Yet the question remains, what does this passage have to say about man's post-regenerate state?

In describing his ongoing struggle with sin, Paul appears to employ the same agonizing hyperbole as we saw earlier in David's own tortured lament (Psalm 51). Of one thing we can be sure: it has nothing to do with any vestigial remains of a some pre-regenerate state of depravity–otherwise how could Paul even *desire* to do what is good?[123]

Should it be suggested that Paul's desire to do good is the result of his being divinely regenerated, what does it tell us but that his regeneration did not fully relieve him of his struggle with sin? Are we to believe, for either Paul or ourselves, that it's a matter of "once depraved, always depraved"?

---

[123] The same hyperbole is seen in Psalm 14:1-3; 53:2-3. At certain points in the discussion, most Calvinists acknowledge that, by God's common grace, even the unregenerate often do what could be called "good."

In this regard, consider Paul's tantalizing observation in Romans 7:20 (following hard on the heels of the described struggle he has with his sinful nature). "Now if I do what I do not want to do, it is no longer I who do it, but it is sin living in me that does it."

Is Paul implying that he is not responsible for whatever unrighteous acts he commits—that his inability to do what he knows to be right is solely and utterly the work of some alien, roguish sin-force living inside his body? (Wouldn't we all like to believe that!) Yet, were that the case, how very strange it is that Paul confides (in 1 Corinthians 9:27): "I beat my body and make it my slave so that after I have preached to others, I myself will not be disqualified for the prize."

If Paul has desires of the flesh that attempt to get out of control (and often succeed), it looks for all the world that he is taking personal responsibility for getting them back under control. Does that sound like a man who, on one hand, is totally depraved; or, on the other, is fully regenerated from death to life?[124]

To the contrary, does it not sound like a man who has been endowed with the free moral choice either to pervert legitimate natural instincts or to rise above such perversion pursuant to nobler self-discipline and prayerful appeals to the power of the Holy Spirit within him?[125]

Like Calvinists, non-Calvinists are in no doubt about sin remaining in the life of the converted believer. As we all agree, that's what sanctification is all about: moving us to greater and greater heights of holiness and purity. But none of this helps resolve the insoluble problem that Calvinists

---

[124] That Paul took "personal responsibility" over his sins is not to suggest that he didn't look to the Holy Spirit for a power beyond himself, as in Romans 8:13: "For if you live according to the sinful nature, you will die; but if *by the Spirit* you put to death the misdeeds of the body, you will live...." Yet he takes seriously the call to self-control implicit in Christ's admonition: "If your right eye causes you to sin, gouge it out and throw it away. It is better for you to lose one part of your body than for your whole body to be thrown into hell," (Matthew 5:29).

[125] In the larger context of the letter to the Romans, of course, Paul is contrasting how the flesh was actually victimized by the law in some ways, but is now set free in Christ to live on a higher plane. Paul uses his personal struggle with sin to showcase the contrast between the competing systems of law and grace about which he is speaking. Under the law alone, it was always a frustrating reality that nothing judicially good could live in him; whereas, in Christ, the genuine goodness of Christ's righteousness could actually be appropriated into his own life. So he implores the Romans (and us) not to live as slaves to mere rules, but to be enslaved—mind, body, and spirit—to the One who can set us free from the endless cycle of spiritual deadness which results from trying futilely to overcome our baser selves chiefly by not breaking any rules.

have when trying to transform a passage pertaining to Paul's "post-regenerate" struggle into proof of man's "pre-regenerate" universal depravity. Nor does it provide any basis for saying that, even after we are regenerate, we necessarily continue to sin out of some innate human instinct.

The Not Insignificant Matter of Jesus

As suggested previously, shoe-horning Jesus into Calvinism's understanding of man's persistent "sin nature" is incredibly difficult. For if Jesus had been exempt from struggling with the "desires of the sinful nature" or "lusts of the flesh," then he would have been an exception to our supposed human depravity and inherent sinfulness. But, if he's to be an exception, then there is no meaningful way it could be said that he was "tempted in every way, just as we are–yet was without sin" (Hebrews 4:15).

Given the fact that Jesus fully shared in our humanity *through Adam* (as confirmed in numerous passages, not the least of which is Luke's genealogy of Christ, Luke 3:23-38), are we prepared to say that Jesus was constitutionally inclined to sin, or was either partially or totally depraved? More to the point of this chapter, how could Jesus have escaped sin so completely if, inherent within human nature, sinning is a moral necessity?

Even granting Jesus' unquestionably divine nature, Jesus clearly had a "fleshly" human nature. (What is the significance of the Incarnation if not the wondrous truth that "The Word became *flesh* and made his dwelling among us"?) But if the thought that Jesus had a "sinful nature" makes you uncomfortable, you are in good company. It's hard to think of Jesus having a "sinful nature" when we know that, despite being tempted in every way as ourselves, he was "without sin."

As it happens, nothing could better highlight the NIV's unfortunate translation of "flesh" as "sinful nature," with its misleading connotation suggesting innate, ongoing sinfulness. If your belief in man's depravity is bolstered to any degree by the NIV's use of the phrase "sinful nature," you may wish to consider that virtually all other translations render the Greek word *sarx* as "flesh." And nothing whatsoever in the word *flesh* has any biblical connotation suggesting that man is innately inclined toward sin, much less compelled to sin out of some moral necessity.

Sola Scriptura...In Context!

As with all theories, "the devil is in the details." And as with all worthy theology, the truth is in the Scriptures. Yet sometimes even what Scripture tells us is a matter of niggling details as well. Consider, for example, Ephesians 2:1-3, which Calvinists cite for support–drawing especially from the phrases "our sinful nature" and "we were by nature objects of wrath." Take a close look at this passage:

> *As for you, you were dead in your transgressions and sins, in which you used to live when you followed the ways of this world and of the ruler of the kingdom of the air, the spirit who is now at work in those who are disobedient. All of us also lived among them at one time, gratifying the cravings of our sinful nature and following its desires and thoughts. Like the rest, we were by nature objects of wrath.*[126]

To say that, before accepting Christ and repenting, it was our nature to sin (in the way of the world), is hardly the same as saying we were born with some inherent "sin nature" which predisposes us to sin. Are we talking about our inborn "nature to breathe," for example, or a particular person's acquired "nature to lie"? In the former, it's innocently doing what comes naturally. In the latter, it's repetitive misbehavior that has become one's normal practice. Huge difference, that!

As between those two options, which one is intended by the opening line: "You were dead in *your transgressions and sins* in which you *used to live*"? Do those words suggest a passive, inborn "sin nature;" or rather an active state of rebellion which has become one's natural mode of operation? It's all the difference between saying, "I can't help myself" and "I jolly well *can* help myself!"

This crucial distinction also explains what Paul is talking about in Romans 8:5-8.

---

[126] The King James Version is even less supportive of the Calvinist spin: "And you [hath he quickened], who were dead in *trespasses and sins*; Wherein in time past ye *walked according to the course of this world*, according to the prince of the power of the air, the spirit that now worketh in the children of disobedience: Among whom also we all had our conversation in times past in the lusts of our flesh, *fulfilling the desires of the flesh and of the mind*; and were by nature the children of wrath, even as others."

Those who live according to the sinful nature have their minds set on what that nature desires; but those who live in accordance with the Spirit have their minds set on what the Spirit desires. The mind of sinful man is death, but the mind controlled by the Spirit is life and peace; the sinful mind is hostile to God. It does not submit to God's law, nor can it do so. Those controlled by the sinful nature cannot please God.

As before, we mustn't forget to whom Paul is addressing these remarks. It's not to unregenerate people outside of Christ, but to brothers in Christ who are in danger of slipping back into the ways of the world that are hostile to God—back into their former nature as those who lived in rebellion to God before they were converted.

Therefore, brothers, we have an obligation—but it is not to the sinful nature, to live according to it. For if you live according to the sinful nature, you will die; but if by the Spirit you put to death the misdeeds of the body, you will live, because those who are led by the Spirit of God are sons of God. For you did not receive a spirit that makes you a slave again to fear, but you received the Spirit of sonship. And by him we cry, "Abba, Father." The Spirit himself testifies with our spirit that we are God's children. (Romans 8:12-16)

Even for those of us who are God's regenerated children, it stubbornly remains our nature to sin. To our shame, sinning is what we *do*. But someone has brought a deceiving, impersonating "look-alike" to the party to insist that, either before or after Calvinism's version of regeneration, we have a "sinful nature" which compels us to sin because of what we *are*.

Is Depravity Irreversible?

Along with the foregoing passages, Calvinists often cite 1 Corinthians 2:14 as a proof-text for pre-regenerate depravity. As before, however, they are overlooking the fact that Paul is addressing the spiritual struggle of those who are already "sanctified in Christ Jesus" (1:2). Far from targeting fallen, unregenerate man, Paul is rebuking his divisive fellow saints in Corinth for not being more spiritually minded.

"The man without the Spirit does not accept the things that come from the Spirit of God," says Paul sharply, "for they are foolishness to him, and he cannot understand them, because they are spiritually discerned." As descriptive as this analysis might also be of the as-yet-unsaved reprobate, still (in 3:1), it is his fellow elect and regenerate "brothers" Paul is speaking about, not unregenerate reprobates.

It is beyond dispute that, to the extent man remains locked into his worldly, unenlightened, and unspiritual frame of thinking, he cannot truly know God in any meaningful sense. If that's what "total depravity" or "total inability" were solely about, then we could all shake hands and go home. But Calvinism insists further that man's unspiritual framework is so ingrained in his natural constitution, that only a supernatural act of God can heal that innate disability. (And, further still, that out of a world filled wall to wall with people spiritually disabled from birth, God reaches down to miraculously "cure" only a select number of them.)

The problem with that notion, as Paul reminds us here, is that even "miraculously cured" people can lapse back into a worldly, unspiritual framework. Which suggests either that depravity is so irreversibly ingrained in man that God's work in regeneration is of little consequence; or, surely more likely, that your sins and mine were never constitutionally mandated in the first place.

Naturally, those who believe in original sin and depravity are not the only ones who have to explain how regenerate believers can continue in sin. Even if Calvinism's explanation is fraught with problems, those who don't hold to original sin and depravity have to confront virtually the same problem. If God acts powerfully through faith and baptism to bring dead sinners to life, what accounts for the persistence of sin in baptized believers?

A View From Two Universes

I don't know all I know about parallel universes, but it seems to me that the answer to the problem lies somewhere along those lines, in that God operates in one sphere while you and I operate in another. From God's perspective, our justification through faith is an objective, judicial change in our relationship with him. The same is true of our initial sanctification, by which we are called out of the world to be God's holy and elect people.

What's involved here is expiation for sin. *Once*, the guilt of our sins was clinging to us; *now* that guilt clings to the cross. *Once*, we were lost; *now* we are saved. *Once*, we were not in a right relationship; *now* we are redeemed. *Once*, there was no covenant; *now* there is covenant. *Once*, we were dead in sin; *now* we have been made alive in Christ.

While in God's "universe" there now has been a death-to-life *transaction*, in our own "universe" we have yet to fully experience our death-to-life *transformation*. The most we can say at the point of faith and baptism is that we are on our way to being transformed–motivated all the more because of the appreciation we have of the wondrous divine transaction accomplished in God's "universe."

It is the story, really, of the believer's sanctification, which simultaneously is *already complete* and yet *still a work in progress*. Paul tells the saints in Corinth (in past tense): "You *were* washed, you *were* sanctified, you *were* justified in the name of the Lord Jesus Christ and by the Spirit of our God" (1 Corinthians 6:11). Then to the saints in Thessalonica Paul says (in both present and future tense): "It is God's will that you *should be sanctified...*" (1 Thessalonians 4:3). As if to say: Now, but not yet; finished, but only begun.

I suspect Calvinists would not greatly disagree with any of that discussion. Where Calvinism gets caught on the hop is in simultaneously maintaining that the regenerate sinner is no longer under the bondage of depravity yet, even so, cannot help but sin because of left-over corruption from his pre-regenerate sin nature. Consider, for example, this creedal statement from *The Westminster Confession*:

> *When God converts a sinner, and translates him into the state of grace, He freeth him from his natural bondage under sin....yet so, as that by reason of his remaining corruption, he doth not perfectly, nor only, will that which is good, but doth also will that which is evil. (9.4-5)*

Whatever happened to regeneration producing "a real and substantive change in the person's *constituent nature*," as Sproul contends?[127] If one's constituent "sin nature" has been changed fundamentally and constitutionally, how can there be any "remaining corruption" to provide impetus for the believer's ongoing sin?

And how can Boettner in a single breath contend that those who are regenerated "still have the remnants of the old nature clinging to them," yet still maintain that regeneration "removes a man's appetite for sinful things so that he refrains from sin"?[128] (Surely, he can't mean that literally!)

As always, of course, Calvinists have the additional burden of having to explain how any of this fits with their doctrine of predestination. For if a person's eternal destiny has been foreordained from before the beginning of time, then it's all just theory from that point forward.[129]

By the force of logic implicit within Calvinism, it matters not whether man has an indelible sin nature; or if he does, whether it applies only prior to his regeneration or lingers on. Ultimately, whether we freely choose to sin or have it chosen for us is an irrelevance. For both the elect and the non-elect, these issues are rendered completely and entirely meaningless by the sovereign certainty of what already has been declared to be. How many hoops and what kind of hoops must be encountered along the way may fascinate theologians, but the end result is never in doubt.

Saturated, Or Diseased?

If only the issue could be reduced to whether we are thoroughly "saturated with sin." Were that the case, I suspect there wouldn't be a dissenter

---

[127] Sproul, 192 (with my emphasis)

[128] Boettner, 171

[129] When in Romans 16:7 Paul refers to Andronicus and Junias, who "were in Christ before I was," there is an implied sequencing of when and how one comes to be "in Christ." But when that sequencing is a foregone conclusion (as it must be by the doctrine of election), then for all intents and purposes Andronicus, Junias, and Paul were all "in Christ" from the moment of election. Whatever hoops God might ask his elect to jump through during their lifetime, according to Calvinism they were either "in" or "out" all along. Despite all that he writes about predestination and election, Paul never once assumes anything other than that each person is truly and genuinely lost and without hope until he is saved through obedient faith—which happens earlier for some and later for others.

among us. Even Sproul's "radical corruption" could fit comfortably with the idea of our being saturated through and through with sin. Even for those of us who are saved, persistent sin permeates, infiltrates, and contaminates. Like, totally!

It's when the talk turns to our being "diseased with sin" that we part company. If sin *diseases*, still, it is not itself a *disease*. It's all the difference between lung cancer and the habit of smoking which so often causes the cancer. Whereas smoking *diseases*, still, it is not itself a *disease*. Smoking is something a person freely and willingly chooses to do...often with horrendous physiological consequences. Sinning, similarly, is something we've all freely and willingly chosen to do...with horrendous spiritual consequences.

Where Calvinists and others get into trouble is failing to properly discriminate between cause and effect. We don't sin because we're sinners, any more than a person smokes because he has cancer. The smoker smokes for pleasure, escape, or perhaps social camaraderie—all the same reasons, really, why a sinner sins.

No less than smokers, of course, you and I can easily become addicted to sin. (In fact, we all are!) But not even that addiction comes upon us wholly uninvited. Just as nothing in one's genes causes him to pick up that first cigarette, so too nothing in our innate human nature causes us to tell that first lie or entertain that first lustful thought. Nor is there anything in our nature which causes us to *continue* lying and lusting even as redeemed children of God.[130]

The closest we come to having anything like an innate "sin nature" is having a body of flesh with natural instincts, needs, and desires capable of being perverted into sinful acts and intents. (And equally as important, capable of being restrained within the boundaries of legitimate expression.) The problem is that, with each repetition of moral failure, sin becomes so powerfully ingrained that we end up with the personified sin of Romans 7:15-25, which seems to operate independently of the mind that has nobler aspirations. Together with Paul, we too can lament, "In my

---

[130] Matthew 15:19 ("For out of the heart come evil thoughts, murder, adultery, sexual immorality, theft, false testimony, slander...") alerts us to the importance of keeping our hearts pure, but speaks not a word about an innate sin nature which "necessitates" our sinning.

inner being I delight in God's law, but I see another law at work in the members of my body."

Paul's point, of course, is that no matter how in tune you and I may be to God's commands, law itself has no power to transform our sinful minds and bodies. Worse yet, the law's insistence on moral uprightness only tends to discourage us, like a mirror constantly held up before us, reminding us of our many flaws. Indeed, the law provides occasion for "loophole lifestyles," since we are notoriously clever enough to find the gaps and exploit them. There is also the problem of Pharisaical arrogance where one convinces himself that he has kept the law in its entirety.

All of which explains Paul's lament that what was designed for good (the Law) "became sin!" By felicitous irony, the perversion of Law into sin is a perfect picture of how *sin itself* becomes sin: It's the unnatural perversion of that which is naturally good. Do we have an innate fleshly nature that gives rise to sin? Absolutely. But not because it is naturally evil or bent toward sin. The evil bit only comes when we take what was meant to be wholesome and beautiful and turn it into moral graffiti...and then leave it there so long that the ugliness seems normal. It's what results from *this* perverted process that then becomes our "sinful nature"—our rebellious, now-deep-seated, habitual nature to sin.

Mark it well: Paul does not leave either himself or us as helpless victims of the law's impotence, nor yet at the mercy of some sin force inherited from "the Fall." In Romans 8, it's not about weakness or wretchedness, or inborn depravity, but about the power (and obligation) to live according to the Spirit. Listen to it one more time: "Therefore, brothers, we have an obligation—but it is not to the sinful nature, to live according to it. For if you live according to the sinful nature, you will die; but if by the Spirit you put to death the misdeeds of the body, you will live" (Romans 8:12-13). You mean, Paul, that the sinful nature can be defeated? Not only *can* be but *must* be!

Thinking Through the Sin Problem

What do you think of the proposition that all sin is a twisting of that which is good? Have you ever before considered that the evil desires of man's "flesh" or "sinful nature" are perversions of the *legitimate* desires of the body? (Chapter 1 of Romans is the definitive treatise on inversion of the natural, created order from good to evil.) Gifted with a life-sustaining desire to eat and drink, for example, we pervert that desire into drunkenness and gluttony. Gifted with the natural desire for sexual expression, we pervert it into all sorts of sexual immorality. Having the need for at least minimal possessions, we pervert that innate need into covetousness, greed, and theft.

To say that we have a "sinful nature" is to say that we have a nature that is capable of being perverted from the legitimate to the illegitimate, from the natural to the unnatural, from the pure to the polluted. (To borrow from Augustine: "Evil is making a bad use of a good thing."[131])

As Screwtape explains to Wormwood, "There are things for humans to do all day long without His minding in the least–sleeping, washing, eating, drinking, making love, playing, praying, working. Everything has to be *twisted* before it's any use to us."[132]

It's crucial to note that not everyone "twists what is natural" in precisely the same way as everybody else. Some struggle with sex or drunkenness; others with idolatry; still others with hatred, jealousy, or anger. Even within genetic lines of offspring, the sins of the family vary widely from generation to generation and from individual to individual. Have you ever wondered why that is? Or, indeed, why some individuals persist in sinning more often or more heinously than other individuals?

Surely something other than some nebulous, amorphous, universal "sin nature" is going on here. If all of us have inherited from Adam the same depravity and sin nature that inevitably inclines us toward sin, how does one explain the fact that our commonly-shared "sin nature" manifests itself in such diverse ways?

Even more to the point, how does the theory that "we sin because we are sinners" actually work? When you move from theory to practice, in what way does one's supposed natural inclination to sin actually end up making sin happen in one's life? Is there some intangible power force

---

[131] Augustine, *Confessions and Enchiridion*, trans. and ed. by Albert C. Outler (Philadelphia: Westminster Press, n.d.), 326-338, section 36

[132] C.S. Lewis, *The Screwtape Letters*, 118

coursing through my body influencing me to entertain lustful thoughts? Or some inner instinct compelling me to tell lies? Or some evil inclination in the innermost part of my moral fabric seducing me into envying what my neighbor has?

The closest we come to a scriptural answer to all these questions is found in James 1:13-15: "When tempted, no one should say, 'God is tempting me.' For God cannot be tempted by evil, nor does he tempt anyone; but each one is tempted when, by his own evil desire, he is dragged away and enticed. Then, after desire has conceived, it gives birth to sin; and sin, when it is full-grown, gives birth to death."

Which merely begs the further question: If we are enticed by our own evil desire, where does *it* come from ? Does it arise *of necessity* out of an innate, inherited depravity and deviously sinister "sin nature," or does it come from the free, voluntary, and wilful perversion of legitimate desires?

Undoubtedly the most objective way to test these two competing explanations is to roll the tape of history back before original sin, depravity, and any supposed inherited "sin nature" ever came on the scene. Since the culprit behind your sins and mine supposedly is a debilitating depravity resulting from "the Fall," how do you explain the sins committed by two individuals who unquestionably were *not* burdened with such depravity? How, if at all, is the supposed progression from one's depravity to one's sin (or from one's pervasive "sin nature" to specific, identifiable sins) to be distinguished from whatever process prompted Adam and Eve to sin *before "the Fall"*?

As all agree, Adam and Eve did not sin because they were sinners; they became sinners because they sinned. Wholly unshackled by original sin, depravity, or some necessitating "sin nature," the first couple were dragged away by their evil desire to eat forbidden fruit. In precisely the same way, you and I are dragged away by our evil desire to taste of forbidden pleasures and set ourselves up as superior to our Maker.

Striving For Perfection

What do you think? Does the fact that we sometimes (though not inevitably) pervert some (but not all) natural, legitimate human desires necessarily imply that we have a built-in nature that can't help but sinning–that simply by virtue of our human nature somehow we are bound to sin? If so, what are we to conclude from all the times and circumstances when, despite clear opportunity and strong temptation, we do *not* pervert our natural, legitimate human desires?

The really crucial question is this: Does the fact that we *do* sin (even after regeneration) necessarily imply that we *must*? If so, what is the overpowering force that compels us to commit acts of sin against our will? Is it innate depravity? Is it Satan...or even God?

If you checked any of the above as the irresistible, overpowering cause of your sin, what explains your ability to look certain temptations in the face and yet choose *not* to yield to them?

Think for a moment about the many temptations which come your way. Isolate on them one at a time. With temptation A, do you not agree that you have a simple choice, either to yield or not to yield? And the same goes for temptation B, temptation C, temptation D, and so on down the line.

I suspect I can say with some assurance that you are like everybody else–most often choosing what's right, but at other times choosing what's wrong. Is there any evidence anywhere suggesting that some external spiritual power or innate human trait is *forcing* any of us either to sin or not to sin? When you do what's right, is it only because you're forced to? And when you do what's wrong, is there anyone or anything you can blame?

The truth is, with each temptation, we all have a choice. Each and every time. It's up to us.

In theory, we could make the right call from A to Z for a lifetime. As it happens, only one person has ever done that. Refusing to use his *divinity* as a crutch when tempted by the devil in the wilderness, Jesus robbed the rest of us of any excuse to use our own *humanity* as a crutch. In the wake of the incarnate Jesus, no longer can anyone say, "But I'm only human." Or, "Nobody's perfect." Or, "The devil made me do it." (Nor yet take false comfort from the exonerating mantra: "We're not sinners because we sin; we sin because we're sinners.")

Living a sinless life *in the flesh*, Jesus laid down the gauntlet, calling us to "be perfect, therefore, as your father in heaven is perfect" (Matthew 5:48).

Then he suffered and died, knowing full well that we would *not* make the right call every time; that we would fall far short of the goal of perfection. Which is not to say that sinning is inevitable; nor, certainly, unavoidable. (Are your sins *unavoidable*?)[133]

One might challenge the whole idea of theoretical perfection by suggesting that successfully evading all sin over the span of a lifetime is like dodging raindrops in a thunderstorm: possible in theory but impossible in practice. Perhaps. But it's important that we get this right. The moment we convince ourselves that perfection is *not* possible, we immediately have a built-in excuse for our sins. And at that point we've lost the plot.

So Why Have *All* Sinned?

Of course, the theoretical possibility of moral and spiritual perfection just makes understanding the problem of sin all the harder. It's easy to explain our sins when we have a notorious villain in residence constantly prodding us to sin. As long as we have a depraved "sin nature" lurking within us, we can point the finger of blame at a condition over which we have little or no control ("We sin because we're sinners!"). But if there is no inbuilt moral handicap to which we can point an accusing finger, what option remains but that we are sinners because we sin?

Yet if that is so, you ask rightly, how is it that, out of the multiplied billions of humankind from Adam until now (including all the saved, redeemed, and regenerate believers throughout history), not a single one apart from Jesus Christ has managed to avoid sinning many times every single day of their lives!

At least a partial answer may be found in the picture Paul paints in Titus 3:2-7 of the contrast between our sin and our salvation. "At one time," says Paul, "we too were foolish, disobedient, deceived and enslaved by all kinds of passions and pleasures. We lived in malice and envy, being

---

[133] One might ask, Was it inevitable that Adam would eventually sin? (If so, the "Garden test" hardly seems fair.) My own response, of course, is that Adam's sin was no more inevitable than our own. It's Calvinists who have a real problem with this question—first, because of Calvinism's affirmation that everything that's ever happened was ordained by God before it ever came to be; and second, because it's yet another reminder that Adam succumbed to sin despite not having the innate depravity which supposedly makes our sin inevitable.

hated and hating one another. But when the kindness and love of God our Savior appeared, he saved us, not because of righteous things we had done, but because of his mercy."

Particularly pertinent to the present discussion, note Paul's reference to our having been "enslaved by all kinds of passions and pleasures." Is that not the key to why we continue in sin even after we have been saved, redeemed, and regenerated? Whatever our specific, personal, and repetitive struggles with sin, the problem is that, by the time we are saved objectively through God's mercy, we are so deeply ingrained in patterns of sin that the melody lingers long after the song has ended. Not that we can't give up forbidden passions and pleasures, for "such *were* some of you" (1 Corinthians 6:11). But still we struggle.

As for those "patterns of sin," there is no denying that they begin early on, long before we are even aware of sin. In fact, therein lies the core problem of moral character. By the time a person is mature enough to realize "what a wretched man I am," the traces of sin are deep indeed. It all begins naturally enough when, out of necessity, the dependent child must be self-focused in order to survive. ("I need to be fed...now!" "I need to have my diaper changed...now!")

But then we encounter "the terrible two's" in which an unconscious self-focus becomes transformed into a more conscious self-centeredness, and even selfishness. ("Mine!" "I want it!") From that point forward, we seem never to leave "the terrible two's," continuing for a lifetime to pervert legitimate desires and needs into their sinful variants.

Is it not this cultivated, persistent, and hardened nature–acting within the members of our body–to which Paul refers as "the flesh" or "the sinful nature"?

Since everyone agrees that sin persists even beyond the point of one's redemption, perhaps you might think this all this palaver is much ado about nothing. But it is all the difference between sinning because we *must* sin, and sinning because we *do* sin. Under the former, sinning is a foregone conclusion, even with the power of God at hand. Under the latter, sinning may be a continuing struggle with a deeply ingrained, sin-stained character, but it is never theoretically or practically outside our control. By the grace of God, those who truly wish to overcome sin may do so–one sin at a time.

Calvinism's only significant contribution to this discussion turns out to be less than helpful. Beginning with its assumption of a universal depravity that prevents every human being from trying to overcome sin (or even wanting to), Calvinism holds that selective regeneration enables the elect both to want and to try. But perhaps the lion's share of humankind, being left helpless in their depravity, can do absolutely nothing about the problem of sin. They cannot respond to the call for righteousness, nor obey God's command to reject sin, nor have any hope of salvation when they inevitably fail to do so.

Worse yet, even those who have been specially regenerated, converted, and saved are still compelled of necessity to sin. Despite their spiritual status having been changed from being lost to being saved, that fact doesn't change in the least their fundamental fallen nature.

Where Pelagianism Went So Wrong

Calvinism's insistence that we have an aggressive, inborn sin nature from which it is not possible to escape reveals what an extreme, distorted view Calvinism has of both the nature of sin and the nature of man. What else explains Calvinism's implicit altering of the text from "All *have* sinned" to "All *must* sin."[134]

By contrast, the ancient Pelagians and so-called "semi-Pelagians" were absolutely right to reject the doctrine of original sin, and to affirm man's unfettered freedom of choice over sin. They were right to insist that moral responsibility comes packaged with moral ability, and equally right to insist that (whether we are unregenerate or regenerate) there is no inherent depravity within us that *predisposes* us to sin.[135]

However, as with so many doctrines developed in response to one extremist view or another, Pelagianism did a 180-degree pendulum swing

---

[134] Should Calvinists object that Calvinism has never taught that "All *must* sin," I would urge you to recall Sproul's contention that there is a "moral necessity" to sin—that "we simply are unable to live without sinning." His view is logically consistent with the premise that man's innate corrupt nature is the explanation for even post-regenerative sin, and is necessarily implied by the teaching that we sin because we are sinners.

[135] Pelagius himself argued that if we are unable to keep each and every one of God's commands, it would be unfair of him to require it of us. "Whatever I ought to do, I can do," was the watchword for Pelagius. [Steele, Thomas, and Quinn, *The Five Points of Calvinism*, 2d Edition (Phillipsburg, NJ, P & R Publishing, 2004), 210]

altogether as extremist as the Augustinian "Calvinism" against which it was reacting. You could almost predict that if Augustine saw nothing but depravity in man, Pelagians eventually would say that there is nothing but good in man. As Pelagianism reached it ultimate extreme, no middle ground seems to have been left wherein man is not predisposed either way, whether toward good or toward evil.

With equal predictability came the hard-line (hyper?) Pelagian view that, because there is nothing in man which inherently rules out his being perfect, then man's salvation doesn't depend in any way on God's grace (though we'll certainly take all the help we can get, thank you very much!). In fact, one of Pelagius' students, Celestius, went so far as to claim that there were others besides Jesus who were sinless![136] (It's one thing to argue the theoretical possibility of moral perfection; another altogether to deny the factual truth that "all have sinned.")

Drawing back from that outrageous extreme, semi-Pelagians such as Cassian acknowledged that even man's theoretically-achievable perfection does not solve the obvious problem that man has *not* achieved perfection, and thus the ongoing need for God's grace to provide justification unto salvation.

Not altogether surprising considering their Roman Catholic heritage, many semi-Pelagians even accepted the notion of original sin, but believed that God's grace was given to all men to overcome their depravity and freely choose good over evil.

Faced with a sketchy historical record, it's sometimes hard to know exactly what the various disciples of Pelagius believed. Apart from a grace-based plan of salvation, for example, one wonders to what extent semi-Pelagians saw grace involved in the believer's day-to-day struggle against sin. Did they view as important the distinction Paul makes (in Romans 6 and 7) between living by the law and living by the Spirit? Did they accept that how a person views God's grace makes a radical difference in how one effectively uses his freedom to avoid sin?

To whatever extent even semi-Pelagians might have left man entirely to his own human devices to make upright moral decisions, then to that extent they robbed man of the very motivation which Paul sees as the key

---

[136] Steele, Thomas, and Quinn, 211

to conquering sin. "For sin shall not be your master, because you are not under law, but under grace" (Romans 6:14).

Whereas law *compels* (with only grudging success), a full appreciation of God's grace *impels* (prompting a heart even more willing). And to say *law*, of course, is as much to say *man*; whereas to say *grace* is of necessity to say *God*.

If Erasmus understood Pelagius correctly, even Pelagius himself was far off the mark. Says Erasmus: "Pelagius taught that no new grace was needed once grace had liberated and healed the free will of man. Thus the free will by itself was deemed sufficient to achieve eternal salvation."[137]

It's all a matter of truths and half-truths. The human quest for perfection of which Jesus himself spoke is itself not a futile quest. It is only futile as long as it remains solely and wholly a *human* quest. In the end, such humanism supplants all seeking after God. Not only can humanism not save, but it cannot even be the antidote to sin, for it exchanges the truth of God for a lie, worshiping the creature rather than the Creator. So, when Calvinists vociferously object to the arrogance and futility of humanism, they are unquestionably on solid ground to do so.

I can't speak for others, but when I contend that you and I are not predisposed to sin by some "diseased" fallen nature, and that we are not compelled to sin by any force external to ourselves, and that therefore nothing but our own misdirected will prevents us from a life free from sin, I hold no brief for the idolatry of humanism. Or for the notorious extremes of Pelagianism, which went so wildly off track. Or, God forbid, for anything like a merit-based, works-oriented, do-it-yourself salvation.

What I contend is that, like Cain, we are called to master sin. Plain and simple. When that call is considered as a *sovereign order*, we must do no less. When it is considered as a *human response*, would you be willing to argue in God's very presence that we are somehow constitutionally, psychologically, physiologically, situationally, morally, or spiritually *incapable* of obeying anything that he has commanded of us? YES/NO?[138]

---

[137] Desiderius Erasmus, *A Diatribe or Sermon Concerning Free Will*, sec.18. See *Erasmus and Luther–Discourse on Free Will*, trans. and edited Ernst F. Winter (London, New York: Continuum, Frederick Ungar Publishing Co., 1961, 1989, 2005), 23

[138] If the answer is that the *regenerate* are capable, but not the *unregenerate*, are we to believe that God's commands are only for the elect?

If this very day you were called before the Judgment Seat of the Great High God to answer for your sins, is this the case you'd feel comfortable presenting?

May it please the Court. I would beg Your Honor to take judicial notice of the fact that, as with all of humankind, I was born into the world inherently bent toward sin and with a depraved sin nature from which I could not escape. With all due respect, Your Honor, you yourself would have had far more to do with that than I. Surely, then, you can appreciate that I sinned throughout my life (even after I was saved) because I was a condemned sinner to begin with. I concede, Your Honor, that with each and every temptation I had a clear choice. And as you know (indeed, even by your own grace), I very often made the right choice. But on those occasions when I failed to make the right choice, I can only plead the defense of innate human depravity, and therefore moral necessity.

Given Calvinism's explanation as to how and why we sin, could any other defense reasonably be presented? How do you think the Righteous Judge would view such a defense?

The Path To Overcoming Sin

As against a morally handicapping fallen nature (with its built-in excuse for sin), Scripture speaks of a Spirit-enhanced redeemed nature (with its built-in motivation for holiness). Under the first option, man *cannot help but sin*; under the second option, man *need not* and *must not sin*.

May I suggest that this distinction goes a long way toward explaining how, despite his humanity, Jesus was uniquely able to remain sinless. If there is anything to be learned from Jesus' temptation in the wilderness, it is that Jesus (the man) never cheated by resorting to the supernatural power of his divine nature. That being the case, it seems likely that his power over sin lay chiefly in his higher self-awareness. Knowing beyond all doubt *who he was*, he acted accordingly. As God-man, it would have been beneath him to sin. He was made for finer things.

Jesus' relationship to sin is not altogether unlike our own relationship to sin. As called-out children of God, saved by grace and filled with his Spirit, we too are made for finer things than sin. This is precisely Paul's point in Ephesians 4:1, where he pleads: "I urge you to live a life *worthy of the calling you have received*."

How then can we overcome sin? By following Jesus' own example in remembering, not *who* we are, but *whose* we are. If with the approach of each and every temptation we stopped long enough to remind ourselves that we are the blood-bought, lovingly-adopted, washed-and-cleansed children of the King, I dare say there is not a sin in the world that could have mastery over us.

If there is anything on which we can all agree, surely it is that, when faced with sin, you and I have a moral responsibility to choose the right and refuse the wrong. Even if you happen to believe you are *predisposed* to sin, surely it is safe to say that you don't claim to be *indisposed* to overcoming it. Nor yet, unable to do so.

No Visible Means of Support?

I don't know about you, but I can certainly attest that the desires of the flesh are a formidable foe. Persistent pockets of spiritual rebellion in my own life make me doubt the strength of my own spiritual resolve as much as anyone. But that's a far cry from contending we are physically or spiritually constituted in such a way as to be perpetually bent toward sin; or even that when we face temptations we do so like a golfer with a handicap or a jockey carrying extra weight.

For children of God, the only thing that tilts the scales one way or the other is having our Father on our side. As Paul reminds us, "God is faithful; he will not let you be tempted beyond what you can bear. But when you are tempted, he will also provide a way out so that you can stand up under it" (1 Corinthians 10:13).[139]

---

[139] The Calvinist twist on this passage is dumbfounding. Says Boettner (speaking of the elect): "Their removal from certain temptations which would be too strong for them is an absolute and free gift from God, since it is entirely an arrangement of His providence as to what temptations they encounter in the course of their lives and what ones they escape." (Boettner, 200.)

Does this match your own experience? Have you not (like myself) repeatedly succumbed to many temptations rather than escaped them?

Far more troubling: How could God providentially have chosen each and every one of our temptations without being personally responsible for them—contrary to James' pointed assertion that God himself does not tempt us (James 1:13)? (That Boettner's statement is entirely consistent with Calvinism's insistence that God, as sovereign, is the primal cause of all things must surely warrant a yellow caution flag.)

And what is that "way out"? For openers, it is the ever-present free and unfettered choice to do what is right. We are not helpless sinners at the mercy of "the Fall," or total depravity, or original sin. We are not victims, or inevitable sinners by nature.

Yet, neither are we alone in the battle against sin. "God is our refuge and strength, an ever-present help in trouble," says the psalmist (Psalm 46:1). Not everyone could say this, I suppose, but the closest I've ever personally come to experiencing anything like that is in my own earthly father. Little wonder that I am as comforted as I am mystified that the sovereign God of the universe should deign with such unexpected familiarity to identify himself as our heavenly "Father."

Who, more than a parent, could provide the kind of invisible support we need when we falter? As we think back, was it not our parents who reached out to safeguard our first tottering steps? And who but our parents steadied the bike when our tiny little legs could barely reach the pedals? No, their "grace" didn't do the walking or riding for us. It just kept us going. Behind the scenes. Without our even knowing.

So too, I suggest, is the work of the Spirit. Were there ever such a thing as "enabling grace," surely *this* is such grace! Beyond the parental analogy I've just shared, I confess I'm at a loss to fully explain it. Maybe it's a matter of doors that open and doors that close. Or "a word fitly spoken"–perhaps by a stranger–that somehow changes our direction. Or even an extraordinary event we might otherwise pass off as sheer chance. All I know is that the Bible is replete with examples of God working in the lives of his people, so I trust it is true in my own life. Indeed, I depend on it.

As both revelation and experience testify, the soul who reaches up to God in the struggle against sin will grasp a power far beyond his own...from One who has looked temptation in the face and overcome it each and every time. If that's just so much God-talk for many, for some it is the only thing in all the world that gets them through the night.

Can An All-Controlling God *Not* Be the Cause of Sin?

In light of man's ongoing sin, one wonders whether Paul was right, after all, about there being some alien, roguish sin-force living inside his body. If Calvinism is correct in attributing to God's divine sovereignty *absolutely everything* that happens, then Paul's persistent "sin-force" could be nothing other than the work of God himself—surely, a troubling thought to any serious student of the Word.[140]

Indeed, as if anticipating such an argument, Jesus himself seems to make a point of refuting it. As we see in his parable of the weeds (Matthew 13:24-30), it is clear that Jesus—speaking on behalf of the Godhead, as it were—is taking no responsibility for the existence of sin. "If you sowed nothing but good seed," the servants of the landowner ask, "where did the weeds come from?" Jesus' response is adamant: "An enemy did this," not me!

Calvinists, of course, are well aware of this troubling conundrum—at times denying God is the cause of man's sin, but at other times boldly defending it as part of God's "mysterious" decrees. As an example of the former, the Westminster Confession explicitly states that "God from all eternity did...ordain whatsoever comes to pass; yet so as thereby neither is God the author of sin...."

Yet, the great apologist for that Confession, Loraine Boettner, nevertheless insists that, since Christ's own evil crucifixion was part of the eternal plan, "then plainly the fall of Adam *and all other sins which made that sacrifice necessary* [my emphasis] were in the plan, no matter how undesirable a part of that plan they may have been."[141] (Foreseeing sin and providing a

---

[140] Many Calvinists (though by no means all) feel unfairly impugned when anyone points out that if God has absolute sovereign control over every act, event, thought, and motive, it logically follows that he must be responsible for sin. The conversation goes something like this: "Do you believe that God has ordained in eternity all that will come to pass?" "Yes, I do." "Then, you hold God responsible for sin!" "No, I do not." "Of course, you do! It is a logical conclusion from your understanding of God's foreordination." "No, it is not." "You have to!" "No I do not."

Certainly, a person need not believe that God's will is logical, for often it defies man's logic. But one cannot so easily evade the obvious dictates of logic merely by claiming that, according to a higher truth, a patently illogical conclusion is logical. Logic may be trumped, but not simply dismissed—especially by those who happily employ logic to argue from Scripture that God—though in total, complete control of absolutely everything—is *not* responsible for sin. He who lives by logic opens himself up to dying by logic.

[141] Boettner, 24. Calvin agrees (*Institutes* 3.23.7): "Whence does it happen that Adam's fall irremediably involved so many peoples, together with their infant offspring, in eternal death unless because it so pleased God? ...The decree is dreadful indeed, I confess. Yet no one can deny that God foreknew what end man was to have before he created him, and consequently foreknew because he so ordained by his decree."

means of dealing with it is light years away from God purposely *planning* that man would sin!)

Undoubtedly in aid of rehabilitating this "undesirable" feature of God's sovereignty, Boettner attempts to nuance the issue by citing God's "permission" of sin (the very position which non-Calvinists would take.) Yet, this virtually unavoidable concession militates against Calvinism's bedrock assertion that nothing whatsoever happens but at the hand of God.

When the subject changes to God's foreknowledge, Boettner seems to forget what he has said earlier about sin's being "permissive." Only a few pages along, Boettner cites R. L. Dabney for the proposition that, "If any other cause or agent is ever to arise, it must be by God's agency....In willing these other agents into existence, with infinite prescience, God did virtually will into existence, or purpose, all the effects of which they were to be efficients."[142]

In other words, even if it happens through secondary causes, the all-seeing, foreordaining God of heaven remains the direct cause of all things...which, of course, necessarily includes not only man's total depravity, but also your sins and mine.[143]

By Calvinist logic, certainly, that conclusion is inescapable (leaving no room for "permission," only direct control). And heaven knows there are plenty folks out there who (following that very logic) have said to God: "Don't blame me for my sins. After all, it was *you* who made me this way!" But what do you think? Is it even remotely biblical that God himself is the cause of the very depravity, rebellion, and corruption he condemns and punishes?

So the second of the two conflicting Calvinist positions simply has to be the case: that God is *not* the cause of sin. The problem for Calvinism is that it is already locked into the first position by virtue of its claim that God has absolute control over all things temporal or eternal, great or small, moral or immoral. By Calvinism's sacrosanct doctrine of God's all-encompassing, micro-managing sovereignty, God is not just the *First Cause* of all things, but the predestining, foreordaining *Only Cause*.

---

[142] Boettner, 45, citing R. L. Dabney, *Theology*, 212

[143] In his *Institutes* (3.23.8), Calvin rebuffs those who would draw a distinction between permission and God's will. "Here they have recourse to the distinction between will and permission. By this they would maintain that the wicked perish because God permits it, not because he so wills. But why shall we say 'permission' unless it is because God so wills?"

When viewed biblically, however, what decisively breaks the chain of divine causation is the exercise of God's own sovereign will to create us with the wholly independent option either to obey or disobey, and then hold us accountable for how we choose. In this sense alone can it legitimately be said that God "permits" sin without in any way being its cause.[144] Biblically speaking, God is beyond all doubt both the *First Cause* and the *Last Cause*, but not the *Only Cause*.

By the power and right inherent within himself as the *First Cause*, God declared that man was to have complete and total responsibility for how he would respond to God's commands. By the power and right inherent within himself as the *Final Cause*, God will hold man accountable for how he has exercised that responsibility. And between the *First* and *Final* Cause, there is no discontinuity whatsoever of God's overarching, eternal purpose.

If a person chooses to disobey God's commands, living a life of rebellion instead, God is not the cause of that rebellion, nor are God's divine plans for mankind as a whole in the least bit frustrated by it. Despite man's being the sole, volitional cause of his own sin, the ultimate salvation and predestined role of God's called-out elect remains firmly intact–all to God's glory.

No one has to tell Calvinists what a predicament they are in, teetering between the "devil" of God's absolute sovereign control over all things and the "deep blue sea" of man's being exclusively in control of *anything*, even if it's his own sin and depravity. Like deer caught in the headlights, Calvinists desperately want to run in the direction of blaming sin and depravity on man himself (thereby justifying God's wrath). But their pre-commitment to God's absolute, all-encompassing control forces them to make the simultaneous claim that both original sin and all subsequent sin is a God-imposed consequence of "the Fall." As Sproul puts it so breathtakingly: "God in some sense desired that man would fall into sin....he created sin."[145]

---

[144] When non-Calvinists argue that Calvinism's absolutist view of God's sovereignty must logically include even sin itself, suddenly we hear talk of divine "permission." But if we dare suggest that God has given his divine permission for man to have faith or reject it, all we hear is that such "permission" would rob God of his sovereign control. A wax nose can be twisted back and forth only so much before it breaks.

[145] Sproul, *Almighty Over All* (Grand Rapids: Baker Books, 1999), 53-54

Resort to Mystery

For those Calvinists who adamantly insist on an incoherent mixture of those two mutually-exclusive positions (believing that God is in total, unqualified control of all things *except sin and depravity*) the usual explanation is that, being finite, we humans simply cannot grasp the obvious mystery involved. Yet in this case, "mystery" seems but a desperate dodge. Despite all that remains unknown about God, genuine mystery is no excuse for what otherwise is simply bad theology.

If it's a good mystery you're after, I highly recommend that best-selling whodunit titled, *The Problem of Sin.* Just when you think the butler did it, it was also the butcher, the baker, and the candlestick maker. It was Lee Harvey Oswald, for sure, and both Jack Ruby and "Jack" Kennedy. But it was also C. S. Lewis, our Baptist deacon and Episcopalian housewife, and every single one of those Methodists, Pentecostals, and Presbyterians. Not to mention you and I, as well. Each in our own way, we all have "dunit."

The mystery, if mystery there be, is that some of us have "dunit" without ever having been regenerated (by any definition of the term), while others of us have "dunit" even after unquestionably having been regenerated. If Calvinists and others are right to attribute the sins of the saved to some residual "sin nature" left over from pre-generation depravity, then the effectiveness of God's regenerative power comes into serious question. Which is to say that the problem of sin is really God's problem.

If on the other hand it is our persistent pattern to sin, yet we are without any inherent "sin nature" which makes sinning inevitable, then the problem of sin is strictly, wholly, and solely *man's* problem.

...Which leaves God's saving grace as the only possible solution to man's problem.

Interesting how it all works out. Sounds intriguingly Calvinistic, doesn't it?

Be perfect, therefore, as your heavenly Father is perfect.

Matthew 5:48

Chapter Summary

- Calvinism's insistence that the saved continue to sin because of left-over corruption from one's original state of total depravity runs counter to Calvinism's own teaching that, in the act of regeneration, man's "sin nature" is constitutionally altered.

- To say that it is our nature to sin is only to say that it is our practice to sin. Paul's reference (in the NIV) to the "sinful nature" must not be interpreted to mean that man sins because he is innately sinful, if for no other reason than that the sinless Jesus shared that same nature.

- Although even the saved remain thoroughly saturated with sin, it is not as if sin were a disease over which we have little or no control.

- With each and every temptation, both the saved and the unsaved have it within themselves to make the right choice every time for a lifetime. Nothing so predisposes us to sin that sinning inevitably is a moral necessity.

- No matter how vociferously its adherents insist that God is not the cause of sin, Calvinism's extremist view of God's micro-managing sovereignty can have no other result.

Reality Check: If in fact God determined the eternal destiny of every soul from before Creation, then our attempts to master sin will succeed or fail on the strength of that foreordained destiny alone. In such a case, the question of whether man has a "sin nature" which makes sin morally necessary even for the saved amounts to little more than hypothetical debate points for sparring theologians.

Chapter 6

Predestination: The Standard Revised Version

All things turn out according to divine predestination:
not only the works we do outwardly,
but even the thoughts we think inwardly.

–Philipp Melanchthon

Forever etched in the history of global conflict, the D-day invasion of Normandy, on June 6, 1944, stands as a timeless monument to the courageous defense of freedom in World War II. While movies periodically keep the memory alive for younger generations, the events of that momentous day are still fresh in the aging minds of the last of those valiant young men who survived the withering fire coming from the German defenders along the French coast.

To be sure, there was courage and sacrifice beyond measure among those who comprised the greatest invasion force ever assembled. But no amount of bravery or fire-power would have won the day had it not been for the little-known, behind-the-scenes genius of a flamboyant Spaniard named Juan Pujol Garcia, who served as a double-agent on behalf of the Allied Forces.

So successful were his hundreds of radio transmissions to the German high command that no one in the Third Reich ever caught on, not even after the D-day invasion. With Hitler's approval, the Nazis even awarded their "valuable spy" the Iron Cross! For their part, British intelligence changed Garcia's codename from Bovril to Garbo in recognition that he was "the greatest actor in the world."

Beyond question, Garbo's most significant deception was convincing the Germans that the Normandy invasion was merely a decoy for a major assault planned further along the coast near Calais. As a result, the Germans maintained the bulk of their strength too far from Normandy to help repel the Allies on D-day. Even months later, the Germans were still anticipating an attack from Garbo's two fictitious Anglo-American armies!

What was the key to Garbo's success? It was as simple as it was ingenious. In the midst of mountains of disinformation, he actually told a lot of truth! Verifiable truth. So much truth, in fact, that the Germans had no reason to distrust him.

Never was Garbo more clever in making creative use of the truth than on D-day itself. After the invasion forces were already on the beach, Garbo sent the Germans what appeared to be frantic messages asking for confirmation of his "earlier warnings" about an imminent assault on Normandy (giving full details of the Allies' invasion plans). Of course, he had never sent any such warning, but by his asking for confirmation that he had, the Germans were duped into believing Garbo had desperately *tried* to warn them!

More Than A Kernel of Truth

The story of Garbo's remarkable role in the Allies' victory reminds me of a valuable lesson I first learned as a young District Attorney: Behind every successful fraud lies a lot of truth. Otherwise, nobody would ever fall for it! In fact, the greater the fraud, the more truth in which it is wrapped.

Now remove the element of intentional deception involved either in criminal fraud or in military espionage and permit me to make an application pertinent to our present discussion. In the same way that the hugely speculative Theory of Evolution continues to have widespread credibility because it is based on the truth of observable evolution within distinct species, I suggest that Calvinism's historic success is largely due to the undeniable elements of truth which it contains. And I'm talking *big* truths. *Major* truths. *Important* truths.

One of those great, indisputable truths–that man could never be saved by works, but only by the grace of God–has already been covered in some detail. If anyone lays claim to that doctrine, then sign me up too. I want to be on their side! But for the very reason that salvation by grace is such an important truth, I'm equally wary of anyone turning that truth into any kind of disinformation about how God saves his elect, no matter how noble one's motives might be for doing so.

Another of the hugely important truths contained within Calvinism is the fact that God has predestined his chosen "elect" to adoption, justification, sanctification, and eternal glory. If you want a proof text for that, how about the entire thrust of Paul's Ephesian letter! And much of Romans! And Peter's first epistle!

Just begin, for example, with this powerful passage from Paul's letter to the saints in Ephesus. The amazing message is that, before the beginning of time, God's chosen ones were predestined to be holy and blameless, adopted as sons of God by sheer grace in order that they might show forth God's glory.

> *Praise be to the God and Father of our Lord Jesus Christ, who has blessed us in the heavenly realms with every spiritual blessing in Christ. For he chose us in him before the creation of the world to be holy and blameless in his sight. In love he predestined us to be adopted as his sons through Jesus Christ, in accordance with his pleasure and will–to the praise of his glorious grace, which he has freely given us in the One he loves. (Ephesians 1:3-6)*

Only a few verses later, Paul reiterates the fact that God had an eternal plan in mind for his chosen ones, and even now is doing whatever it takes to make that plan work.

In him we were also chosen, having been predestined according to the plan of him who works out everything in conformity with the purpose of his will, in order that we, who were the first to hope in Christ, might be for the praise of his glory. (Ephesians 1:11-12).

In his magisterial epistle to "all in Rome who are loved by God and called to be saints," Paul brings this comforting assurance: Having known beforehand everything that would transpire in the history of the world, God called to himself all those who would love him, and he planned even then to make provision for their justification unto glory.

And we know that in all things God works for the good of those who love him, who have been called according to his purpose. For those God foreknew he also predestined to be conformed to the likeness of his Son, that he might be the firstborn among many brothers. And those he predestined, he also called; those he called, he also justified; those he justified, he also glorified (Romans 8:28-30).

Finally, Peter's introduction to his first epistle points us especially to the work of the Holy Spirit in God's master plan, bringing God's elect to obedience to Christ, through whose blood they are to be saved.

Peter, an apostle of Jesus Christ, To God's elect, strangers in the world, scattered throughout Pontus, Galatia, Cappadocia, Asia and Bithynia, who have been chosen according to the foreknowledge of God the Father, through the sanctifying work of the Spirit, for obedience to Jesus Christ and sprinkling by his blood....(1 Peter 1:1-2).

In these and other passages, both Peter and Paul are showing us God's magnificent scheme of redemption from the highest vantage point possible. Finite and time-bound as we are, we find it ever so difficult to stretch our minds around the idea of eternity. Or eternal purpose. Or eternal will. Or how we ourselves fit into that eternal purpose and will.

Perhaps only those who have ever been expectant parents can begin to appreciate the excitement God must have felt when anticipating the joy he would experience one day with his children. If you have children, do you remember what it was like when they were still in the womb—yet there you were, already painting the nursery pink or blue and choosing baby's first clothes?

And how that marvelous expectation must be elevated all the more when a couple anxiously awaits word of their receiving a child for adoption. With what special child will they be blessed? What will he or she look like? What genetic or cultural "baggage" might the new arrival bring to the family? Depending on the child's age, are there any already-developed character traits that will make for interesting times?

Is it mere coincidence that God speaks of having *adopted* his chosen ones? (And to think that he already had an incomparably perfect Son!)

Whether it be adoptive or natural parents, acts of joyous anticipation in preparation for arriving children are sublime acts of faith. "Now faith is being sure of what we hope for and certain of what we do not see" (Hebrews 11:1).

What Did God Foresee and Foreknow?

Yet herein lies a great mystery...as well as the nub of the controversy over Calvinism. For unlike earthly parents, God acted not upon what he did *not* see, but what he actually *saw* and *knew*. (Indeed, not just *what* he saw and knew, but *who* he saw and knew.) Remember that operative phrase in Romans 8:28-30? "For those God *foreknew* he also *predestined*," says the text; and only then, "those he *predestined*, he also *called*."

Look closely at the progression here:

Foreknew. Predestined. Called.

Do you detect any significant distinction between that progression and this one?

Predestined. Called. Foreknew.

Which comes first in Paul's own listing: foreknowledge or predestination?

And tell us again, Peter: How were God's elect chosen? They were "*chosen according to the foreknowledge of God*," says Peter. Yet, if that's the case...if

God based his selection of the elect upon what (and whom) he foreknew...just exactly what (and whom) did he know?

Before we attempt to answer that, is it possible from Peter and Paul's discussion of predestination that we all could agree on at least one thing? That there was *some rational basis* upon which God would choose those whom he would call and justify? That his choosing was not whimsical, fortuitous, or capricious? That he didn't simply choose his elect by lottery?

It would not be overstating the issue in the least to say that the whole case for Calvinism hinges on your answer here, even if you believe that God's choices were based on those whom he "foreloved" (as Calvinists often insist). Was even *that* choice merely whimsical, or did he choose, as do we, to love individuals for what he saw in them?

To say the very least, if the word "foreknew" has nothing to do with God's prescient "foreknowledge" of future human response, but rather God's *decision to foreknow* those whom he would arbitrarily elect, then Romans 8:29 is reduced to meaningless redundancy. Did Paul really mean to say, "For those God *predestined* he also *predestined*...."? Is there any compelling reason why we should not take the word "foreknew" at face value as the verb naturally associated with the noun "foreknowledge"?

Reformed theologians have dubbed the five key verbs in Romans 8:28-30 as "the golden chain of salvation," arguing that each verb is both active and past-tense, which is to say that each verb speaks to something God himself did without any human input whatsoever. (Those five verbs are: foreknew, predestined, called, justified, glorified.) Crucially, say Calvinists, the first of those verbs, "foreknew," is no less purposeful on God's part than the last four. God didn't just passively foresee the future in the abstract and react to what he saw, as if bound by it. Rather, he actively "foreloved" those whom he would predestine and call–and in that sense "foreknew" them.

I have no quarrel with the argument that the word *foreknew* speaks to something other than God's simply looking into a crystal ball and planning eternity accordingly. That would be putting the cart before the horse. From the very beginning, God's predetermined plan was to bring into being a special elect people, to be conformed to the image of Christ. And by what process would that happen? The elect would be called to faith through the preaching of the gospel of Christ; be justified by Christ's death on the cross; and be glorified in and through Christ, the firstfruits from the dead.

Given the combination of that plan and his divine omniscience, God would have foreseen each and every person down through time who would respond obediently to the gospel's call. Accordingly, it was those righteous saints, individually and collectively, whom God specifically and purposefully had in mind to be predestined according to his eternal purpose.[146]

That God could foresee and foreknow who among all his creatures would freely and willingly respond to him in faith takes nothing away from the fact that the whole scheme of redemption and glorification was God's from start to finish. It's what he passionately envisioned in his mind's eye. It's what he desired. It's what he intended. It's what he predestined.

The Challenging Idea of Limited Omniscience

You may have noticed that I just now included an assumption (regarding God's omniscience) which until recent times would have been almost universally agreed. Calvinists and non-Calvinists alike have believed uniformly that before the beginning of time God simultaneously foresaw every event and action that would occur in both time and eternity–past, present, and future.[147] Lately, however, some thoughtful neo-Arminians have begun to espouse what they term "open theism," or "free will theism," or "the openness of God," which calls into question this venerable understanding of God's omniscience. While historical precedent for this view is not lacking, never before has it enjoyed this much attention.

"Open theism" (sometimes called Neotheism or New Theism) is a view which, while emphasizing God's genuine openness to interaction with a decision-making mankind, has the effect of limiting God's exhaustive knowledge to events which have already occurred. How else, they ask, can we explain God's changing his mind (at the behest of Moses, for

---

146 Consider 1 Peter 1:2 and Ephesians 1:4-6.
147 Consider Psalm 139:1-24; 147:5; Isaiah 45:1; 46:5-11; Daniel 2 and 7; Hebrews 4:13.

example), or truly responding to our prayers (as if he's never before heard our requests)? How else can man make any free choices whatsoever if God already knows in advance what decisions he will make? (On that note, of course, Calvinists would applaud their logic, if not their opening premise.)

In this intramural sidebar among Arminians who otherwise agree on man's free will, it seems like a reasonable enough concern on its face. If God's foreknowledge is complete and infallible, how indeed could what God foresaw from eternity fail to happen? How could limitless foreknowledge accommodate any future personal freedom?

To be fair, "open theism" does not suggest, for instance, that David was wrong when he said, "My frame was not hidden from you when I was made in the secret place. When I was woven together in the depths of the earth, your eyes saw my unformed body. All the days ordained for me were written in your book before one of them came to be" (Psalm 139:15-16).

Were it not for what they perceive to be a limitation on man's ability to act freely, proponents of "open theism" likely would have little concern that God could see into the future. (For that reason, one suspects that "open theism" is just another in a long line of doctrines born out of over-reaction against some other doctrine—in this case, Calvinism, or perhaps any theology suggesting an impersonal, aloof God.)

The obvious response to the concerns prompting "open theism" is that there is a huge difference between what is *known* and what is *necessary*. Doris Day's old hit song, "Que será, será" (what will be, will be), is hardly the equivalent of "Que debe ser, será" (what will be, *must* be), though one must admit that "Que será, será" makes for far catchier lyrics! And though we all agree with the song's punch line: "The future's not ours to see," the question remains whether the future was for God to see.

As for "what will be," how could anyone take issue with the rather mindless redundancy that what will happen will happen! Surely, it doesn't take a rocket scientist to figure that out. So if we merely take another step further to suppose that God actually foresaw all that would happen in the future, does his foreknowledge tell us anything more than the fact that it will happen...as it happens?

We are left, then, with the only questions that really count: Did it *have to happen* that way? Could it have happened in any other way? And if it *did* happen in some other way, is not that changed eventuality what God would have foreseen instead?

Perhaps a simple illustration will help to introduce the distinction. You drive up on the scene of an accident and witness the carnage. Had the accident never happened, you never would have seen it. Right? So are you to conclude that, simply because you saw the accident, it inevitably *had* to happen? Of course, not.

But, still, some will insist that what applies to past events does not apply equally when speaking of future events. How could God, in particular, know events and actions in advance without his foreknowledge robbing human actors of their volition?

Another way of putting this is to ask: Is *foreknowledge* tantamount to *foreordination* (as Calvinists would affirm)?

Suppose for a moment that, in the vast reaches of eternity before time began, God had the divine ability to get into a time machine and set the date ahead to June 6, 1944. Suddenly, there God is, looking down on Omaha Beach watching the Americans fighting their way onto the shore against formidable German resistence. Assume also that God is simply there as a neutral observer. Contrary to the claim of virtually all combatants that "God is on our side," in our supposed hypothetical, God's hand isn't in the conflict either way.

Is there anything about the mere fact that God is able to watch the D-day landings from his "time machine" that necessarily determines whether or not the invasion will be a success? Is there any theoretical reason why the Germans might not have won both the battle for Normandy and ultimately the war itself? And if, in fact, this had happened, isn't *that* outcome, instead of an Allied victory, what God would have witnessed?

Of course, if we change our hypothetical to assume that God really was on the side of the Allies and, despite the odds, had already foreordained that the Americans would take Omaha Beach, nothing in all the world could have changed the outcome. In that instance, what God would have witnessed is what God already wanted. What he had decreed. What he had purposed, planned, and provided. And were that the case, his eternal fore-knowledge would have been based directly upon what he had foreordained.

But do you not agree that it is only by adding our second assumption that we get this particular connection between foreknowledge and foreor-dination? As we plainly saw, no such connection is logically necessary.

Maybe the problem is that we are so focused on *foreknowledge* that we are overlooking the obvious about God's *knowledge*. Screwtape helps us think more laterally as he counsels Wormwood that his patient "supposes that the Enemy, like himself, sees some things as present, remembers others as past, and anticipates others as future." Indeed, "He doesn't really think...that things as the Enemy sees them are things as they are!" And your point, Screwtape? "The Enemy does not *foresee* the humans making their free con-tributions in a future, but *sees* them doing so in His unbounded Now. And obviously to watch a man doing something is not to make him do it."[148]

So the key question is: Unless one makes further assumptions, is there anything inherent within either knowing or seeing that *necessitates* that which is known or seen? Yes? No? For Calvinists, Arminians, and all the rest of us, it's important to decide.

If in fact there is nothing inherent within *knowledge* itself that necessi-tates what is known, then how can there be any difference when what we're talking about is the *fore*knowledge of God? As Erasmus argued in his essay *On Free Will*: "Foreknowledge does not cause what is to take place. Even we know many things which will be happening. They will not hap-pen because we know them, but vice versa. An eclipse of the sun does not occur because astronomers predict it, but it can be predicted, precisely because it will take place."[149]

Time now to answer that really crucial question: Is God's foreknowl-edge necessarily to be equated with any purposed, planned, and provided foreordination on his part? Yes? No? Make sure you're on firm ground here. The implications are huge.

What an irony that, in their quest to counter Calvinism's skewed under-standing of predestination, Arminian proponents of "open theism" virtu-ally concede by inference one of the most bedrock arguments of

[148] C. S. Lewis, *The Screwtape Letters*, 149-150
[149] Erasmus, *Concerning Free Will*, sec.33.

Calvinism. Whereas Calvinism insists that foreknowledge presumes fore-ordination, "open theism" insists that foreknowledge precludes free will. In the end, it's a distinction of emphasis with little practical difference.

Both sides, it seems, have failed to see the illogic in their parallel assumptions. While Calvinists wrongly limit man's free will in order to maintain their deterministic understanding of foreknowledge, the propo-nents of "open theism" wrongly react against any foreordained determin-ism by severely limiting God's eternal foreknowledge.

A Way Out Of All the Confusion

I wonder if there's not a simple illustration that can lead us out of all this confusion. Think of it this way. It's the day of the big game, and you're sit-ting in front of the television in a state of hypnotic euphoria watching your favorite college team play its arch-rival. As the time clock winds down to the final two seconds in the game, your team is on their opponent's fifteen yard line, but behind by four points. A field goal won't do. Gotta be a touchdown. With the national championship in the balance (did I fail to mention that?) and time left for only one more play, your team comes to the line while the stadium rocks with the roar of screaming fans. You're screaming, too.

So here comes the moment of truth. The center hikes the ball to the quar-terback, who steps back into the pocket. Meanwhile, the wide receiver runs deep into the end-zone, covered like a blanket by a hulk of a linebacker. Spotting his receiver, the quarterback quickly cocks his arm and releases the football. As the ball flies toward its target, both the receiver and the defender leap high into the air. At that point, the whole stadium is holding its collective breath in anticipation, and everybody in the room is riveted to the action. Will he catch it or not? If he catches it, your team wins! If he doesn't, you lose!

For one split second, the defender's hands tip the ball ever so slightly, but suddenly it's clear that the wide receiver has somehow hauled in a quite unbelievable catch and come down with the ball firmly in his grasp. Touchdown! You win! The stadium crowd goes crazy, and there are high fives slapping all over the living room as the excitement explodes.

Okay, so it's just a game. But, you already know what's coming next: the obligatory instant replays of that dramatic, game-winning catch, over and over again from every conceivable angle in stop-action, slow motion. Unlike disputed plays where the umpire takes a sideline look at the instant replay to decide the proper call, these replays of the "miracle catch" were sheerly for the fun of reliving the moment time and time again!

And what's the one thing you can be sure of with each replay of that incredible catch? No matter what the angle, the wide receiver comes down with the ball...every time! Forget any anxious anticipation at this point. Because of instant replay, you can absolutely, positively know in advance that he's going to catch the ball.

But *might he have dropped it?* You bet. Was there any absolute guarantee that he wouldn't drop it? Not with this guy's spotty record this season! Even so, no one in his right mind is going to think that our game's hero might possibly drop the ball in one of the scores of replays being flashed on the screen.[150]

As you can already guess, what I'm suggesting from this illustration is that God's foreknowledge is much the same as instant replay; only that what God had in the far reaches of eternity was "instant *pre*play." At the push of a divine button, God was able to roll the tape of history and see every person who would ever live and know their every thought and deed. For both better and worse, even before he created the universe, he knew you and me inside and out–the good, the bad, and the ugly.

---

[150] With apologies to Norman Geisler, who uses a similar illustration in *Chosen But Free*, 2nd Ed., 45. I have been using this illustration for many years, unaware until the writing of this book that it was anywhere in print. If I unwittingly picked up this illustration from anyone else, I gratefully acknowledge the contribution.

Yet it must be said that Geisler backs away from this very illustration in attempting to maintain his peculiar "third way" of "moderate Calvinism." Having first established that what God foresaw (the results of man's free choice through time) was thus "determined"(fixed) once and for all (as if permanently captured on a video tape of a game), Geisler then argues that God simultaneously "determined" (arbitrarily decreed) each soul's destiny independently and without recourse to the results of man's free choice (as if God himself scripted in advance every block, tackle, pass, and run of the game). This second, distinct "determining"(meaning predestination) was necessary, says Geisler, in order to maintain the doctrine of grace, sovereign election, and God's own indivisible nature.

In trying to reconcile the irreconcilable, Geisler has lost the plot of both divergent explanations. "Chosen but free" works well when election is based upon foreknowledge, but loses all credibility when the chosenness is then said to be set in stone independently of man's own free choice. Geisler would have been on safer ground employing his logic to help explain how God's sovereign control could providentially assure the final score of the game without imposing himself moment by moment on each player on the field (the *real* mystery). As it is, Geisler is vulnerable to his own indictment when he argues: "The strong Calvinist's position must be rejected because it is contradictory"(p. 21).

Disquieting as it may be, before time began God already would have foreseen your reading the words in this sentence at this very moment...as well as what you are thinking about these words.

Although undoubtedly pained by the thought, God must also have foreknown that Adam and Eve would sin, as would even spiritual giants like Abraham, Moses, and David. And yes, of course, God knew even before you and I were ever born that we too would live in rebellion against his divine sovereignty. Not that he desired that. Far from it! Nor that he in any way pre-programmed us to sin. It was simply the risk he took in choosing to create us with free will.

Being created in God's image meant not only that we would be spiritual beings having a potential for immortal existence, but also that we would have both free will and the capacity for genuine, free moral choice. Choice that all too often we would exercise badly, defiantly, and sinfully. (Has that same prospect stopped any wanna-be parents from having children?)

On a more positive note, it also meant that God knew in advance all the good things that would happen, as well as the identities of all those who would respond to the preaching of the gospel. Remember Paul's nighttime vision in the city of Corinth? Only through his divine prescience could God have said to him: "Do not be afraid; keep on speaking, do not be silent. For I am with you, and no one is going to attack and harm you, because I have many people in this city" (Acts 18:9-10).

But it gets even better. Ever experience watching yourself on a video tape? One of the most amazing things about God's "instant preplay" is that God could see himself as well, interacting with mankind within the time-space continuum of a universe he had yet to create. That includes even those occasions when he changed his mind at Moses' behest, and had second-thoughts about appointing Saul king, and relented from bringing the punishment he had promised against Nineveh.[151]

---

[151] Exodus 32:11-14; 1 Samuel 10:15, 35; Jonah 3:10.

Is this to suggest that God himself is not immutable? Hardly! God's character and nature do not change. "I AM WHO I AM" (Exodus 3:14). "I the LORD do not change" (Malachi 3:6). See also Psalm 25:27; Hebrews 1:10-12; 13:8; James 1:17.

As is clear from the three examples cited in the text, God can certainly change his mind. What God can *not* do is renege on a promise. "God is not a man, that he should lie, nor a son of man, that he should change his mind. Does he speak and then not act? Does he promise and not fulfill?" (Numbers 23:19). To the same effect, see: 1 Samuel 15:29 and 2 Timothy 2:13.

Want Proof of God's "Instant Preplay"?

And just how can we be sure that God had such "instant preplay"? First and foremost, because God not only works within the bookends of time, but, as the Eternal One, also stands outside of time. Since therefore God sees past, present, and future *simultaneously*, nothing, strictly speaking, is "future" anymore than it is "past." (Where is Einstein when we need him!)

Along the time-line on which temporal history has unfolded, of course, we rightly speak of "future events" and "future actions" on the part of both God and man. On that same time-line, for instance, Resurrection and Judgment are yet to be. They are *future*. But that's only in our finite, time-bound frame of vision. By contrast, the infinite, eternal God of heaven even now sees it all–from beginning to end. "I am God, and there is none like me. I make known the end from the beginning, from ancient times, what is still to come" (Isaiah 46:9-10).

Beyond that, we also know that God had "instant preplay" because of his divine power of prophecy. No, not just prophecy about what God himself promised to do (which would have been totally within his own control); or how he could predict his reaction in response to whatever man's own independent action might be.[152] Rather, it's the incredible *details* of prophecy, including the volitional actions of individuals which might have gone one way or other, that give us such convincing evidence of God's foreknowledge.

Consider, for example, the regulations laid down for Israel's kings, long before Israel (contrary to God's warnings) would demand a king. And also God's knowing in advance that the period of captivity would last for precisely 70 years (quite incredibly, whether calculated from the first deportation in 605 B.C. to the first return and completion of the temple's foundation in 536 B.C., or from the destruction of Solomon's temple in 586 B.C. to the full restoration of the temple in 516 B.C.!). And God foretelling the very name of Cyrus, the Persian leader, before he was ever born...and 150 years before he came to power! And, of course, there was also Jesus predicting that Peter would deny him three times before the cock crowed; and that Judas would betray him.[153]

---

[152] See, for example, Deuteronomy 31:16-18

[153] Deuteronomy 17:14-20; 2 Kings 24:1; Ezra 3:8-9; 2 Kings 25:8-10; Ezra 6:14-15; Isaiah 45:13; Matthew 26:75, 25

Most wondrous of all, even before there was a world for sin to enter into, God already planned an altogether marvelous scheme of redemption in which he would wrap himself in human flesh in the person of Jesus of Nazareth and shed his own blood for your sins and mine. No less than you or I watching ourselves in a family video, God would have seen himself on the giant screen of divine foreknowledge as the suffering Savior on the cross of calvary. Which, when you think about it, makes it all the more amazing that he did not shrink back from the path of destiny leading to that awful agony.

Hoping Against Hope

Whatever else we might disagree about regarding God's foreknowledge, all sides surely can agree with our earlier premise that God acts both outside of time and within time, simultaneously. That being true, I am intrigued by the possibility that God is not just omnipresent and omniscient, but is also what we might call "omni-hopeful."

This fascinating possibility is raised by such passages as Jeremiah 3:7, where God says of Israel, "I thought that after she had done all this she would return to me but she did not...." And in 3:19 there's that hopeful cry: "How gladly would I treat you like sons and give you a desirable land, the most beautiful inheritance of any nation," followed by that poignant line once again: "I thought you would call me 'Father.'"

And who could possibly overlook the hopefulness of Jeremiah 26:3? "Perhaps they will listen and each will turn from his evil way. Then I will relent and not bring on them the disaster I was planning because of the evil they have done." Unfortunately, Judah remained entrenched in evil, and so her threatened punishment was inevitable.

In each instance, what God fervently *hoped* was not what actually came to pass. And yet there is no question but that, even in the face of eternal, *out-of-time* foreknowledge, there was still hope within the present *in-time* framework. Or to bring us back to our "instant preplay" analogy, what God could foresee on the tape of history was not always what he hoped for as he viewed himself interacting with his creatures. It's like watching your favorite movie over and over, and finding yourself crying at the same point every time!

This must also surely explain why God would appear to be so dumbfounded when he lamented: "They have built the high places of Topheth in the Valley of Ben Hinnom to burn their sons and daughters in the fire–something I did not command, *nor did it enter my mind."* (Jeremiah 7:31).

It's possible, of course, that we were never meant to take those words literally–that they provide yet another example of hyperbole, intentionally used to exaggerate the point. At the very least, Calvinists must surely agree that an omniscient God would have foreseen such a monstrous abomination (despite being hard pressed by their insistent linkage between foreknowledge and foreordination to say that God himself didn't foreordain it). Even if taken literally, however, God's lament only demonstrates all the more that divine foreknowledge does not rule out God's eternal hopefulness.[154]

Have you ever stood at the bedside of someone you knew was hours, minutes, or perhaps moments away from an inevitable death, yet you still hoped against hope that somehow the inevitable would never happen? I have. And so I wonder if that is not how God himself must feel as he looks from *within time* at what he has already seen from *outside of time.*

Above all, we dare not miss that crucial reference to calling God "Father." For without doubt the King Eternal would know his own decrees. And the Judge Almighty would be certain of the eventual outcome. But at the bedside of the lost and dying (count on it), the Loving Father would still be hoping....

A True Case of Predestination

If you really want a case in which God not only foresaw but also foreordained, then believe in Him who was "the Lamb that was slain from the creation of the world" (Revelation 13:8). As Peter tells us, Christ was the predestined, chosen, elect Savior of the world:

---

[154] Calvinists put forward a similar argument to explain how God could *wish* that the predestined lost would be saved, even knowing they are eternally damned. The colossal difference is that, under Calvinism, God himself not only foresaw that result, but unalterably and irresistibly foreordained it. How, then, could God possibly remain hopeful for an obedience which, by his own sovereign will, has been absolutely ruled out?

You know that it was not with perishable things such as silver or gold that you were redeemed from the empty way of life handed down to you from your forefathers, but with the precious blood of Christ, a lamb without blemish or defect. He was chosen before the creation of the world, but was revealed in these last times for your sake. (1 Peter 1:18-20)

Unique among men, Jesus of Nazareth was predestined, called, and foreknown...in that order. Given his life-saving, sin-atoning purpose, first came the foreordaining, and only then the foreknowing. First came his predestined purpose, and only then the glorious, incarnational calling forth![155]

In fact, the only objective, solid assurance we can have of our own election is by being in the Elect One, Jesus Christ. If election depended upon what God may or may not have done in the secret, unrevealed recesses of eternity, how could we possibly know whether or not we are among the elect? By contrast, when our election is wholly and solely through Christ's eternal election, no mystery remains as to whether or not we are chosen. For we are chosen *in him*!

A "God-centered" election enshrouds us in the often obscure, meta-physical nature of God, whereas a "Christ-centered" election can be known as surely as the redemptive history which has been revealed in and through the person of Jesus—the crucified Lord, the risen Christ, and Savior of all who trust him in obedient faith.

If there is any mystery, it is that this called-forth "Word made flesh," is said by the Hebrew writer (in 2:14) to have "shared in our humanity." To the saints in Philippi, Paul explains how that happened:

Who being in very nature God,
    did not consider equality with God something to be grasped,
but made himself nothing,
    taking the very nature of a servant,
    being made in human likeness.
And being found in appearance as a man,
    he humbled himself

---

[155] See Isaiah 49:5-7; Acts 2:23; 3:18; 4:28.

and became obedient to death—
even death on a cross! (Philippians 2:6-8)

And just that quickly, we come face to face with a profound question. At the very mention of the word *obedient*, we are drawn back to Jesus' incomparable inner struggle in Gethsemane. With sweat drops of blood rebuking any thought that it was all a sham or a clever pretense, Jesus fervently prays to his Father: "Not my will, but yours be done."

Do you believe that, there in the garden, Jesus had a genuine, honest-to-goodness choice either to obey or not to obey? To submit or to succumb? To fulfill his predestined purpose or to frustrate it? Did Jesus really and truly have a personal will of his own to yield to his Father?

If your answer to all these questions is "yes," can we not begin to see through the person of Jesus himself that there is nothing either logically or theologically inconsistent between being predestined in purpose, yet still being free to choose? No, I'm not talking here about Calvinism's tortuously-contrived "pretend version" of free will; nor even, for the moment, about "open theism's" legitimate concern about how God's chosen elect could retain a genuine freedom of will if God both foresaw and foreordained the eventual outcome.

Far more important—and profoundly so—is what we learn from reversing the logic. If in fact all men and women have genuine freedom of will, then surely predestination has to mean something other than arbitrary, unconditional selection of the elect.

What God Foresaw

Which brings us full circle back to our original question: On what basis apart from sheer capriciousness or fortuity did God predestine us? If, as Peter tells us, we were *chosen according to the foreknowledge of God*, what *was* that "something" he foresaw on which he based our election?

The answer, I suggest, is that he foresaw which hearts would respond to the good news of salvation in Christ and which would not. He saw what would actually happen in one life after another when the gospel was preached. Far from having already predetermined our eternal destiny with no reference whatever to our own action, God says explicitly: "I the LORD search the heart and examine the mind, to reward a man according to his conduct, according to what his deeds deserve" (Jeremiah 17:10). That's hearts, minds, conduct, and deeds—all of which God would have seen from eternity.

Jesus himself shows us the connection between man's belief and God's eternal foreknowledge, saying, "'Yet there are some of you who do not believe.' For Jesus had known from the beginning which of them did not believe...." (John 6:53-54).

In the battle for the souls of man, God in his sovereign, divine omniscience stood on the "Normandy Beach of time," as it were, and watched as sinner after sinner came ashore—some with the spiritual resolve to throw themselves under God's own protective wing, and others who were determined to do it on their own—to "do it or die," which sadly they have done in their millions, and to their eternal destruction.

Who, then, has been justified in Christ? All those who have been called to God's purpose. And who has been called? All those whom God has predestined. And whom has he predestined? All those whom he foresaw from the dawn of eternity would respond in obedient faith to the gospel of salvation.[156]

In light of that progression, one of Calvinism's favorite texts (John 17:2) loses considerable punch. Praying to his Father, Jesus says (with reference to himself): "You granted him authority over all people that he might give eternal life to all those you have given him."

Standing alone, this passage tells us nothing about the basis upon which the Father determined "those he had given him." Were they given because they were predestined and then foreseen, or foreseen and only then predestined? If we put this passage alongside Paul's own progression, then those who were given to the Son would have been determined on the basis of what the Father had foreseen in them.

---

[156] In fact, more than just the elect have been "called." In a death-blow to Calvinism's doctrine of particular election, Jesus himself said: "Many are called, but few chosen" (Matthew 20:16 NKJV). Either this means many *elect* are called but only a few are chosen (which would make no sense even for Calvinists), or it means that the *non-elect* are also called, but are not chosen because they refuse to believe.

Have you ever considered closely what we are told about how and when the evangelist Timothy was called? Paul gives us more than a clue when he encourages his young protégé, saying, "Fight the good fight of the faith. Take hold of the eternal life *to which you were called when you made your good confession* in the presence of many witnesses" (1 Timothy 6:12). No mention here about a calling taking place before Timothy was ever born.

Saved sinners don't come to Christ because they are predestined. Saved sinners are predestined because, as God could already see from eternity, they are the ones with hearts willing to passionately seek God. As David counseled his son Solomon, "the LORD searches every heart and understands every motive behind the thoughts. If you seek him, he will be found by you; but if you forsake him, he will reject you forever" (1 Chronicles 28:9). What God sees now is what he has seen from the beginning: even the motives behind our thoughts!

But this only begs the more important question: For what *purpose* are the foreseen elect saved?

A Purposeful Predestination

Mostly lost in all the debate over predestination is the fact that when the Scriptures speak of our being predestined, it is not as an end in itself, but as a means to an end. The question is not *who* is predestined, but *why* are we predestined? And the "why" is never left in doubt. Just look again at all the predestination passages and how terribly far we seem to have missed the point.

He chose us [WHY?]...to be holy and blameless....

He predestined us [WHY?] to be adopted as his sons...to the praise of his glorious grace.

Having been predestined [WHY?]...in order that we...might be for the praise of his glory.

Predestined [WHY?] to be conformed to the likeness of his Son.

To God's elect...who have been chosen [WHY?]...for obedience to Jesus Christ....

Thinking in terms of *who* is predestined and *who* is not misses the whole point of predestination. To speak in terms of the *elect* as opposed to the *non-elect* is far wide of the mark. When the issue of salvation is in question, Scripture talks about the saved and the unsaved; or the saved and the lost; or the redeemed and the unredeemed. But, despite the ultimate truth of it, there's not a word to be found about the *elect being saved* and the *non-elect being lost*, as if that were the point of all the talk about predestination.

When, on the other hand, the focus is squarely on those who are saved, redeemed, and forgiven, (as it is invariably in Peter and Paul's epistles) then and only then the talk turns to that which is relevant to those who are assumed to be among the chosen. Then and only then do we begin to hear about the *predestined purposes* to which they have been called as God's elect.

If, indeed, the elect in Ephesus, Colosse, Philippi, and Rome had been predestined, called, and justified, they needed to be reminded of their high calling and the eternal purpose behind it. As we too are being reminded even today, Christ's disciples are to be a "purpose-driven church," predestined individually to live purpose-driven lives.

Lest they forget, Peter reminds his own readers that they are "a chosen people, a royal priesthood, a holy nation, a people belonging to God," *so that they might "declare the praises of him who called [them] out of darkness into his wonderful light"* (1 Peter 2:9). What a heritage! What a legacy! What a privilege!

Individual and Corporate Predestination

Have you noticed over the last few paragraphs that we've begun to see a subtle shift from *individuals* who are foreseen and predestined, to a *collective group* which is foreseen and predestined. Instead of just one believer here and another believer there, it's *all* the saved. *All* the redeemed. *The church. The body of Christ. A chosen people, a royal priesthood, a holy nation.*

To be predestined as an individual is to be predestined as part of a collective whole with all other predestined individuals. No less than with the human body itself, the elect body of Christ is not merely incidental to the election of its individual members. Quite to the contrary, our election as individuals is of only incidental importance to our being part of Christ's elect body, which from eternity was predestined to bring glory to God. In terms of election, the corporate, universal *ekklesia* is primary, while those who happen to comprise her are but secondary.

It is through *the called-out church* that the mystery of the unsearchable riches of Christ is being revealed, especially in the joining together of Jew and Gentile. "His intent was that now, *through the church*, the manifold wisdom of God should be made known to the rulers and authorities in the heavenly realms, according to his eternal purpose which he accomplished in Christ Jesus our Lord" (Ephesians 3:10-11).

As we shall see in the following chapter, there is a crucial distinction to be made between how God has foreordained his elect *as a collective whole* compared with how he has foreordained us as his elect *individually*. For the moment, however, that significant difference should not obscure the glorious truth that those whom God individually foreknew were predestined, called, justified, and glorified!

So are we suggesting that Calvinists are right to believe in predestination? Of course, they're right. Just not their standard revised version of it. Their version of predestination and Scripture's version of predestination are as different as Garbo's fictionalized version of the D-day invasion and its true reality. Beginning with the same basic truth, all it takes is a slight twist in a different direction and suddenly you've got a completely different picture.

The truth is that God created mankind with free moral agency with which he does not interfere, even if at times he providentially intervenes. Yet, not even his periodic providential forays into the lives of nations and individuals in order to bring about his eternal plan ever rob anyone of their own responsibility for moral choice. (And, in case you're wondering, yes, that includes Pharaoh and Judas Iscariot.)

Like everyone who's ever lived, you and I must choose between spiritual life and spiritual death. Between honoring God and pleasing ourselves. Between obedience and disobedience. Between faith and unbelief. Between morality and immorality. Between good and evil; right and wrong.

Depending upon how each and every human being personally chooses, says Paul, eternal life or God's wrath is in the balance:

> God "will give to each person according to what he has done." To those who by persistence in doing good seek glory, honor and immortality, he will give eternal life. But for those who are self-seeking and who reject the truth and follow evil, there will be wrath and anger. There will be trouble and distress for every

human being who does evil: first for the Jew, then for the Gentile; but glory, honor and peace for everyone who does good: first for the Jew, then for the Gentile. (Romans 2:6-10)

In fact, how *we* decide to choose, is precisely how *he* decides to choose. And, indeed, it is in that sense that he has *already chosen.*

For, through his divine power, the omniscient God of the universe foresaw that you and I would...

Choose to honor his sovereign will for our lives; and
Commit ourselves in faith to his leading; and
Acknowledge our sins before him; and
Accept his free offer of grace to all who seek his mercy; and
Trust only in Christ's atoning blood for our salvation; and
Obey his call to repentance and baptism and holy living.

And *because God saw all that before time itself began*—even then, he...
Chose us to be his very own adopted children;
Honored us as his elect people; and
Predestined us to holy works of righteousness...

All to his rightful glory!

What more could we ask of a God who, even now, has already set the table for the resplendent feast of love he is planning to share with us in the heavenly realm?

Say you believe in predestination? So do I!

For we are God's workmanship, created in Christ Jesus to do good works, which God prepared in advance for us to do.

Ephesians 2:7

Chapter Summary

- The doctrines of election and predestination are unquestionably biblical and altogether wonderful. By contrast, the Calvinist version of those two doctrines could hardly be more unbiblical.

- The predestination of God's elect is not based upon any arbitrary choice of God, but rather upon God's foreknowledge of those who would respond to the gospel of grace.

- That God in his omniscience knew from before Creation whether or not specific individuals would respond in obedient faith in no way means that God himself was in control of that personal decision, as Calvinism teaches.

- Nor does man's exercise of genuine free will mean that God's foreknowledge must necessarily be limited in any way, as "open theism" contends.

- As presented in Scripture, the discussion of predestination and election has nothing to do with who is chosen and who is not, but rather the eternal purposes to which God has called all those who would become his chosen ones through faith and obedience.

Reality Check: If Calvinism is right in saying that every aspect of your life has been predestined from eternity, then whatever you think, believe, say, or do has no intrinsic meaning beyond mechanically implementing the predetermined result.

Chapter 7

Headline:
"Hanging Chads" Put Election in Doubt

The elect of God are chosen by Him to be His children,
in order that they might be made to believe,
not because He foresaw that they would believe.

—Augustine

Remember the controversy that dogged the 2000 Presidential election when the contest between George W. Bush and Al Gore came down to a relative handful of disputed ballots in the State of Florida? For most of us, it was the first time we had ever heard of those ghastly creatures called "hanging chads." (Hanging *what?*)

Then came the pictures of all those beleaguered election officials closely examining each and every ballot to see whether or not the holes in the punch-cards were obstructed by tiny bits of paper that hadn't quite been removed–those dreaded hanging chads. As Al Gore might hasten to tell us: Beware of hanging chads! No election is safe when those gremlins are about.

Especially is that true of the Doctrine of Election. Just when you think you've got a winner, close reexamination of a number of "hanging chads" in Scripture casts serious doubt on Calvinism's idea of unconditional election.

In the previous chapter, we examined the biblical concept of predestination and compared that with the radically different version presented to us by Calvinism. Ask most people to tell you what Calvinism teaches, and you'd probably hear the single word: *Predestination*. But, surprisingly, this key feature of Calvinism is not the "P" in *TULIP*. (That "P" stands for perseverance of the saints.)

Calvinism's view of predestination is linked hand in hand with the "U" of *TULIP*, which stands for unconditional election. Whereas predestination, properly understood, is an altogether wondrous biblical truth, the idea of unconditional election could not be further from the truth.

Although the two concepts go hand in hand, it is important to understand that the idea of unconditional election brings Calvinists to their unique understanding of predestination, not the other way around.

Beginning with the fundamentally flawed assumption that man cannot be asked to meet any conditions whatsoever in the process of salvation without threatening salvation by grace, Calvinists are led to the conclusion that one's election simply *has to be* unconditional. Were there any conditions attached at all, then man would be participating in his own salvation, and that would never do. Which leaves us with the only alternative: it must have been God alone who decided each man's eternal destiny.

At that point, Calvinism desperately needed a convenient biblical vehicle to convey the novel idea of unconditional election. Whether wittingly or unwittingly, Calvinism hijacked the legitimate concept of predestination, painted it a completely different color, and drove it miles away from the word's original meaning—all in aid of a cause deemed sufficiently worthy as to justify the felony.

This undoubtedly goes a long way toward explaining why predestination usually gets top billing in the popular press. Once Calvinism's peculiar version of predestination became the means of conveyance for unconditional election, most folks began to talk only of the hijacked vehicle, and not so much about its less-visible driver. Nor did it hurt that the familiar biblical vehicle had a presumed legitimacy which the unauthorized driver clearly lacked.

In this chapter, therefore, we need to explore more closely the core concept of unconditional election. To do so, we'll look at a number of problematic biblical passages. While undoubtedly some could be understood to favor the Calvinist view, others unambiguously argue against it. On both sides, then, are hanging chads demanding a closer look.

As we go along, incidentally, don't forget that the issue is not whether God's chosen people are "elect" (that's a given), but whether or not our election is solely and unconditionally God's decision, or conditioned in some way upon how we ourselves respond to God's grace.

It Sure Looks Like Election Is Conditional!

To begin, let's take a quick look at just three passages which certainly look as if salvation (which invariably is linked with God's chosen elect) is conditioned upon how you and I respond to the gospel. Consider, for example, this compelling admonition from the writer of Hebrews that...

> *Without faith it is impossible to please God, because anyone who comes to him must believe that he exists and that he rewards those who earnestly seek him. (Hebrews 11:6)*

From this passage, what does it appear we must do in order to please God?
a) Nothing (because God's elect are unconditionally chosen); or
b) Believe in God and earnestly seek him.

When Paul addresses the Greek philosophers on Mars Hill in the great city of Athens, explaining who the true God of heaven is and what he expects of man, we hear Paul saying:

> *From one man he made every nation of men, that they should inhabit the whole earth; and he determined the times set for them and the exact places where they should live. God did this so that men would seek him and perhaps reach out for him and find him, though he is not far from each one of us. (Acts 17:26-27)*

Calvinists would certainly rejoice at the first part of this text, suggesting as it does that God predetermined when and where men would live.

(Left to reasonable doubt, of course, is whether this is referring to individual souls, or instead to nations, societies, or perhaps various cultures.) Even so, whether God predetermined each soul's eternal destiny is another (gigantic) question altogether.

In that regard, there seems to be only desire and hope, not certainty, that individual men and women would reach out for God and actively seek him. Does this sound as if God pre-selected some folks, but not others, without any conditions whatever being imposed?

And what are we to conclude from Paul's mention of a universal command for men to repent?

> *Therefore since we are God's offspring, we should not think that the divine being is like gold or silver or stone—an image made by man's design and skill. In the past God overlooked such ignorance, but now he commands all people everywhere to repent. For he has set a day when he will judge the world with justice by the man he has appointed. (Acts 17:29-31)*

From this passage, what would you say will be the basis upon which God will judge the world?

a) On God's unconditional election of certain people to be his saints; or

b) On the basis of whether individuals, themselves, repent before God.

And finally, we have what is often referred to as "the Great Commission." As Jesus anticipates his imminent ascension, we see him giving parting instructions to his apostles:

> *He said to them, "Go into all the world and preach the good news to all creation. Whoever believes and is baptized will be saved, but whoever does not believe will be condemned." (Mark 16:15-16)*

If you'd never heard a word about Calvinism and were trying to understand what this passage is telling us, what would you think a person needs to do in order to be saved?

a) Nothing whatsoever (since already unconditionally elected); or

b) Believe and be baptized.

As undoubtedly you are aware, these are but three representative passages among many others which could be presented that unequivocally call for faith, repentance, and baptism...all in connection with salvation.

Whatever else we may understand about the process of salvation, are you prepared to defend the proposition that God has absolutely no expectations for man himself? No conditions man must satisfy? No commands to be obeyed? No righteous life to be lived?

It has to be said, of course, that Calvinism would quickly agree that sinful man needs to believe and repent. (Maybe even to be baptized.[157]) Yet, Calvinists insist that neither belief nor repentance can occur without God initiating those responses through the regenerating work of the Holy Spirit. And it is this inner prompting–given only to the elect–which is unconditional. How, Calvinists ask, could it be anything other than unconditional since God chose his elect before the world was even created?

Not only is that reasoning so circular as to be unhelpful, but it would make a complete nonsense of the passages cited above, none of which suggests in the slightest that–for some folks, but not others–the cards are already stacked in favor of faith and repentance. Were that the case, why would Paul tell the Athenians: "...but now he commands *all people everywhere* to repent"? Why command *all people* to repent when God knows some people couldn't possibly repent?

What do you think? Does it make any sense for there to be a consistent biblical emphasis on man's obedience to God through belief and repentance while, all along, there is another level on which the question of whether any given individual will believe and repent is already decided?

If one's election has already been determined unconditionally in heaven, why does the Bible talk in terms of salvation and election being dependent upon clear conditions on earth?

If the elect are called to be saved without any condition on their part, why are we told:

---

[157] Curiously, the call to submit to baptism seems to be virtually lost on many believers, despite baptism's inescapable pairing with faith, as in the "Great Commission." Because immersion involves a visible, physical act, as compared with the mental act of faith and often-behind-the-scenes acts of repentance, apparently baptism just *looks* way too much like "work"! The irony is that, since the candidate for immersion is, in that moment, *acted upon*, rather than *acting*, baptism itself is the most passive, submissive, humbling, "non-working" response possible.

1. That it's not possible to please God without having faith? (Hebrews 11:6)

2. That God has called all men to repent? (Acts 17:29-31)

3. That salvation is promised to those who repent and are baptized? (Acts 2:37-38)[158]

Ezekiel's Treatise on Calvinism

As we further consider Calvinism's premise that God's election of the saints was based not upon man's own actions but solely upon God's choosing, how are we to explain the three generations of Ezekiel 18? In this hypothetical scenario involving father, son, and grandson—the first generation "father" is righteous, the second generation "son" is unrighteous, and the third generation "grandson" is righteous like his grandfather.

Does not the central message of this compelling chapter ("The soul that sins is the one who will die") teach that salvation is based, not upon God's arbitrary election of one man over another, but upon how one chooses to live his life?

Perhaps you might respond: "Well, yes, but how each of these three men chose to live was already predetermined from eternity." Or perhaps, "It's only regeneration by the Holy Spirit, gifted unconditionally, that makes possible a life of righteousness."

Yet, if either of those were the case, what purpose would be served by a series of warnings obviously directed to those who would incline themselves toward being unrighteous? If conceivably an elect person might be drawn to his salvation through such warnings, what possible good would warnings do for the non-elect, who couldn't heed the warnings even if they wanted?

Calvinists often argue that, because all mankind was in Adam's loins when he sinned, we thereby share in his punishment of spiritual death. If the same logic were applied to the hypothetical in Ezekiel 18, the righteous third-generation "grandson" would have shared in the punishment of death

---

[158] To make sense of Acts 2:39 ("The promise is for you and your children and for all who are far off—for all whom the Lord our God will call"), one has to back up to verse 38, which clarifies the means whereby God calls. There is no hint here of a calling through eternal pre-selection, but rather through the preaching of the gospel and our obedient response to that good news in repentance and baptism. Importantly, that call goes out to both Jews and Gentiles, which is to say *everyone*.

applied to his wicked father, simply by virtue of having been in his loins. But nothing could be clearer than the teaching point of the hypothetical:

> *The son will not share the guilt of the father, nor will the father share the guilt of the son. The righteousness of the righteous man will be credited to him, and the wickedness of the wicked will be charged against him (Ezekiel 18:20).*

If that principle were applied in the case of Adam, the doctrine of original sin would be a non-starter. In fact, one is hard-pressed to see how the doctrine of election can stand at all in light of the plain teaching of the opening preamble of this crystal clear text:

> *The word of the LORD came to me: "What do you people mean by quoting this proverb about the land of Israel: 'The fathers eat sour grapes, and the children's teeth are set on edge'? As surely as I live, declares the Sovereign LORD, you will no longer quote this proverb in Israel. For every living soul belongs to me, the father as well as the son—both alike belong to me. The soul who sins is the one who will die." (Ezekiel 18:1-4)*

The first obvious point emerging from this passage is that sin is not passed along from generation to generation (a faulty assumption made when Calvinists cite Psalm 51:5 in support of original sin). The second, equally-clear point is that whether one is crowned with eternal life or banished to eternal death has nothing to do with an arbitrary election of individual destinies wholly unassociated with a person's own spiritual decisions. Each one of us has a choice either to live righteously before God and reap his blessing or to live wickedly and suffer the death penalty.

The Calvinist Conundrum of Election's Timing

Important as it is, the problem of individually-chosen sin is the least of Calvinism's worries. Far more important is the stubborn problem of timing that just won't go away. While election generally focuses on the saved, we mustn't forget that election also applies to the lost. (As Boettner admits: "The chief difficulty with the doctrine of Election, of course, arises in regard to the unsaved....")[159]

Apparently never stopping to realize that election of the lost would have taken place long before sin and rebellion entered the world, Calvinists argue with equal insistence that the lost *deserve* God's wrath for living in rebellion to him. But if that were so, how could their election to destruction be anything other than *conditional*? If because of prior *unconditional* election the "saved elect" cannot possibly deserve their salvation, how can it be said in the same breath that the "lost elect" most certainly deserve their destruction?

When the Westminster Confession declares, regarding the rest of mankind, that "God was pleased...to ordain them to dishonor and wrath *for their sin* [my emphasis]...," it argues against its own prior assertion that God "hath not decreed anything because He foresaw it as future, or as that which would come to pass upon such conditions."

Given those conflicting affirmations, Calvinism's own insistent sequencing is critical. First, of course, comes the predestining decree of unconditional election for those who are to be saved, as well as the consequent lostness of those who will remain unsaved. At that point, we'd do well to take a red felt pen and draw a broad, indelible line right there. For only then comes Creation, followed by Adam's sin and "the Fall," bearing with it the original sin and depravity whereby, supposedly, each newborn is innately rebellious toward God and worthy of his wrath.

Am I missing something, or does it seem to you also that–at the point of election–no one would yet have sinned personally or been imputed with sin vicariously? Still believe that the predestined lost *deserve* God's wrath?

For that matter, not even the election of the saved is consistent with Calvinism's pivotal sequencing. Calvinist J. B. Mozley reminds us that, as the whole race after the fall was "one mass of perdition...it pleased God of His sovereign mercy to rescue some and to leave others where they were."[160] But in light of the sequence issue, do you see any problem with God's "rescue plan" for the elect? Exactly! Election already would have taken place long before there was any "mass of perdition" from which to rescue the elect.

Remember that bold red line we just drew? It hasn't budged a fraction.

---

[159] Boettner, p. 104
[160] J. B. Mozley, *The Augustinian Doctrine of Predestination*, 287. (Cited by Boettner, p. 104.)

Troubling Questions for Non-Calvinists

One of the interesting aspects of the hanging-chad crisis in Florida was the way in which the questionable ballots were examined by election officials. To insure fairness through a system of checks-and-balances, each ballot was carefully scrutinized, not just by one, but by two officials. Before a ballot was accepted or rejected, both officials had to agree as to whether there was a hanging chad, and, if so, whether the ballot was likely to have been miscounted as a result.

Not a bad idea. Whenever that much is at stake, objectivity is always a good thing. Even considering a hotly contested presidential race, of course, the stakes could hardly be higher than in a discussion of Calvinism, in which the issues are nothing less than the very essence of God, man, and salvation!

So in the spirit of objectivity, it has to be said that there are some "hanging chads" in Scripture which, on their face, would certainly seem to support the doctrine of unconditional election. Given those challenging passages, it's time to turn the tables and let Calvinists ask some troubling questions of the rest of us.

Would it be weaseling to ask if the questioning could begin with what I consider to be one of the easier passages? The question is, Doesn't Jeremiah 1:5 give us a great personal illustration of unconditional election? Calling Jeremiah to his mission as a prophet, the Lord says: "Before I formed you in the womb I knew you, before you were born I set you apart; I appointed you as a prophet to the nations." Since Jeremiah's selection had taken place long before he was born, doesn't this prove that God's pre-selection *had to be* unconditional?

Absolutely. Without a doubt, Jeremiah's appointment as God's prophet was unconditional. It certainly wasn't based on his faith, his proven character, or any "work" great or small that he might have done. His predestination as a prophet was purely arbitrary. Indeed, his prophetic office wasn't just foreknown, but foreordained.

What's more, all the same things could readily be acknowledged regarding Moses and Aaron; Abraham, Isaac, and Jacob; Saul, David, and Solomon;

Isaiah, Ezekiel, and Daniel; and even poor ol' Jonah. Perhaps *especially* poor ol' Jonah! Talk about irresistible grace in the face of human resistance![161]

From the New Testament, too, we would certainly include John the Baptist, Peter, and, of course, Paul.[162] Speaking of his chosen apostles, Jesus said: "You did not choose me, but I chose you and appointed you to go and bear fruit...." (John 15:16). Nor could we possibly overlook that supreme example of an unconditionally-chosen vessel: Mary, the highly-honored mother of Jesus.

God's sovereign right to providentially choose whomever he wishes for "special duty" is without controversy. What's truly amazing is that the God of Heaven has broken into our own time-and-space world to strategically move pieces on the chess board toward the completion of his own end-game. Behind it all, there is a plan and a purpose to our universe. We are not alone. History is not adrift. Of one thing we can be sure: Whatever extraordinary means it takes to fulfill his divine design, even now God is making it happen![163]

So, does God intervene in the lives of individuals when necessary to the accomplishment of all that he has intended from the far reaches of eternity? On this, Calvinists and non-Calvinists couldn't be more agreed.

Yet, as we all know, the question dividing us goes one giant step further. In that regard, is there anything in Jeremiah 1:5 to suggest that, from Jeremiah's special calling as a prophet, we can extrapolate a universal rule of unconditional election? Strange as it might be, is there anything in pure Calvinist theory that would prevent the Sovereign God from using Jeremiah as a prophet, then consigning him to hell as one of the non-elect?

Certainly, we know that God providentially used any number of *wicked* individuals whom we would expect to end up in hell. (Then again, by Calvinist theory, how can we safely presume that these same individuals were *never later regenerated* as being God's elect all along?) The point is that how God uses men and women as instruments in his providential working remains a separate issue altogether from Calvinism's unconditional election.

---

[161] See especially 1 Samuel 10:6, 9-10.

[162] Galatians 1:15-16; 1 Corinthians 1:1

[163] Consider Joshua 11:20 as an example of how God has worked directly through nations to bring about his sovereign purposes.

Israel, A Specially-Chosen Nation

There is no better illustration of this crucial distinction between divine providence and unconditional election than Israel herself—God's elect nation. As with Jeremiah and all the other specially-selected individuals through whom God has worked to implement his eternal plan, Israel, too, was chosen for a special role in bringing the world to Christ.

Did God choose Israel because she was a mighty nation? Quite the opposite. "The LORD did not set his affection on you and choose you because you were more numerous than other peoples, for you were the fewest of all peoples" (Deuteronomy 7:7).

Did he choose Israel because of any foreseen faithfulness she would exhibit? Are you kidding? "Understand, then, that it is not because of your righteousness that the LORD your God is giving you this good land to possess, for you are a stiff-necked people" (Deuteronomy 9:6)! Given Israel's infamous spirit of rebellion and almost unquenchable penchant for chasing after other gods, one simply has to believe that her election was unconditional and arbitrary. Certainly, there is no question that it was undeserved.

But we're talking here about Israel *as a nation*. As a *chosen people*. As *corporate* Israel. When you consider the children of Israel one by one, as individuals, we know that some were faithful to God and others were not. As Paul put it: "For not all who are descended from Israel are Israel. Nor because they are his descendants are they all Abraham's children. On the contrary, 'It is through Isaac that your offspring will be reckoned.' In other words, it is not the natural children who are God's children, but it is the children of the promise who are regarded as Abraham's offspring." (Romans 9:6-8).

What made a true Jew was not Abraham's blood in one's veins, but Abraham's faith in one's heart.

So, despite Israel's unrelenting obstinance as a nation, there was always a remnant of the faithful (as God reminded a discouraged Elijah about the seven thousand who had not bowed their knee to Baal). Of that faithful remnant, says Paul, significantly: " What Israel sought so earnestly it did not obtain, *but the elect did*" (Romans 11:7).

That last line, with its reference to "the elect," may sound Calvinistic, but don't forget that the word *elect* itself tells us nothing about the question in issue: whether that election was conditional or unconditional. The point is that these particular "elect" of Israel, like the Christian "elect" after them, were God's faithful remnant.

More crucial for the moment, don't overlook the important distinction Paul is making here between an elect nation (chosen unconditionally despite being notoriously unfaithful) and those individual Jews who were said to be "elect," as specifically marked out by their faithfulness.

A Tale of Two Brothers

One of the most fascinating examples of how God intervened supernaturally in the lives of individuals in aid of his grand design is found in the story of Jacob and Esau, the twin offspring of Isaac and Rebekah. By providentially reversing the natural order of succession from the older to the younger, God worked through these two brothers to bring about his selection of Israel as his chosen people. "Before the twins were born or had done anything good or bad–in order that God's purpose in election might stand: not by works but by him who calls–she was told, 'The older will serve the younger.' Just as it is written: 'Jacob I loved, but Esau I hated'" (Romans 9:11-13).

Was there unconditional election in this case? No doubt about it...if what we're talking about is God's *providential* working to bring about his eternal plan. In that sense alone, this passage is the very definition of unconditional election. However, it is by no means the smoking gun proving the case for unconditional election *unto salvation*. Is there anything at all here about Jacob's being elect *unto salvation* or Esau's being predestined *to reprobation*?

Solely from what the text tells us, this particular "election" was simply about the older son (and his descendants) serving the younger (and his descendants). How do we know that? We have it on the best of authority, from the mouth of the Lord himself. When Rebekah asked the Lord why her twins were in such turmoil in her womb, the Lord replied: "Two *nations* are in your womb, and two *peoples* from within you will be separated; one *people* will be stronger than the other, and the older will serve the younger" (Genesis 25:23).

If anyone wants to know why there is so much turmoil over Romans 9, it's because Calvinists have missed the obvious message of Genesis 25.

Romans 9 is not about Jacob and Esau, but about Israel and Edom, and, in the wider frame, the Jews and the Gentiles. Think *nations*, not *individuals*.

Consider in this regard that other set of brothers, Isaac and Ishmael. Although the son of the handmaiden (Ishmael) was banished in favor of the chosen son of promise (Isaac), Ishmael's descendants were also blessed. First, as a great nation in themselves, then eventually as co-recipients of the grace shown to all the world through Christ.

As for God *loving* Jacob and *hating* Esau, Paul's specific reference is to Malachi 1:2-3, where (1600 years after Jacob and Esau had died) Malachi reminds those who were beginning to doubt God's love that his love has never failed from the moment he providentially chose Jacob's descendants over Esau's. It is clear, therefore, that Paul's use of this passage has nothing to do with Jacob and Esau's eternal destinies, but everything to do with post-exilic Israel and—far more important—both Israel's redemptive future and that of the whole world.

It is not terribly helpful when Calvinists protest that the entire context of Romans 9-11 is not about providence and chosen nations but about salvation. You'll get no dissent from me on that score. In fact, as I'm sure we all agree, the entire *epistle* is about salvation! But it begs the further question of what particular aspect of salvation Paul is addressing when he focuses on Jacob and Esau, and Pharaoh, and Israel, and the Jews and the Gentiles.

The question is: What, specifically here, is Paul telling us about salvation? Is it, as Calvinists contend, that we are saved through special election, in the same way as Jacob and Esau were "elected"? Or is it, as non-Calvinists contend, that we are saved through our personally choosing to trust in the very Christ who sovereignly and providentially (as with Jacob and Esau) has made that choice possible not only for the Jews but also for Gentiles? Not surprisingly, I believe it is the latter.

How About Pharaoh, and What About the Potter?

Yet, even if that's the case, Calvinists would be right to ask about Paul's follow-up discussion.

*What then shall we say? Is God unjust? Not at all! For he says to Moses,
"I will have mercy on whom I have mercy, and I will have compassion on whom
I have compassion." It does not, therefore, depend on man's desire or effort, but
on God's mercy. For the Scripture says to Pharaoh: "I raised you up for this very
purpose, that I might display my power in you and that my name might be proclaimed in all the earth." Therefore God has mercy on whom he wants to have
mercy, and he hardens whom he wants to harden." (Romans 9:14-18)*[164]

There is no mystery why Calvinism has its adherents. Wrest this passage
from its context, and it certainly *looks* like God arbitrarily, perhaps even whimsically, bestows his saving mercy and compassion on whomever he wills.[165]

However, I suggest that Paul's mention of Pharaoh and the hardening of
his heart is meant to signal a completely different message. What do you
think? Is Paul intending here to tell us that, for his own inexplicable reasons,
God withheld his mercy from Pharaoh as being one of the non-elect (and to
that end hardened his heart)? To the contrary, is not Paul telling us that, just
as with Jacob's selection instead of Esau, God providentially raised up
Pharaoh as an instrument through whom he was to bestow his mercy *on Israel?*

You might be surprised to learn that this distinction is not just a biased,
ill-informed view coming from non-Calvinists. In his commentary on
Calvin's First Catechism, John Hesselink notes that "even a conservative
Calvinist such as G. C. Berkouwer believes that Calvin fails to understand
part of Paul's argument in Romans 9:17f. For in the hardening of
Pharaoh's heart Calvin sees a revelation of eternal damnation, whereas

---

[164] When Calvinists cite the parable of the laborers in the vineyard (Matthew 20:1-16) to refute
the argument that God would be unjust to elect some and not others, they disregard the context
altogether. Far from addressing the justness of selective salvation, Jesus is responding to Peter's
prideful insinuation that the apostles would surely reap a greater reward than others for having left
all to follow Christ. As is obvious from the two virtually-identical verses between which the parable is sandwiched ("So the last will be first, and the first will be last"), Jesus' point has to do with
humility of service, not arbitrary, sovereign election of the saved and the lost.

[165] Throughout this book, I use the words "arbitrary" and "arbitrarily" to indicate that God's
choice of the elect had nothing to do with man's faith, desires, actions, or righteousness. It doesn't
necessarily imply that God had no rational basis whatsoever for making his choices. To that extent,
my use of these words is not unlike the meaning which Calvinists attach to the word *unconditional*
in "unconditional election." On the other hand, if God in fact acted with complete whim and
caprice in his choice of the elect, surely Calvinists would be among the first to acknowledge his
sovereign right to do so.

Berkouwer (and most exegetes) maintain that Paul here 'is not concerned primarily to expound the "ruin of the wicked" which is "ordained by his counsel and will" [so Calvin], but rather to point to God's power and freedom in the history of salvation as he proceeds to manifest his mercy.'"[166]

Despite this crucial acknowledgment by many Calvinist scholars, other Calvinists invariably ask: "But what about the potter and the clay?"

One of you will say to me: "Then why does God still blame us? For who resists his will?" But who are you, O man, to talk back to God? "Shall what is formed say to him who formed it, 'Why did you make me like this?'" Does not the potter have the right to make out of the same lump of clay some pottery for noble purposes and some for common use?

What if God, choosing to show his wrath and make his power known, bore with great patience the objects of his wrath—prepared for destruction? What if he did this to make the riches of his glory known to the objects of his mercy, whom he prepared in advance for glory—even us, whom he also called, not only from the Jews but also from the Gentiles?

As he says in Hosea:

"I will call them 'my people' who are not my people;
    and I will call her 'my loved one' who is not my loved one,'
and,

"It will happen that in the very place where it was said to them,
    'You are not my people,'
    they will be called 'sons of the living God.'"

                                   (Romans 9:19-26)

To whom, do you think, is Paul referring as the "clay"? Is it *individuals* who are at the Potter's mercy as to whether he will shape them beautifully and save them for his own treasured collection, or perhaps, instead, toss them aside simply because he doesn't like how they've come out of the "throwing" process on the potter's wheel?

---

[166] I. Hesselink, *Calvin's First Catechism, A Commentary* (Louisville: Westminster John Knox Press, 1997), 96. [Citing G. C. Berkouwer, *Divine Election* (Grand Rapids: Wm. B. Eerdmans Publishing Co., 1960), 213-14.]

To the contrary, is it not clear from the context (from Romans chapter one onwards) that Paul is talking about how God has every right to extend his mercy to the *Gentiles* just as he had extended it to the *Jews*? And if that universal grace is the will of "the Potter," who are we as "the clay" (especially the Jews) to object?

Had God so desired, Paul argues, he could have dismissed all Israel with a curt, "not my people." Period! Fortunately for the Jews, what God actually said was more to the effect of: "no longer my people by virtue of ethnic heritage, but now—whether Jew or Gentile—my people by virtue of Christ-confessing faith." Instead of the Jews *losing* and the Gentiles *winning*, it was a win-win for both. No longer was there mercy just for some; now mercy was being extended to all.

Sadly, lost somewhere in the black hole of Calvinism are Hosea's words of universal grace: "I will call them 'my people' who are not my people." Are those the first words that come to mind when you think about arbitrary, exclusive election?

In this regard, have you ever considered the irony of the Calvinist argument for unconditional election, which asks defensively: *Why not* election for some but for not others, since God can have mercy upon whom he will have mercy? Whereas in Romans 9-11 Paul uses those words to champion the widest possible expanse of God's mercy, Calvinism (by espousing exclusive, limited election) ends up actually restricting God's mercy![167]

We mustn't forget, of course, that there is another significant "potter and clay" story in Scripture. It's the one where God tells the prophet Jeremiah to go and observe a potter working in his shop, and then says to him, in effect, "I'm like that potter. I can do what I wish with the clay in my hands." Yet, just when you think it's all about God's unassailable, unalterable sovereignty, God is emphatic that how *he* acts depends on how *his creatures* act. Listen closely as God speaks to Jeremiah:

---

[167] If it ends up that "many are invited, but few are chosen" (Matthew 22:14), or that "small is the gate and narrow the road that leads to life, and only a few find it" (Matthew 7:14), still, it is not because of God's choice, but man's. The invitation remains universal: "Come to me, all you who are weary and burdened, and I will give you rest" (Matthew 11:28).

Then the word of the LORD came to me: "O house of Israel, can I not do with you as this potter does?" declares the LORD. "Like clay in the hand of the potter, so are you in my hand, O house of Israel. If at any time I announce that a nation or kingdom is to be uprooted, torn down and destroyed, and if that nation I warned repents of its evil, then I will relent and not inflict on it the disaster I had planned. And if at another time I announce that a nation or kingdom is to be built up and planted, and if it does evil in my sight and does not obey me, then I will reconsider the good I had intended to do for it. (Jeremiah 18:1-10)

Is this not extraordinarily amazing: God actually changing his mind depending upon how mankind responds to him? What could be further from the teaching of Calvinism? Yet, what could be more breathtakingly biblical?[168]

What Paul *Really* Says About Calvinism

What seems to be confusing to so many is Paul's intricate interlacing of two apparently separate issues: 1) faith versus works, and 2) the sensitive matter of Gentile acceptability in light of the Jews' historical chosenness.

What's eminently exquisite about Paul's argument is that, by blending the two distinct issues into one discussion, he is able to demonstrate all the more forcefully that Gentiles are now just as loved and "chosen" as the Jews.[169] Why? Because the key to the Gentiles' chosenness is personal faith, not their national or ethnic identity as it was for the Jews (as symbolized so significantly by the Law and law-keeping). In fact, Paul argues that, from Abraham onward, it was always *faith* not *law-keeping* (much less Hebrew ethnicity for its own sake) that was the arbiter of true chosenness, even for the Jews.

---

[168] Note that God is not speaking here about individuals, but of nations and kingdoms.

[169] The Gentiles also "chosen"? Writing to former pagans who had "turned to God from idols," Paul says: "For we know, brothers loved by God, that he has chosen you, because our gospel came to you not simply with words, but also with power, with the Holy Spirit and with deep conviction" (1 Thessalonians 1:4-5). What Paul experienced among the Thessalonians was a reprise of what Peter had experienced in the house of that first Gentile convert, Cornelius. The Holy Spirit had come in confirming power! (To the same effect, see also 2 Thessalonians 2:13-14. From eternity, the plan of salvation involved God's initiative through the Spirit and man's response through belief.) And with this dramatic inclusion of those who once were "afar off" and "unclean," God's chosen ones have ever since been called out from among both Jews and Gentiles (Romans 9:24).

Most amazing of all about this passage is how Paul's argument brings us to the core of our current controversy. For every Jew who thought he could "work his way to heaven" by slavish law-keeping, it seems there were just as many Jews who were placing their trust for their salvation in their very Jewishness. *They* were God's chosen people, not the Gentiles. How dare Paul suggest otherwise! Had not Israel been the vessel of beauty unconditionally chosen for noble purposes by the Potter? Were they not God's people, and they alone?

I say this in tough-love, but I suggest that the exclusivist, Pharisaical spirit of Calvinism was in evidence among the Jews long before Augustine and Calvin ever formulated or articulated the doctrine of unconditional election. In that regard, I submit that, far from supporting the notion of unconditional election, Paul's argument is aimed specifically at refuting such a misguided doctrine with its temptation to unworthy conceit. Just look at his conclusion....

How, Paul, does one come into a saving relationship with God? Not through arbitrary chosenness or unconditional election, but through a personally-chosen faith.

> *"The word is near you; it is in your mouth and in your heart," that is, the word of faith we are proclaiming: That if you confess with your mouth, "Jesus is Lord," and believe in your heart that God raised him from the dead, you will be saved. For it is with your heart that you believe and are justified, and it is with your mouth that you confess and are saved. As the Scripture says, "Anyone who trusts in him will never be put to shame." For there is no difference between Jew and Gentile—the same Lord is Lord of all and richly blesses all who call on him, for, "Everyone who calls on the name of the Lord will be saved." (Romans 10:8-13).*

That's Gentiles as well as Jews. In fact, that's *everyone* who calls on the Lord, not just a pre-selected number.

But don't you mean, Paul, that God himself has already decided whom he will regenerate through the Holy Spirit so as to have the ability to call on him and be saved? Didn't you quote Isaiah's prophecy: "I was found by those who did not seek me; I revealed myself to those who did not ask for me" (Romans 10:20)?

As we've seen from the context, Paul is not talking about unconditional election of individuals, but rather about the inclusion of the Gentiles in God's eternal plan. Yet, even if one were to insist otherwise, take a close look at the clear implication of the very next verse: "But concerning Israel he says, 'All day long I have held out my hands to a disobedient and obstinate people'" (Romans 10:21). Even assuming Israel was an unconditionally elect nation, does this sound as if individual Jews were powerless to resist God's election? (As is plain from Acts 7:51, Stephen didn't seem to think so!)

If God had already irreversibly chosen his elect from among Israel, would there have been any need for him to patiently hold out his hands to the wicked among Israel, hoping that they would submit to his loving embrace? Is this the picture you would paint of a God who, from before the foundation of the earth, had already exercised absolute, sovereign control over the eternal destinies of every soul?

Is this not, instead, the picture of a loving God who, from before the beginning of time, had unconditionally decided to extend his arms in mercy and grace to all of rebellious mankind through the person of Jesus Christ? As Paul told Timothy, "This grace was given us [not because of anything we have done but because of his own purpose and grace] in Christ Jesus before the beginning of time" (2 Timothy 1:9).

I realize, of course, that Calvinists claim this particular passage as their own, saying that surely this passage shows God's grace to be unconditional. But if you take a closer look at this "hanging chad," Paul is only saying of the saved that we are saved by grace and not by works. He doesn't say "This grace was given to us *but not to the non-elect*."

Yet, even that secondary truth pales by comparison with Paul's primary point, which powerfully proclaims the unconditional election from eternity of the One who makes undeserved, unmerited saving grace possible: Jesus Christ.

A New "Chosen People"

You know what I love about the theological puzzle presented to us in Scripture? It's the way all the pieces fit, whether we're listening to Paul or to Peter or to any of the other inspired writers. Their overlapping, inter-twined imagery, especially, is absolutely fascinating.

For example, in Romans 9-11 we've just seen Paul talking about the chosen nation of Israel and how God worked providentially through spe-cially-designated persons to introduce the saving grace of Jesus Christ to both Jews and Gentiles. The felicitous result? Once, the Gentiles had not received mercy, but now they have. Once, the Jews had received a special mercy, but now they share that special mercy with the whole world.

From among both Jews and Gentiles, then, has emerged a whole new, *spiritual* "nation"–a special people of God's own choosing. Like Israel, this "nation" too is an elect nation and a chosen people. Yet, unlike Israel (in which there was a distinct remnant by faith of "true Israel"), when it comes to the kingdom of God, the "holy nation" and those who comprise her are one and the same. In Christ, the remnant of faith *is* the "nation"!

Nor was the chosenness of this new "nation" based on any human merit or worth, anymore than with Israel herself. In a striking parallel to Deuteronomy 7:7, Paul reminds us that our chosenness is not about us, but about God. "Brothers, think of what you were when you were called. Not many of you were wise by human standards; not many were influen-tial; not many were of noble birth. But God chose the foolish things of the world to shame the wise; God chose the weak things of the world to shame the strong" (1 Corinthians 1:26-27).

And does it get any better? Just as Israel–as a nation–was chosen unconditionally from before the beginning of time, so too this new "holy nation"–*as a nation*–was chosen unconditionally. Says Peter: "You are a chosen people, a royal priesthood, a holy nation, a people belonging to God, that you may declare the praises of him who called you out of dark-ness into his wonderful light. Once you were not a people, but now you are the people of God; once you had not received mercy, but now you have received mercy" (1 Peter 2:9-10).

From before the beginning of time, God purposed that he would have a special people, brought together from the ends of the earth and throughout all generations, who would comprise a spiritual kingdom of righteousness, exalting his divine glory through lives of holiness and praise. Beginning with the faithful patriarchs, continuing in the faithful remnant of Israel, and culminating in the faith-filled disciples of Jesus Christ, the Kingdom of God was foreseen and foreordained *from* eternity *for* all eternity.

Indeed, as we saw previously, this is the very "mystery" of which Paul wrote in his letter to the Ephesians—"this mystery, which for ages past was kept hidden in God, who created all things. His intent was that now, *through the church*, the manifold wisdom of God should be made known to the rulers and authorities in the heavenly realms, according to his eternal purpose which he accomplished in Christ Jesus our Lord" (Ephesians 3:8-11).

Where Conditional and Unconditional Election Meet

Clearly, there was never a time when the whole church as a collective group of believers was not a part of God's eternal purpose. In fact, given the role for which the church was intended (glorifying God), it was the very object of the exercise. For, "in him *we* were also chosen, having been pre-destined according to the plan of him who works out everything in con-formity with the purpose of his will, in order that *we*, who were the first to hope in Christ, might be for the praise of his glory" (Ephesians 1:11-12).

That's the *we* part (the collective-body-of-the-saved part) that has been unconditionally predestined eternally. Which is to say: the body of Christ, the church universal. But what about the *you* part? Says Paul: "And *you* also were included in Christ when *you* heard the word of truth, the gospel of your salvation. Having believed, *you* were marked in him with a seal, the promised Holy Spirit..." (Ephesians 1:13).

There is, then, the (unconditionally) elect *body of Christ*, to which the (con-ditionally) elect members of that body are "added daily," as penitent, baptized believers, just as in that inaugural Pentecost week (Acts 2:47). Yet, you may ask: How could the church as the body of Christ be unconditionally elect without the individual members of that body also being unconditionally elect?

Is that really so difficult or unusual? Suppose, for instance, that Congress proposed to raise an army for a particular mission, and deter-mined in advance the benefits to be awarded to the members of the mili-tary. Would the proposed army itself be any less (unconditionally) intend-ed if, instead of an involuntary draft, it were to be an all-volunteer army?

And assuming the forces were "all volunteer," would not the intended benefits accrue only on the condition that one willingly signed up?

That God foresaw from eternity all those individual men and women who would end up comprising his foreordained church does not detract from their volitional choice to put their faith in Christ, thereby becoming members of Christ's body. (Remember our discussion of God's "instant preplay"?) Nor, as we've already seen, does that free and voluntary choice make them any less "the elect," nor any less "predestined" in the marvelous sense that Scripture uses those terms. It just means they weren't elected or predestined *unconditionally*.

The Most Challenging "Chads" of All

I've saved to the last what I consider to be two of the most difficult "hanging chads" for those of us who are non-Calvinists. If you take most translations of these two texts at face value, they would seem to run counter to the case for conditional election which has been presented thus far.

The first text is Luke's observation that "When the Gentiles heard [that the gospel had been extended to them as well as the Jews], they were glad and honored the word of the Lord; and *all who were appointed for eternal life believed*" (Acts 13:48).

In the war of words over this passage, typically we are at the mercy of various translations of *tetagmenoi*, with proponents on each side pointing to whatever translation happens to fit their respective theological assumptions.[170]

As compared with the translation above, for example, some scholars would render the crucial clause from Acts 13:48, not as "appointed" or "ordained," but as "were found disposed to" eternal life.[171] Naturally, that would completely change the crucial *source* of one's faith from God him-

---

[170] In Acts 13:48, the Greek word at issue is *tetagmenoi*, which the King James Version (following the Latin Vulgate's controversial choice of *praeordinati*) renders as "ordained." As in pre-ordained. Most other English versions follow suit. Interestingly, the "Eastern Fathers," more naturally conversant with the original Greek, rejected the addition of *prae* (or pre-) in the Vulgate and maintained that in the original Greek there was no connotation lending itself to foreordination, or to unconditional election as Calvinists today would understand it.

[171] See, for example, Bartlet's comments on Acts 13:48. J. Vernon Bartlet, *The New Century Bible: The Acts*, edit. by Walter F. Adeney (Edinburgh, T. C. & E. C. Jack).

self to the individual believer. But I confess I am wary whenever hotly-contested translations enter into any doctrinal fray. If there is sufficient lack of consensus as to allow for a battle of translations, surely we are all called back to context, context, context.

While I would never urge my own understanding as settling a matter over which so many scholars have come to blows, I can't help but think that, by some irony, the meaning of Acts 13:48 is best explained by the Calvinists' own argument that–in a variety of other passages–the word "all" means nothing more than "both Jews and Gentiles." Whereas that argument is plainly fallacious in passages where the Jew/Gentile issue is not even remotely present, it makes perfect sense here where the Jew/Gentile issue is specifically being addressed (from verse 46 on).

Consistent with that clear context, Paul and Barnabas seem to be saying that, when the Gentiles believed, they were taking part in a universal offer of salvation which God had purposed, ordained, and predestined from before Creation. Hence this reasonable rendering that, "among the newly-included Gentiles, there were those who were now gladly believing, just as there had already been those among the Jews who believed–all of whom would be saved pursuant to God's eternally appointed plan."

In the second text, which addresses the flip-side, Peter tells us that: "[Those who reject Christ as the cornerstone of faith] stumble because they disobey the message–*which is also what they were destined for*" (1 Peter 2:8).

In the ongoing battle of translations, some believe that J. B. Phillips' translation of 1 Peter 2:8 best captures the essence of the original text: "Yes, they stumble at the word of God, for in their hearts they are unwilling to obey it–which makes stumbling a foregone conclusion."

While I wouldn't go to the wall for either translation, I do suggest it is not outside the bounds of reason to understand 1 Peter 2:8 as referring to God's foreknowledge of those whose rejection of the gospel demonstrates their eternal destiny as known by God from before Creation. Were that the case, of course, the persistent question remains whether God's foreknowledge is tantamount to foreordination, as Calvinists claim.

At the very least, one must not overlook the obvious: that their destiny is directly tied to *their own disobedience* of the gospel–not to an unconditional election taking place before the beginning of time, before they were born, and before they had ever heard the gospel being preached.

It has to be said, certainly, that if the usual renderings of these two controversial passages is correct, then Calvinism would appear to have a couple of strong texts in their favor. However, one of the first rules of exegesis is that the ambiguous is always controlled by the unambiguous. Following that rule, what can be more unambiguous than texts like Titus 2:11–"For the grace of God that brings salvation has appeared to all men." Or 2 Peter 3:9–"[The Lord] is patient with you, not wanting anyone to perish, but everyone to come to repentance." In neither of these texts is there any wiggle room for battles of translation.

Although at times the accuracy of a particular translation can be crucial to theological discussion, rarely, if ever, is the controversial rendering of a couple of passages out of scores of others going to win the day. Solely from a sense of fair play, I, for one, would be willing to allow both of these "hanging chads" to be counted in the balloting in favor of Calvinism. Even so, in terms both of sheer numbers and obvious clarity, when all the scriptural "ballots" are cast, the accumulated biblical texts lacking any hint of a "hanging chad" prevail by a landslide.

Election Only, Or "Double Predestination"?

Finally, no discussion of unconditional election can end without at least passing reference to the debate among Calvinists as to whether they should believe only in predestination of the elect or in so-called "double predestination," whereby the non-elect were just as intentionally and purposely predestined to their condemnation as the elect were predestined to salvation.

Actually, it gets somewhat more complicated. Some Calvinists, including R.C. Sproul, acknowledge that election and reprobation are two sides of the same coin. In that sense, at least, there cannot help but be such a thing as "double predestination." Says Sproul, "It is manifestly obvious that if some people are elect and some are not elect, then predestination has two sides to it. It is not enough to speak of Jacob; we must also consider Esau."[172]

---

[172] Sproul, 157

Yet Sproul rejects what is usually put forward as the "double predestination" view (sometimes known as "equal ultimacy") whereby God not only positively chose his elect but also positively chose to condemn the non-elect. Most Calvinists would agree with Sproul, saying that God merely left the lost in their original fallen state as he was rescuing the elect.

Obviously, I don't have a dog in this particular fight, as the saying goes. But it does seem to me that "double predestination" is a more honest and forthright approach to the troubling, but logical implications of unconditional election. After all, is it not a fundamental assumption of Calvinism that God visits condemnation upon all mankind via the imposition of original sin and total depravity? (Would any Calvinist claim that *man* is responsible for universally imputing original sin and depravity to the human race in the wake of Adam's sin? Who, then, but God?)[173]

According to Calvinists (citing Psalm 115:3 and 135:6, "he does whatever pleases him"), is not *everything* that happens identical with what God has pleased? Does not everything that is, or ever has been, or ever will be, reflect exactly and minutely what God himself has done? (To borrow the Calvinists' own argument, how could any outside interference with God's sovereign will not serve in some way to thwart it?)

Even if, therefore, the idea is that God has chosen to save his elect from among the condemned, nothing in that changes the fact that those who are *not* among the elect are eternally damned only because they are acting pursuant to God's eternal plan in the first place. Is there any way, then, to get around the fact that deliberate, intentional, foreseen (and thus foreordained) reprobation simply has to accompany election in a two-sided "double predestination"?

Well, actually, there is a way around it...sort of...if you're willing to go a *long way* around it. Throughout the history of Calvinism, the harsh ring of premeditated, purposeful reprobation of the non-elect has sent Calvinists scurrying for some way to soften the blow and rationalize the result. Over the centuries, that effort has devolved into what those of us on the out-

---

[173] John Calvin had no doubt but that the Fall was God's idea. "Scripture proclaims that all mortals were bound over to eternal death in the person of one man [cf. Rom. 5:12 ff.]. Since this cannot be ascribed to nature, it is perfectly clear that it has come forth from the wonderful plan of God." [*Institutes* 3.23.7]

side might see as a tempest-in-a-teapot debate over which came first, the "chicken" of unconditional election or the "egg" of "the Fall." (If you're not already familiar with this debate and its unusual terminology, brace yourself for a couple of tongue-twisters soon to surface.)

Tongue-Twisters and Brain-Teasers

As if well aware of the conundrum we explored earlier regarding the awkward timing of election, Creation and "the Fall," some (typically strict, or hyper) Calvinists have held that God's election had no reference whatsoever to the sinful state that would result from "the Fall." At a given moment in eternity, the divine Potter decreed to himself which of his vessels would be created for honor, and which for dishonor. If perhaps he had his own reasons, no future contingency whether of sin or of goodness had anything whatsoever to do with the Potter's unilateral, wholly unconditional decision.

"Supralapsarianism," as that position is called, is derived from the root words "lapse," meaning *a fall*, and "supra," *before*. Thus, the disquieting, unpalatable idea of a wholly arbitrary *double-predestining* of both the saved and the lost taking place *before* "the Fall." Which is to say, the election results were in and the winners and losers declared before anyone had sinned personally or fallen victim to sin's universal condemnation. (Hence the disturbing "ouch factor.")

While this position serves to safeguard the arbitrary sovereignty of unconditional election in its purest sense (and most closely reflects Calvinism's classic assumptions), embarrassingly it also means that "the Fall" cannot escape being seen as God's chosen means of facilitating that foregone result. Implying as this does that "the Fall" is directly attributable to God isn't exactly the best public relations for predestination. If it's true that "the Fall" was *necessary* in order to fulfill God's already-determined election, then the question naturally arises how God could be just in condemning those whose fallen nature necessarily results from his own plan.

Perhaps for that reason, most Calvinists today assert that God's election actually anticipated "the Fall," thus allowing God to positively and affirmatively rescue the elect from their reprobate condition while merely passing over the reprobate non-elect. So there was election, it is said, but not double-election. Whereas the election of the saved was *intentional*, the reprobation of the lost was *incidental*. God simply chose not to interfere with their status quo. Which brings us to the second of our tongue-twisters, "infralapsarianism," indicating that election follows *after* the idea of "the Fall."[174]

Not surprisingly, we are told that this sequence is not to be understood chronologically (as if God made one decision followed in time by another) but logically. Yet, the moment of election itself cannot help but be prior to both Creation and the sin of Adam, which supposedly inaugurated man's fallen and condemned state. So to whatever extent "the Fall" was seen and anticipated by God, Calvinist logic itself tells us that "the Fall" would have been, not just foreseen, but foreordained. (Certainly, that was John Calvin's position.[175])

All the more intriguing is Loraine Boettner's insightful observation that "Since [God] knows their destiny before they are created, and then proceeds to create, it is plain that the saved and the lost alike fulfill His plan for them; for *if He did not plan that any particular ones should be lost, He could at least refrain from creating them.*" [Emphasis mine.][176] Which only begs the excellent question: Why *did* God create the lost, knowing all along that, based on no fault of their own, he would damn them eternally?[177]

What's baffling about Boettner's argument (made in the context of defending God's sovereign foreordination) is that it proceeds from the

---

[174] A variation on theme known as "sublapsarianism" contends that God's eternal decrees provided actual universal atonement, but thereafter decreed salvation itself only for the elect. (By contrast, infralapsarianism contends that God's decrees first declared salvation only for the elect, and thereafter an atonement that–if perhaps *sufficient* for all–was not *provided* for all, but only for the elect.) Among the advocates for sublapsarianism is the systematic theologian Millard J. Erickson. This view is used to support the anomalous "Calvinist" position which accepts unconditional, particular election while rejecting limited atonement. Not only is there a patent inconsistency between particular election and unlimited atonement, but there is also no reason to decree the provision of atonement unless and until there is a decree to save at least some, if not all, sinners. [See Marcelo Souza's critique of sublapsarianism: http://www.thecenters.org/Marcelo/Is_Sublapsarianism_Tenable.html.]

[175] "God not only foresaw the fall of the first man, and in him the ruin of his descendants, but also meted it out in accordance with his own decision." [*Institutes* 3.23.7]

[176] Boettner, 46

[177] The usual answer–that it would cause the elect to treasure their salvation all the more and encourage them to give even greater praise to God–is spurious indeed. Just as easily, anyone believing that a loved one is among those who have been eternally damned before ever personally committing sin would have as much reason to blame God as to praise him. It is at least arguable that non-Calvinists have more reason to treasure their salvation, knowing that a loving God was willing to take such a great risk that we might not love him in return. And should it be that our own loved ones do not respond to the good news of the gospel, at least we have the assurance that God gave them every opportunity to do so.

supralapsarian assumption that God *elected* before he *created*. Yet, pages later, when attempting to explain the perplexing details of election, Boettner does a screeching u-turn. Arguing that "just punishment" can be imposed solely where there is sin, Boettner maintains: "only the infralapsarian scheme is self-consistent." That is to say: *creation* was contemplated first (together with man's post-Fall depravity), and only then *election*. Speaking of consistency...or the lack of it![178]

Resort to Calvinism's Arcane Secrets

That this bundle of issues presents such a mind-numbing dilemma for Calvinists must surely explain the intense search for a backup explanation as to how God could anticipate "the Fall" without being directly responsible for it, much less violating the cardinal rule of election: that it must be solely and entirely unconditional.

And what is that backup explanation? Suddenly, we are confronted with a whole system of secret, unrevealed, eternal "decrees" (somehow conveniently perceived by Calvinists).[179] By blending these decrees in a kind of theological alchemy, God's direct, hands-on causation of all things becomes merely remote-control "permission" if that helps to soften the apparent harshness of his arbitrary decisions. (Hence, if we're talking about *election*, then "the Fall" was merely anticipated, and not God's idea at all.) Yet by those same decrees, "anticipation" somehow wondrously transforms into direct, sovereign causation, if that is needed to put control back into God's hands. (Hence, if we're talking about *original sin and total depravity*, "the Fall" is God's purposeful, divine, and just punishment of mankind for the sin of Adam.)

Just as love covers a multitude of sins, limitless creative rationalization covers a multitude of inconsistencies. Or actually *uncovers* them. Any time

---

[178] Calvinist inconsistency knows no bounds. Boettner says, for example, that "In regard to the first fall of man, we assert that the **proximate** cause was the instigation of the Devil and the impulse of his own heart; and when we have established this, we have removed all **blame** from God" (251). Yet Boettner maintains with equal confidence: "Even the works of Satan are so controlled and limited that they serve God's purposes" (243). And finally that "God fore-planned and fore-saw the fall" which was "a necessary part in the plan" (235).

[179] For example: "Even the fall of Adam, and through him the fall of the race, was not by chance or accident, but was so ordained in the secret counsels of God." (Boettner, 234)

this much rationalization has to be conscripted to defend a particular doctrine, one is looking at symptoms of a far more systemic disorder lying beneath the surface.

In the end, the battle between supralapsarianism and infralapsarianism (or even sublapsarianism) is wasted ink. Whatever the logical or chronological order between election and "the Fall" itself, by Calvinism's own doctrine of sovereignty, God alone is the trial judge who handed down to the entire human race the death-penalty sentence of original sin and total depravity. Any talk of God's simply leaving the lost where he found them can only mean he left them exactly where he himself *put* them. In any court in the land, the unjust entrapment in such a scheme would be an absolute defense.

Whereas non-Calvinists face a similar question of reprobation (since God promises to save those who respond in obedient faith and to condemn those who do not), the difference is that, for non-Calvinists, God is not responsible for man's sin in the first place. There are no fail-safe secret decrees playing both ends against the middle to produce, then rationalize away, the obvious inconsistency that man's sinfulness is, at once, both his own responsibility and yet precisely as God created him to be.

Without denying the profound mystery of the gospel, still, the more complex and arcane one's theology, the more suspicious. Most suspicious of all, of course, is when that theology runs completely counter to the obvious, uncomplicated, unmistakable theme line running throughout the panorama of Scripture: *the salvation of the lost.*

In Paul's impassioned words, "Here is a trustworthy saying that deserves full acceptance: Christ Jesus came into the world to save sinners..." (1 Timothy 1:15). If *all* of mankind is under the condemnation of sin (as Calvinists rightly insist, but for all the wrong reasons), then it cannot help but follow that Christ did not come into the world to save only a select number of souls.

Under the tutelage of Calvinism, we are asked to take a quite incredible journey, all the way from legitimate concerns about not being able to "work our way to heaven" to the ultimate, quite-incredible conclusion that the lost wouldn't be able to get to heaven under any conceivable circumstances. Is this what your Bible says?

As we have suggested time and again (because it's importance simply can't be overstated), the true test of unconditional election is not what happens to those who are fortunate enough to be among the elect, but what happens to everybody else. It's *the other side of the story* that tells the tale. For no matter how ingenious the attempt to deflect the implications, the logical and necessary flip-side of unconditional election is *unconditional reprobation*–which cannot help but entail a darkened view of both God's sovereignty and character.

Dress it up all you will. Disguise it if you must. Tell us again how marvelous it is that Christ came into the world to save his chosen elect (in effect, the *already-saved*). Despite all the impressive theological argumentation, Calvinism's most blithely rationalized embarrassment remains the same. While the elect march triumphantly upward to heaven having done absolutely nothing to be so fortunate, billions of men and women, condemned unconditionally before they were ever born, are arbitrarily, necessarily, and irreversibly predestined to hell. And it's all God's doing from start to finish. All to his glory!

Such a picture not only robs God of his righteous glory but makes a mockery of the gospel's call to lost souls. The lost may certainly refuse the saving grace that comes through Christ, but any scenario where the eternally saved could never be lost, nor the eternally lost ever be saved, could not be further from the redemptive story-line of Scripture. If ever you believed that the doctrine of unconditional election was a winner, tell me that this vaunted teaching isn't invalidated by the one hanging chad that matters most...

———————————

"For the Son of Man came to seek and to save what was lost."

Luke 19:10

———————————

Chapter Summary

- Although Calvinism is more popularly associated with the word *predestination*, the core doctrine of Calvinism is *unconditional election*: the idea that, for his own reasons before the Creation of the world, God arbitrarily chose who would be saved. Hence, salvation is not conditioned upon anything you or I might do, not even having faith in Christ.

- It has to be said that Calvinism would never have gotten off the ground had there not been at least some apparent textual support. On their face (especially when taken out of context), a number of passages certainly *look like* they support unconditional election.

- Many of the core passages used by Calvinists to argue the case for unconditional election are addressing the issue of Gentile inclusion in God's plan of salvation–not whether you and I were chosen, or not chosen, from the dawn of eternity.

- There is no question but that God unilaterally and unconditionally chose and foreordained both the nation of Israel (as a nation), and individuals such as Abraham and Moses and Jesus' mother Mary, to bring about his eternal purposes.

- Yet God's providential intervention into the lives and events of individuals and nations is a far cry from God unconditionally choosing whom to save, or–by implication–whom to condemn.

- The acid test of Calvinism's legitimacy is not the supposed unconditional salvation of the elect, but the unconditional condemnation of the non-elect, whose damnation is solely the result of God's own sovereign rule.

Reality Check: If God's arbitrary election of the saved and unsaved was based in the far reaches of eternity upon no identifiable acts of obedience or disobedience that you might possibly manifest during your lifetime, then you can have no objective basis whatsoever for knowing whether you are among the saved or lost.

Chapter 8

Limited Atonement, Or Unlimited Affront?

*The doctrine that Christ died for the purpose of saving all men
logically leads to absolute universalism,
that is, to the doctrine that all men are actually saved.*

–Louis Berkhof

For many years during my life as a law professor, I taught a seminar called Law and Morality. Although I enjoyed teaching Criminal Law, Trial Practice, and other traditional law school courses, this unusual seminar was an altogether more exhilarating experience. Exploring topics where law and morality naturally intersect, we fiercely debated such hot-button issues as abortion, euthanasia, gay rights, gambling, prostitution, and drugs. Given the robust conversations around the table, I'm sure I received far more insight than I imparted. But there was one shocking insight I was not prepared for the first time I heard it. Nor did I ever cease to be taken aback by it, even though it kept reoccurring year after year.

In the first session each year, I set out to help the students distinguish between law, morality, and ethics. As part of that discussion, I queried them as to whether there was a hierarchy of moral authority with anything like an overarching natural law at the top. Did they believe there was such a thing as natural law? If so, what was it, and how did it trickle down to morality, group ethics, and positive law?

To stir their thinking, my opening question was: Is there any "capital-'T' Truth" out there? Anything in terms of morality that is *absolute*? Invariably, a number of students would respond (with sweet irony): "Absolutely not!" For them, the only thing that was absolute was the fact that absolutely *nothing* is absolute!

This almost comical, if woefully deluded, answer was not the one I found so shocking. (In an age of pervasive moral relativism, what else should I expect from many young people?) It's what happened when I further tested their adamant response that rocked me on my heels the first time I heard it.

"If no morality is absolute," I pressed, "is there anything that's inherently evil?" Again came the confident reply: "No way!" That's when I pulled out my trump card, thinking with equal confidence that I had them in a corner. "If nothing is inherently evil," I began (relishing the trap I was laying), "then what about the Holocaust? Was it not inherently evil?"

Surely, I had them on the ropes with that question. Surely, they'd have to run up the white flag and surrender. But to my utter amazement, one student after another firmly insisted that not even the Holocaust was inherently evil! And how could this possibly be? The stock answer was that, if the Nazis found it acceptable to kill millions of Jews, then *for them* it wasn't evil! And if not evil *for them*, then obviously it wasn't *inherently* evil.

I couldn't help but wonder how these future guardians of law and order would react to the courtroom argument of gang members that *for them* it wasn't wrong to kill a rival gang member in a drive-by shooting. Or if they, themselves, would ever be tempted to defend an accused rapist on the grounds that *for him* rape wasn't all that evil. For the moment, however, I was struggling to understand how they could possibly say that the genocide of six million Jews wasn't evil in and of itself.

Maybe, just maybe, hearing some of my non-Jewish students parade out such drivel might not have been so surprising. Incredibly, though, even my

Jewish students had joined in the chorus. Surprised and stunned, I asked one of my Jewish coeds how she could possibly take such a position. I'll never forget her reply: "Well, of course, Professor Smith, I wouldn't want the Holocaust to happen to me or to my family or to any other Jew, but [get ready for this...] I can't impose my morality on anyone else." Wow!

Then again, why was I so easily taken off guard? Why should it be so shocking that children of the relativism revolution were simply taking their spoon-fed philosophy to its logical conclusion, no matter how unthinkable?

If everything is relative, there can be no absolutes.

If there are no absolutes, there can be no ultimate, universal morality.

If there is no ultimate, universal morality, then there is nothing that is inherently evil.

And if there is no universal truth, then your truth is just as valid as mine.

And if each of us is free to choose our own moral standards, then I have no right to impose my own morality on others.

The most interesting thing about this discussion each year was always the increased level of defiance in their voices at the point when they finally realized what an unthinkable position they ultimately were forced to defend. Intuitively, they knew they had ended up in no-man's land, light years away from what they actually believed. But, given their relativist world view, consistency was forcing them to defend the absurd...and, worse yet, the morally outrageous.

So what's a person to do at that point but become all the more insistent that he's right. Predictably, even their voices suddenly became shrill, giving credence to that time-honored legal maxim: The weaker the case, the louder the argument!

Affirming the Unthinkable

If you've not already anticipated where I'm going with this, I have to say that there is one point, in particular, where the debate over Calvinism gives me a distinct sense of déjà vu. Whenever I read a book or article defending the doctrine of limited atonement, I keep thinking I see the same heightened defensiveness I saw in my students. And no wonder! The proposition that our Lord and Savior came to earth to give himself as a ransom only for a select group of sinners is—to say the very least—breathtaking!

One senses that Calvinists intuitively know they are defending a proposition that is biblically scandalous, but having committed themselves to the doctrine of unconditional election, they have no option but to take a big gulp and boldly affirm the logical extension of that premise. For, if in fact God has unconditionally predestined the elect to salvation through Christ, and *only* those elect, then it follows as night follows day that the intended effect of Christ's atoning blood on the cross is limited to those very same elect.

Even from Calvinist commentators comes the candid acknowledgment: "This doctrine necessarily follows from the doctrine of election....These two doctrines must stand or fall together."[180] (Remember, then, where this necessarily leads if Christ's atonement was *not* limited. If it can be shown that Christ shed his blood as an atonement for *all sinners who, of their own, would turn to him in faith*, then even Calvinists concede that their bedrock doctrine of unconditional election would crumble.)

Naturally, Calvinists attempt to argue beyond simply the internal logic of the system. When the battle of scriptures is joined, Calvinists cite a number of passages which indicate that Jesus died for "his people" (Matthew 1:21); or "the sheep" (John 10:15); or "the church" (Acts 20:28; Ephesians 5:23-26); or "us" (Titus 2:14); or even "us all" (arguably equated with Paul's reference to God's "chosen," or "the elect," in Romans 8:32-33).

Similarly, we are pointed to Matthew 20:28 to the effect that "the Son of Man did not come to be served, but to serve, and to give his life as a ransom *for many*." Their point, of course, is that Christ's atoning blood was shed for the "many" who are God's people.[181]

---

[180] Boettner, 151

[181] In addition, Calvinists often cite Matthew 26:28 and Mark 10:45 (along with Romans 5:15-19), arguing that *many* is limited to the elect, and does not mean *all*. For the proposition that *many* (*polloi*) includes *all* in these redemptive passages, see Gerhard Friedrich, ed., *Theological Dictionary of the New Testament*, vol. VI, trans. and ed. Geoffrey W. Bromiley (Grand Rapids: Wm. B. Eerdmans Publishing Co. 1964-76), 536-45.

In that light, consider Matthew 22:14. "For many [all] are invited, but few [not all] are chosen." As in the parable of the wedding banquet (Matthew 22:1-14), Christ's atonement was provided for all who were invited, even if not everyone accepted the invitation.

Is there anyone who would disagree? Jesus did indeed die for his people, his sheep, his church, and the chosen elect–meaning all "the many" who are in fact saved. But that only begs the crucial question under discussion: Did Jesus die for anyone else? Did he die for the whole world? For *all* the lost–past, present, and future?[182]

If Jesus' sacrifice for *all* sinners is not the central, compelling, and jubilant theme of the gospel, pray tell, what is? Dare we imagine a Calvinist version of Isaac Watts' beloved carol, whereby, instead of "Joy to the World," we sang "Joy to the Elect"? If only Watts had understood that Christ's atonement was limited to certain pre-selected sinners, surely he wouldn't have been so foolish as to include the lines:

> *He comes to make His blessings flow*
> *Far as the curse is found.*

> *Let every heart prepare him room,*
> *And heav'n and nature sing.*[183]

Despite what seems so obvious, Calvinists pose a number of seemingly legitimate questions. For example, if Christ died for all sinners, then why aren't all sinners saved? Either the sin was paid for, or it was not. (And if all sin was paid for on the cross, even the sin of unbelief must surely have been paid for.) In short, how could Jesus stand in the place of a person, pay his sin debt in full, have the Father accept the sacrifice of his son as High Priest, and still that person end up lost?

---

[182] Calvinists argue that, had Jesus died for every living soul, past as well as present, then he would have died for those who were already dead and in hell. In a sense that is true, for everyone living and dying prior to the cross will be judged by what Christ did on the cross. Even the sins of the righteous ancients (already dead and heaven-bound) were atoned for retroactively by the blood of the cross. Without Christ's blood, their salvation would not have been possible. (See Hebrews 11:39-40.) No less true, Christ's atoning blood was the only hope of those who rejected God before the coming of Christ. Had they turned to God in faith even before the cross, they too could have availed themselves of Christ's atoning blood. (Strictly speaking, of course, no one is in hell just yet, since hell's punishment awaits Judgment, which awaits Resurrection, which awaits the Coming of Christ in glory.)

[183] Interestingly, this reference to the Watts' carol was in my manuscript before I read Richard Mouw's *Calvinism In the Las Vegas Airport*, in which (on p. 44), Mouw also cites the carol, speaking of "the expansive scope of what was accomplished for the larger creation." Given the obvious truth of the proposition, it's almost impossible for this carol not to come to mind.

Analogies are not always the best answer, but they can help put us on the right track. To that end, consider a scenario where a wealthy benefactor wishes to emancipate a slave-owner's many slaves. On the condition that the slave-owner never again acquires slaves, the benefactor makes him an offer he simply can't refuse. A deal having been struck, the extravagantly high price is paid, the slaves are free to go, and one after another leaps for joy as they make their way to freedom.

To the amazement of all, however, there are a number of slaves who simply won't budge. Some are fearful at the prospect of a freedom they've never before known. Others, think it must surely be a trick. Still others have an inexplicable sense of loyalty to their cruel master. Whatever their reasons, the price for their freedom hasn't changed their enslaved circumstances in the least. And yet the ransom price remains fully—even lavishly—paid.

It's easy to see why Calvinists would assume that atonement and salvation are coexistent since, once applied to the believer, atonement *does* result in salvation (Hebrews 10:10-18). (Not to mention that—operating from the assumption of predestined salvation—Calvinism naturally equates salvation with atonement.) But provision for atonement through Christ no more automatically saves all mankind than provision for atonement through animal sacrifices automatically brought all Israel into a personal relationship with God.

Provision only makes possible what otherwise would not be possible—in this case redemption, propitiation, and reconciliation. Yet, if never applied, it doesn't provide. Provision must be accompanied by appropriation, no less than when emergency services are provided to victims of a hurricane. If for whatever reason storm victims don't take advantage of the emergency aid that's been provided, can the *mere availability of the provision* possibly do them any good?[184]

Returning to another biblical example, would anyone wish to argue that the blood of the Passover lamb (surely a type of Christ's own atoning blood) would have protected any Israelite who refused to apply it to the doorframe?

---

[184] Compare Numbers 21:8-9, where "The LORD said to Moses, 'Make a snake and put it up on a pole; anyone who is bitten can look at it and live.' So Moses made a bronze snake and put it up on a pole. Then when anyone was bitten by a snake and looked at the bronze snake, he lived." This passage is referenced by Jesus himself in John 3:14-15 where Jesus says: "Just as Moses lifted up the snake in the desert, so the Son of Man must be lifted up, that everyone who believes in him may have eternal life." Standing side by side, universal atonement and contingent individual faith coexist in complete harmony.

And is there any question but that the blood did in fact save from harm all Israelites who applied it? Likewise, the penal substitution of atonement is fully efficacious for any who claim it, but is completely ineffectual for any who refuse it.

To say that Christ's atonement is "fully effective" is to say that–for his part–atonement and justification are a *done deal*. There is nothing contingent, potential, or merely "theoretically possible" about the work Christ has done once and *for all*. (Read: universal, unlimited atonement.) On the other hand, it would be indiscriminate and wrong to conclude that Jesus thereby *saved* all. Universal atonement is not to be confused with "universalism"–a notion so clearly unbiblical that Calvinists and most non-Calvinists join as one to denounce it.

Given, then, that there is universal atonement but not universal salvation, it follows that salvation is necessarily contingent on whether the sinner is willing to claim Christ's atonement for his own.

We've noted previously the irreconcilable clash between unconditional election and being saved by faith. In a variation on theme, if we truly are saved by *faith*, how can we be saved by atonement standing alone? Just as faith without atonement would be a futile exercise, atonement without faith can be of no effect. You can have all the power of a 220-volt line, but it won't do you any good unless you plug into it. How else explain Romans 3:25: "God presented him as a sacrifice of atonement, *through faith in his blood*"?

What do you, yourself, think? Is it the *providing* of atonement that saves, wholly apart from faith; or is it the *trusting in it* that appropriates its saving power to the believing sinner?[185]

In Romans 5, Paul connects these two aspects of atonement in a quite wonderful way. As for the *provision* of atonement, "God demonstrates his own love for us in this: While we were still sinners, Christ died for us" (5:8). And as for our *trusting in it*, just listen to this: "Since we have been justified *through faith*, we have peace with God through our Lord Jesus Christ, *through whom we have gained access by faith* into this grace in which we

---

[185] Although his sublapsarian "Calvinism" suffers from logical schizophrenia, Millard Erickson is correct when he affirms: "Our inheriting eternal life involves two separate factors: an *objective* factor (Christ's provision of salvation) and a *subjective* factor (our acceptance of that salvation)." [Millard J. Erickson, *Concise Dictionary of Christian Theology* (Grand Rapids: Baker Book House, 1987), 832]

now stand" (5:1). Does it get any better? In two complementary sides of the same coin, we have both *redress* and *access*!

When it boils down to it, the question at hand has to do with the sufficiency of Christ's work on the cross. How would you respond to the proposition that, if Christ's atonement was sufficient for *any* sinners, it was sufficient for *all* sinners; or, if *not* sufficient for all, then sufficient for none?

The standard Reformed response is that, either way you slice it, atonement is limited. Whereas Reformed theology limits the atonement to the elect, general atonement likewise limits the effect of atonement to the saved. Under either system, it is argued, only the saved/elect actually benefit from Christ's work on the cross.

Of course, the huge, unacknowledged difference is that, according to Reformed theology, Christ didn't *want* anyone but a predetermined number of souls to benefit from his atoning blood. To the contrary, the Scriptures teach that because Christ was not willing for any to perish he lovingly paid the full price for every soul who's ever lived.

By Reformed reckoning, the number of the elect is like an exclusive, private club with a set membership (not one more, nor one less). However, the scriptural picture is of an open membership available to all comers, whatever number that finally turns out to be. ("Whoever wishes, let him take the free gift of the water of life, Revelation 22:17).

If under both belief systems a certain number ultimately are saved and a certain number lost, still, the likelihood of its being the same number under each belief system is next to nil. Nor would the final tally be tabulated in anything like the same way. By Reformed theology, the precisely-numbered elect are elected before the polls ever open. By biblical teaching, the unprescribed number of elect are not elected until the polls are closed. That God knows the exact number and precise identities in advance does not diminish the fact that he didn't stuff the ballot box or rig the vote. What he did do by his atoning sacrifice is to insure a universal franchise so that no one is automatically disenfranchised.

Perhaps you've heard the Calvinist argument that, as they see it, Christ's atonement is like a narrow bridge extending all the way across the chasm of condemnation, whereas the non-Calvinist view is of a great wide bridge extending only half-way. (This is the tortured result when it is claimed that *everyone* agrees that Christ's atonement was limited–either by God's intent or by man's response.) What this false dichotomy fails to present is the more biblical third alternative of a great wide bridge extending all the way.

Together with Calvinists, non-Calvinists agree that the "bridge" of Christ's atonement is fully sufficient to pay the price for man's salvation. And further still that, without that divine bridge, man could never have the slightest hope of making it across on his own. The question, then, is not the *bridge* (splendidly constructed of one vertical pillar and a single horizontal beam), but the number of those who might cross it.

The problem we encounter is that at the entry to the bridge, as it were, Calvinism's doctrine of election lowers an impenetrable barrier, preventing all but the predestined elect from crossing. By contrast, the universal invitation of the gospel raises the barrier, permitting access to all who in faith would accept the gracious invitation to cross over. That not everyone chooses to cross the bridge says nothing about the sufficiency of the bridge itself, only about those who are foolish enough not to make use of it.

Calvin On Christ's Atonement

For many Calvinists today, it should be cause for pause that Calvin himself did not make limited atonement a key part of his systematic theology. While Calvin's view of the extent of Christ's atonement is hotly disputed, there can be no doubt but that his comments on various relevant passages reflect significantly different nuances from today's hard-line Calvinist view of limited atonement. For example, it was Calvin's belief that, through Christ, "all the sins of the world have been expiated."[186] Does that sound even remotely like limited atonement?

And how about Calvin's commentary on Mark 14:24, where Jesus said regarding the cup: "This is my blood of the covenant, which is poured out for many." Far from limiting the blood of the covenant only to the elect,

---

[186] John Calvin, *Calvin's Commentaries: The Epistles of Paul the Apostle to the Galatians, Ephesians, Philippians, and Colossians*, trans. T. H. L. Parker and eds. David W. Torrance and Thomas F. Torrance (Grand Rapids: Wm. B. Eerdmans Publishing Co., 1979), 308.

Calvin said: "The word many does not mean a part of the world only, but the whole human race."[187]

Many Calvinists will also be surprised to learn what the Reformer had to say with reference to the critical passage: "He is the atoning sacrifice for our sins, and not only for ours but also for the sins of the whole world" (1 John 2:2). Of that passage, Calvin minced no words, saying: "It is also a fact, without controversy, that Christ came to atone for the sins 'of the whole world.'"[188]

So as not to take Calvin out of context, it is important to understand this quotation in its full context. In the larger discussion, Calvin is responding to a man named Georgius, who is a proponent of universalism—the foolish idea that all mankind will be saved.[189] Calvin begins with the testy question which Georgius has posed in an attempt to refute Calvin's idea of limited, rather than universal election:

> Georgius imagines himself to argue very cleverly when he says, "Christ is the propitiation for the sins of the whole world. Therefore, those who would exclude the reprobate from a participation in the benefits of Christ, must, of necessity, place them somewhere out of the world." *Now we will not permit the common solution of this question to avail on the present occasion, which would have it that Christ suffered sufficiently for all men, but effectually for His elect alone.* This great absurdity, by which our monk has procured for himself so much applause amongst his own fraternity, has no weight whatever with me.

In the sentence I have highlighted, Calvin makes a remarkable statement. Rather than take the easy way out, says Calvin, he is not going to respond, as some might, by suggesting that Christ died for all, but only effectually for the elect. And why not simply give that response? Because, says Calvin...

---

[187] John Calvin, *Calvin's Commentaries: A Harmony of the Gospels Matthew, Mark, and Luke and the Epistles of James and Jude,* trans. A. W. Morrison and eds. David W. Torrance and Thomas F. Torrance (Grand Rapids: Wm. B. Eerdmans Publishing Co., 1972), 138-39

[188] Calvin, *A Treatise on the Eternal Predestination of God,* translated by Henry Cole in "Calvin's Calvinism" (Grand Rapids: Reformed Free Publishing Association) 165-167 (sometimes referenced as IX.5). The book itself is out of print. [One may find the full text at: http://www.reformed.org/documents/calvin/calvin_predest_2.html.]

[189] "It is the figment of Georgius, that no man whatever, neither one nor another, is predestinated to salvation, but that God pre-appointed a time in which He would save the whole world." [Introduction to Treatise]

John does indeed extend the benefits of the atonement of Christ, which was completed by His death, to all the elect of God throughout what climes of the world soever they may be scattered. But though the case be so, it by no means alters the fact that the reprobate are mingled with the elect in the world. *It is also a fact, without controversy, that Christ came to atone for the sins "of the whole world."*

There we have Calvin's extraordinary statement cited above, clear as a bell. Christ's atonement, says Calvin, was for the sins of the whole world, both the elect and the reprobate.

Yet if that is true, hasn't Georgius raised a good question about the whole world being saved? Not at all, says Calvin...

But the solution of all difficulty is immediately at hand, in the truth and fact, that it is "whosoever believeth in Him" that "shall not perish, but shall have eternal life." For our present question is, not what the power or virtue of Christ is, nor what *efficacy it has in itself,* but *who those are* to whom He gives Himself to be enjoyed. Now if the possession of Christ stands in faith, and if faith flows from the Spirit of adoption, it follows that he alone is numbered of God among His children who is designed of God to be a partaker of Christ.

Certainly, Calvin and I would need further discussion about how a person comes to faith (whether by predestination or by genuine free choice). Nevertheless, his crisp distinction between Christ's unlimited atonement and the altogether separate issue of how that atonement is finally applied is absolutely correct. As Calvin goes on to point out, it's all the difference between offer and acceptance...

Indeed, the evangelist John sets forth the office of Christ to be none other than that of "gathering together all the children of God" in one by His death. From all which we conclude that *although reconciliation is offered unto all men through Him, yet, that the great benefit belongs peculiarly to the elect,* that they might be "gathered together" and be made "together" partakers of eternal life.

Again, Calvin and I most certainly would disagree about how "the elect" come to be the elect. But otherwise, we are on the same page when it comes to the universal offer of salvation through the atoning blood of Christ. Inconsistent though it may be with his understanding of predestination, Calvin was of no doubt about the universal nature of the *offer*. "He announces salvation to all men indiscriminately," says Calvin in his *Institutes*.[190]

If only more Calvinists were as clear about Christ's atonement as Calvin himself, there would be no foolish talk about Christ's atonement being in any way "limited." That the notion of "limited atonement" has become so entrenched in Calvinist dogma as compared with Calvin's own less than dogmatic thinking is merely testimony to the fact that ideas have consequences. In this case, once Calvin put forward the premise of unconditional election, its logical extension—limited atonement—was bound to follow.[191]

One wonders if Calvin's apparent reluctance to acknowledge the troublesome implications unlimited atonement brings to the doctrine of election might not betray an intuitive sense that he would be well advised "just not to go there." Had he done so, the doctrinal system which bears his name likely never would have flourished.[192] At least it can be said that the overwhelming testimony from Scripture clearly affirming Christ's atonement for the sins of *the whole world* did not escape Calvin, as is reflected in the unequivocal statements we've just seen.[193]

---

[190] See *Institutes*, 3.24.17.

[191] Which may well explain Roger Nicole's argument (summarized by James White) querying how there could be such a "swift move of Reformed thought from an alleged universal view of Calvin to the particular view of the first generation of his disciples." [See White, *The Potter's Freedom*, p. 259, citing Roger Nicole's article: "John Calvin's View of the Extent of the Atonement" in the *Westminster Theological Journal*, Fall, 1985, vol. 47 #2.] In this regard, consider the swift movement of thought from Calvin to Beza, from Arminius to his Remonstrants, and from Pelagius to his more radical disciples. Teachers and authors always run the risk that their students and readers will take seminal ideas to unintended, though often logically valid, extremes.

[192] It is this very inconsistency in Calvin's thinking and writing which prompts authors like Roger Nicole to conclude that Calvin couldn't possibly mean what he actually said. Says Nicole in the above-cited article (p. 220), "It seems difficult to imagine that Calvin would posit as the purpose of Christ an indefinite, hypothetical redemption, when at so many other points it is plainly apparent that the specific elective purpose of God is the controlling feature of his outlook." The problem is that one first has to acknowledge what Calvin *said*, and only then to argue what Calvin *might have meant*—the former being indisputable, the latter being vulnerable to biased, curative speculation.

[193] Along with other Calvinists, R.C. Sproul departs from Calvin's clear exposition, first lamely suggesting that Paul might possibly be referring to the "non-Jewish world," then offering the equally unconvincing argument that Scripture often uses "world" when it doesn't actually mean "the whole world" (as in Luke 2:1). One wonders why Sproul feels compelled here to depart from the rule of hermeneutics he cites from Luther: "We must everywhere adhere to the simple, pure, and natural meaning of the words." (Sproul, 56.)

Beyond A Scriptural Doubt

What about yourself? Have you taken a close look at the atonement passages lately? There's not a lot of mystery to them, whether taken in isolation or in their fuller, proper context. I suggest that if you asked almost anyone unfamiliar with the finer intricacies of the Calvinism controversy to read these passages and tell you what they say, the odds are infinitesimal that they would ever come up with the idea of limited atonement.

So what do you think about the following passages (which in other contexts Calvinists would claim as their own)? Do they indicate to you that the mercy and power of Christ's atoning blood was limited to a predetermined number, or rather that it flowed freely for sinners all?

> "Just as the result of one trespass was condemnation *for all men*, so also the result of one act of righteousness was justification that brings life *for all men*" (Romans 5:18).

> "For God has bound *all men* over to disobedience so that he may have mercy on *them all*" (Romans 11:32).[194]

And even though Paul is specifically addressing the issue of Gentile inclusion in this next passage, just look at the implication of universal grace being provided to atone for universal sin:

"This righteousness from God comes through faith in Jesus Christ to *all who believe*. There is no difference, for *all have sinned* and fall short of the glory of God, and are justified freely by his grace through the redemption that came by Christ Jesus. God presented him as a sacrifice of atonement, through faith in his blood" (Romans 3:22-25).

In each of these first three texts, Calvinists feel ever so comfortable with the half of the passage suggesting their understanding of universal

---

[194] As earlier in his letter, Paul is once again speaking of the inclusion of Gentiles along with Jews. Having condemned sin in all men–Jew and Gentile alike–God has now provided an avenue of mercy to all men–Jew and Gentile alike. "There is no difference, for all have sinned and fall short of the glory of God, and are justified freely by his grace through the redemption that came by Christ Jesus" (Romans 3:22-23). Nothing in this passage suggests either wholesale condemnation through original sin and depravity, nor yet the Calvinist argument that there naturally would be predestination of the elect from among *both* Jew and Gentile. Clearly, the extent of mercy being made available is just as universal as the mass of mankind who need that mercy.

condemnation. But I watch in amazement as they seem to scramble for any possible pretext to rationalize away the other half, which clearly invokes universal grace and atonement (not to be confused with universal salvation, as Calvin himself has reminded us).

Again, what do *you* think? Can the following passages possibly be telling us anything other than that justification and grace are on offer for everyone?

> "But the angel said to them, 'Do not be afraid. I bring you good news of great joy that will be for *all the people.* Today in the town of David a Savior has been born to you; he is Christ the Lord." (Luke 2:10-11)

> "For Christ's love compels us, because we are convinced that one died *for all....*" (2 Corinthians 5:14)

> "But I, when I am lifted up from the earth, will draw *all men* to myself." (John 12:32)

> "For the grace of God that brings salvation has appeared to *all men....*" (Titus 2:11)

> "But we see Jesus, who was made a little lower than the angels, now crowned with glory and honor because he suffered death, so that by the grace of God he might taste death *for everyone.*" (Hebrews 2:9)

> "I will pour out my Spirit on *all people....And everyone who calls on the name of the LORD* will be saved." (Joel 2:28, 32)

> "The Spirit and the bride say, 'Come!' And let him who hears say, 'Come!' *Whoever* is thirsty, let him come; and *whoever* wishes, let him take the free gift of the water of life." (Revelation 22:17)

And, what can one possibly say in the face of these powerful passages identifying *the world*, not just the elect, as the object of Christ's atonement?

"For God so loved *the world* that he gave his one and only Son...to save *the world* through him." (John 3:16-17)[195]

"For I did not come to judge *the world*, but to save it." (John 12:47)

"I am the light of the *world*. *Whoever* follows me will never walk in darkness, but will have the light of life." (John 8:12)

"...God was reconciling *the world* to himself in Christ...." (2 Corinthians 5:19).

"This is good, and pleases God our Savior, *who wants all men to be saved* and to come to a knowledge of the truth. For there is one God and one mediator between God and men, the man Christ Jesus, who gave himself as a ransom *for all men*...." (1 Timothy 2:3-6).

Can there possibly be any question but that Jesus Christ came into the world to save all those who would respond to him in obedient faith?[196]

To get some feel for just how wildly out of touch Calvinism is with Scripture, compare the following two passages:

---

[195] When faced with this extraordinarily powerful text, Calvinists attempt to avoid its clear and compelling implications by resort to the argument that *world* means *all kinds of people*. The original word *kosmos* occurs no fewer than 75 times in John's gospel and never once means *all kinds of people*. To settle this in your own mind, try substituting that phrase wherever kosmos is used, and decide for yourself whether it makes any sense.

Although *world* is sometimes used in a less-than-universal sense, the context invariably is clear enough to put one on alert as to that special usage. And in a verse like Luke 2:1, where *world* obviously refers to the Roman Empire, we even find a different root word: *oikoumene*. There is a world of difference between a geographical usage and a redemptive usage. Not to mention the obvious hyperbole intended in a passage such as John 12:19 ("Look how the whole world has gone after him!").

[196] Especially regarding particular election, Calvinists cite John 17:9 where Jesus says: "I am not praying for the world, but for those you have given me, for they are yours." Even apart from the fact that Jesus has his immediate disciples in mind rather than the elect generally, the many references cited above to Christ's coming and dying for "the world" alerts us to a misuse of this passage whether employed in aid of particular election or particular atonement.

"The Father has sent his Son to be the Savior *of the world.*" (1 John 4:14)

"The Father's ultimate purpose was to save *the elect.*" (R.C. Sproul, 174)

If perhaps there is a sense in which non-Calvinists could agree that the *ultimate effect* of Christ's atonement was to bring his elect to glory, don't be fooled for a moment that this is what Sproul has in mind. Says Sproul, correctly, the crux of the controversy is this: "Did Christ die to atone for the sins of every human being, or did he die to atone for the sins of the elect only?"[197] From that point forward, his entire polemic is sharply focused on proving the latter–that Christ died *only for the elect* and *not for the world.*

That Sproul and other Calvinists are forced to fly so blatantly in the face of crystal-clear scriptures to the contrary is striking testimony to the abject poverty of the doctrine of election which leads them into this shameful theological quagmire.

Viewed in the dim light of Calvinism, John 3:16 cannot help but read: "For God so loved the *elect* that he gave his one and only Son, that *the elect alone shall have access to his atonement,* and thereby not perish but have eternal life."[198] But that's not exactly how the Bible's most memorized verse reads, is it?

Reduced to Unworthy Quibbling

We spoke earlier of the maxim: The weaker the case, the louder the argument. Its corollary is: The weaker the case, the more desperate the defense.

A good example of a desperate defense is seen in the oft-repeated response to the compelling truth of 1 Timothy 2:3-6. "But if God really and truly intended all men to be saved," goes the Calvinist argument,

---

[197] Sproul, 164

[198] Or as John Owen concludes his lengthy exegesis of the text with what he believes to be the "sense" of it: "God so loved his elect throughout the world, that he gave his Son with this intention, that by him believers might be saved." [John Owen, *The Death of Death In the Death of Christ* (Carlisle, Pa: The Banner of Truth Trust, 1995), 214]

"then surely that intent could not be frustrated by man's unbelief." Which only leads to our third maxim: If the case is weak, reframe the question!

As you'll recall (go back and look at the exact words), what Paul tells Timothy is that God *wants* (or *desires*) all men to be saved, not that he *intends* for all to be saved.[199] (When you think about it, this is virtually the same argument Calvinists themselves use, only with a predestinarian twist.) The purpose God *intended* from the beginning–a purpose which cannot be thwarted–was to provide a means to save all those who are willing to come to him in obedient faith.

While, undoubtedly, that is what God would *want* for everyone, in his divine sovereignty he has chosen not to *force* his own will on anyone. What God *wants* and *intends* are two different matters–as different for him as for parents who want the best for their children but realize there are some choices maturing children must make for themselves.

Along a similar line, Calvinists insist that, even if there were no predestination, God nevertheless would have foreknown both the saved and the lost. So what sense does it make, they ask, for Christ's blood to have been shed for the whole world if God already knew that not everybody's name was written in the book of life?[200] The answer, of course, is the same as before–that, from eternity, God was not only omnipresent and omniscient, but omni-hopeful. The cross was as much a gesture of God's hope for man as it was man's only hope.

If having hope against hope seems foolish for an omniscient God, we are reminded by Paul that the message of the cross has always been sheer foolishness to those who are perishing (1 Corinthians 1:18). But, then, foolishness is in the eye of the beholder. If you don't think so, just ask anyone who's ever loved and lost. Unrequited love may have made many a fool, but who among us would say it wasn't worth the risk...as well as, in the case of Christ, worth the unspeakable suffering?

---

[199] Any comfort Calvinists might get from the King James Version's rendering, "Who will have all men to be saved," is immediately snatched away by the realization that any implied desire for universal salvation couldn't be farther removed from the doctrine of election. Archaic as it is, the KJV language indicates nothing more than God's *desire* for all men to be saved, not his intent.

[200] The far tougher question is: If from the beginning of time God had already chosen to save only the elect, why the charade of having Jesus die on the cross at all? Those who are never *truly* lost do not stand in need of saving by any means.

What we see next is yet another quite astonishing Calvinist explanation, this time regarding what Paul meant in 1 Timothy 2:3-6 and Titus 2:11 when he refers to "all men" being the object of Christ's salvation, ransom, and grace. With a straight face, Calvinists argue that "all" means nothing more than all classes or categories of people, whether they be rulers or the ruled, rich or poor, educated or uneducated; and that from all these various kinds of people, God has called out his chosen elect—not to be confused, they insist, with a universal call to all mankind to freely and willingly *become* his elect.[201]

Calvinists base their argument at least partially on Revelation 5:9, where the twenty-four elders are singing praise to the Lamb, saying: "With your blood you purchased men for God from every tribe and language and people and nation." If Christ purchased people *from* every category of men, goes the argument, it obviously means that he didn't purchase the whole lot. Yet, the particular here does not rule out the general. That Christ paid the purchase price for saints from every tribe, language, and nation does not rule out his also having paid the price for anyone else who might have believed and been saved. That they did not avail themselves of the purchase, doesn't mean the price wasn't paid.

The same response applies to Acts 20:28. That God purchased the church with his blood (the particular) does not exclude the fact that he also paid the price for the whole world (the general). That Jesus laid down his life for the sheep (the particular) does not rule out his having laid down his life for any and all who will allow the Good Shepherd to bring them into his fold (the general). Paul simply could not have been more explicit when he spoke of "Christ Jesus, who gave himself as a ransom *for all men*...." To speak, instead, of "all *kinds of* men" makes no sense whatsoever when the reason for the ransom is provided with equal explicitness—that God our Savior "*wants all men to be saved* and to come to a knowledge of the truth."

---

[201] Of this text Richard Mouw says: "It seems obvious to me at first glance that he [Paul] really does mean *everyone*. But then I read some Calvinist theologians who want me to understand that 'everyone' here refers to *every one of the elect*. I understand the theological impulses that push them to this interpretation, but I cannot buy their argument." [Richard J. Mouw, *Calvinism In The Las Vegas Airport* (Grand Rapids: Zondervan, 2004), 47]

That God wants and wills to save men and women from every class and category of people is without dispute. God is no respecter of persons. But it defies understanding how anyone could possibly deny–from 1 Timothy 2:3-6, in particular–that God wants and wills to save all of his creatures, if they will but let him.[202]

It only gets worse when Calvinists are faced with what may be the most powerful of all the passages telling of God's desire that *all* be saved. In 2 Peter 3:9, Peter responds to the sneering cynics who are demanding to know when this long-overdue Christ is going to return as promised. "The Lord," says Peter, "...is patient with you, *not wanting anyone to perish, but everyone to come to repentance.*"

In context, of course, this verse is part of Peter's warning to those who have already been saved not to "fall from their secure position" (which only raises thornier problems yet for Calvinists). Even so, how in the world does one get around the obvious point that God doesn't want *anyone* to perish? Suddenly, we begin to hear all sorts of ingenious terminology being bandied around. Terms like "God's legislative will," or "his decretive will," or "God's constitutional compassion." By his nature, we are told, God would really, really *like* to save everyone. Unfortunately, he himself has issued a decree that will forbid it from happening.

Ironically, that disingenuous rationalization actually has more truth in it than Calvinists have supposed. No, not the unthinkable scenario where God acts contrary to his own inner will (in a kind of Freudian civil war between the ego and the superego), but in implementing his single-minded will to empower man with free moral choice.

We've covered this before, but the issue remains crucial. If man has no such free moral choice, why call him to repentance? (What possible relevance

---

[202] Even Charles Spurgeon takes his fellow Calvinists to task for using such a spurious argument. "'All men,' say they, 'that is, some of all sorts of men': as if the Lord could not have said 'All sorts of men' if he had meant that." Spurgeon's own primary response to the crucial passage is a less than helpful disclaimer: "I have never set up to be an explainer of all difficulties." [*Metropolitan Tabernacle Pulpit*, vol. 26, 49-52.]

Yet, surprisingly, Spurgeon could hardly have explained the passage more perfectly when he adds: "I believe that it is my Father's wish that 'all men should be saved, and come to the knowledge of the truth.' But I know, also, that he does not will it, so that he will save any one of them, unless they believe in his dear Son; for he has told us over and over that he will not." A non-Calvinist couldn't have said it better.

has repentance to a pre-programmed creature?) And why else be patient with man to allow sufficient opportunity to repent? Would individuals pre-selected for salvation and incapable of being lost need extra time for repentance? Sooner or later, all the clever arguments seem to lose their luster.

Charles Spurgeon once faulted his hyper-Calvinist opponent, John Gill, for sometimes letting his imagination run wild "when he falls upon a text which is not congenial with his creed, and hacks and hews terribly to bring the word of God into a more systematic shape."[203] Given the unusually tight systematic requirements of Calvinism, what was true of Gill has all too often been true of Calvinist apologists generally.[204]

Looking back on the years I spent teaching law students how to come up with thoughtful arguments in support of their cause seems like child's play compared to what we are witnessing here. As one whose profession has been spent in the arena of advocacy, my hat's off to them. The creativity with which Calvinist interpreters have tried to explain away the obvious raises the fine art of "spin doctoring" to new heights.

Not Just Your Ordinary Doctrinal Difference

If my own tone in this chapter has become somewhat more acerbic, it's because it's time to do some sober thinking about all this. Just what is it, again, that's being rationalized away so cavalierly? *Only the atoning sacrifice of Christ's blood for the sins of the world!*

Of course, if Calvinism's got that right, then praise be to Christ for even his limited atonement! But if Calvinism's got that wrong...can we even begin to appreciate the full implications of what is being said?

The problem is, not all doctrinal differences are of the same gravity. Recognizing that some are lesser and some are greater (even within the broader debate over Calvinism), it has to be said that the perniciousness

---

[203] *Commenting and Commentaries* (London: Banner of Truth, 1876, repr. 1969), 9

[204] Richard Mouw cites with approval Owen Thomas' account of a Welsh preacher who said to his fellow Calvinist preachers that many a Calvinist colleague "will spend an hour's exegesis upon the word 'world'; it will almost take his breath away to utter 'all'; he will circumnavigate land and sea to avoid meeting 'everyone'." But the fact is, Thomas quotes the preacher as saying, the Bible uses the words "all" and "world" in a fairly straightforward manner. "Trust more in the Bible, I implore you," he concluded. [Mouw, 45, citing Owen Thomas, *The Atonement Controversy in Welsh Theological Literature and Debate–1707-1841*, trans. John Aaron (Edinburgh: Banner of Truth, 2001), 341]

of this particular doctrine is off the charts. I assure you that these words are carefully measured, but *if* Calvinism's got it wrong and Christ did in fact die for the whole world, then how can the doctrine of limited atonement be anything other than rank blasphemy?

Never has so much been put at such risk. Apart from questioning the divine nature of Christ himself, never has fundamental Christian belief been so defiled. Never before through human wisdom has the cross of Christ been so emptied of its power!

And *why*, one has to ask, do Calvinists risk being so utterly blasphemous? I fear it is because, like my relativist law students, they have already taken the wrong fork in the road and only now realize to their horror that consistency demands their defending the shockingly indefensible.

Whereas my culturally-brainwashed students were led by their acceptance of extreme relativism to deny the existence of all absolutes, the most intriguing thing is that Calvinism errs to the opposite extreme, believing in *nothing but* absolutes. It begins with a view of God's sovereignty which is so absolute that it somehow absolutely rules out any possibility that God himself might have sovereignly chosen to make salvation contingent upon man's own freely-exercised faith and obedience. It doesn't end until, for possibly the lion's share of sin-saturated mankind, there is absolutely no hope of participating in the propitiating, redemptive atonement of Christ which is absolutely limited to a predetermined, set number of elect.

And all along we are told that, somehow, some way, this result is supposed to glorify God...?

Would that the only thing at stake was one's moral interpretation of the Holocaust. But by contrast to the millions of lives tragically snuffed out in aid of a morally-twisted cause, what's at stake here is nothing less than the One Life freely given to atone for everyone who has ever gotten themselves caught up in morally-twisted lives. Which includes you and me and every other human being who has ever lived.

Had there never been a pre-commitment to the notion of arbitrary, unconditional election, it's hard to imagine that anyone would have thought (or dared!) to dream up the idea of limited atonement.

Indeed, Calvinists openly acknowledge that limited atonement is made necessary by the fact that saving faith is a gift of God solely for the elect.

Given the crucial interdependence of Calvinism's component doctrines, is not the root of the problem all the more obvious? In light of the overwhelming biblical testimony to Christ's blood being shed for the whole world, something has to be seriously wrong with the underlying premise that faith is supernaturally supplied only to the elect.

It simply has to be asked: If it's the doctrine of unconditional election that's driving the Calvinism bus to its shockingly indefensible destination on the border of blasphemy, surely it's time to park this bus!

Want to hang your hat on something that is positively, absolutely "capital-'T' Truth"? "Look, the Lamb of God, who takes away the sin of the world!"[205]

———————————

For surely it is not angels he helps, but Abraham's descendants. For this reason he had to be made like his brothers in every way, in order that he might become a merciful and faithful high priest in service to God, and that he might make atonement for the sins of the people.

Hebrews 2:16-17

———————————

———————————

[205] John 1:29

Chapter Summary

- Sometimes wrong assumptions and beliefs lead to logical extensions which turn out to be quite unthinkable. The Calvinist teaching that Jesus' atonement on the cross was "limited" to the elect is the best proof yet that its whole system is fundamentally flawed.

- Nothing could be clearer than that God is not willing that any should perish, and that Jesus died for the sins of the whole world.

- Atonement is not the equivalent of salvation, any more than provision is the equivalent of appropriation. Through his death on the cross, Christ has provided the atonement for all who are willing to appropriate it through faith.

- The unworthy quibbling of Calvinists aimed at dismissing the obvious import of passage after passage affirming Christ's universal atonement serves to expose not only the weakness of this particular doctrine but also the underlying doctrine of unconditional election.

- Not all doctrinal differences are of the same importance. The scandalous suggestion that Christ's atonement was in some way limited borders on being blasphemous.

Reality Check: If the eternal destiny of every person who's ever lived was predestined from eternity, Christ's death on the cross would be virtually moot. With salvation and reprobation already a done deal, atonement (and Christ himself) is reduced to little more than a means to a predetermined end.

Chapter 9

Irresistible Grace?
Wonderfully Irresistible!

*Reformed theology does not teach that God brings the elect
"kicking and screaming, against their wills," into his kingdom.
It teaches that God so works in the hearts of the elect
as to make them willing and pleased to come to Christ.*

–R.C. Sproul

Without doubt, there are vast differences; and I assure you I'm not trying to tar Calvinism with the same brush or suggest any guilt by association. Nevertheless, I simply can't escape thinking about certain disturbing parallels between Calvinism and the notion of karma in Hinduism and Buddhism.[206]

---

[206] Nor must one ignore obvious comparisons between Calvinism and Islam. Indeed, so close are the parallels that Loraine Boettner devotes an entire appendix in his classic, *The Reformed Doctrine of Predestination*, to what he calls "A Comparison with the Mohammedan Doctrine of Predestination." Boettner cites Dr. Samuel Zwemer (a zealous missionary to Muslims) for the proposition that "Islam is indeed in many respects the Calvinism of the Orient" (p. 318).

Although Boettner attempts to distinguish the fatalism of Islam from Calvinism's understanding of predestination, he nevertheless draws support from Islam's "doctrine of Fatalism," along with the fact that "the mechanistic and deterministic philosophies have exerted such great influences in England, Germany, and America." Given such universal support, says Boettner, "this doctrine is at least worthy of careful study" (p. 2). On the strength of this evidence alone, it could hardly be said that Calvinism's determinism (whether "hard" or "soft") is simply a straw-man argument unfairly urged by non-Calvinists.

Back in the mid-1980's, the first Christian book I ever wrote was a response to actress Shirley McLaine's best-selling autobiography *Out On A Limb*. (Taking off from that familiar phrase, my own book was titled, *Out On A Broken Limb*.) Far from being a run-of-the-mill autobiography, Ms. MacLaine's spiritual (and predictably earthy) memoir was a primer for the New Age belief system that was becoming ever more popular at that time. "New Age" is the generic label which became attached to this unlikely, eclectic blending of Hindu, Buddhist, and even Christian thought–all wrapped up in a blanket of "me-generation" self-worship.

At the heart of New Age thinking is the ancient, eastern notion of reincarnation, the belief that we live in successive bodies and personalities throughout many centuries until we achieve a kind of spiritual perfection known as Nirvana. At that point, we basically blend back into the oneness of the universe from which, so it is said, all of us originally came.

Calvinists obviously would reject with all their might such a bizarre, unbiblical belief system, and particularly the notion that, through the process of reincarnation, we are *working* our way to perfection. Any idea of grace is notoriously absent from Hindu and Buddhist thinking. And while it is true that Calvinism asserts that Christ's atonement was necessarily "limited" in scope, according to New Age belief there is no room whatsoever for Christ's atonement, only an artfully crafted (if idolatrous) "at-one-ment" with one's own self.

Still, there are disturbing parallels. For instance, by the law of karma each person begins his or her life with a certain amount of bad karma to be worked off. It's not exactly original sin or total depravity, but this innate false-start and inborn negative "energy" is not altogether dissimilar to Calvinism's own version.

Not only that, but like Calvinists, New Agers claim that there are no accidents or coincidences. Nothing happens by chance. For New Agers, it's all been decided by a cosmic computer in the sky. We are just playing out the roles assigned to us. If we are born rich or poor, it's karma. If we are good or bad, that too is karma.

Although (importantly) Calvinism attributes the absence of accidents or chance to a personal, sovereign God, as opposed to the impersonal, cosmic law of karma, there is no real difference in the resulting determinism. In each instance, as if by fate, everything is decided in advance. All is predestined.[207]

Under both belief systems, that preordained determinism takes on a sinister hue when it comes to the problem of evil. By the New Age doctrine of monism, you and I and God, as well as everything else in the universe, are all One—which can only mean, problematically, that God and evil are also one.

Though coming from a different direction altogether, Calvinism gets caught in a similar dilemma. The struggle for Calvinists is explaining how a totally foreordaining God can be sovereign over every thought, action, will, and circumstance without being directly responsible for evil. (Indeed, many Calvinists would even concede that logical conclusion, saying that God's direct, causative role in the existence of evil is simply one of life's deep mysteries we humans can't possibly understand.)

For all this, it is the next intriguing parallel which brings us to the immediate subject of this chapter—Calvinism's doctrine of irresistible grace. For Calvinists, the challenge is in finding room for man to have even the tiniest corner of free will in a space so wholly and totally occupied by God's sovereign control. New Age thinking encounters virtually the same problem, affirming on one hand that karma dictates who and what we will be in our future lives, while on the other hand insisting that we ourselves decide our destiny by the way we live.

It's not just the age-old battle over determinism and free will, wherein the question being asked is which of the two—*determinism* or *free will*—is the ultimate force behind one's actions.[208] For Calvinists, no less than for New Agers, the quite-different problem is trying to explain how both free will

---

[207] Speaking of whether one is born rich or poor, in honor or in shame, with good parents or bad, Boettner declares (at p. 265) that: "the lot of every individual has been determined by the sovereign good pleasure of God." Believers in karma would say precisely the same. But Calvinists take yet a giant step further, saying that it is through one's very "lot" or assigned circumstances that God puts some in a position to be saved and others not. Therefore, it is not just the poor heathen's poverty we should lament, but the predestined and irreversible poverty of spirit into which he was born!

[208] Calvinists are often keen to distance themselves from the word "determinism" in any form, whether "fatalistic determinism" or otherwise. But having already embraced God's sovereign control over every act, event, thought, and motive, how can Calvinism escape the most fundamental dictionary definition of "determinism"—the doctrine that everything, especially one's choice of action, is determined by a sequence of causes independent of one's will?

and determinism can operate simultaneously and in tandem, as each belief system claims.[209]

Where Irresistible Grace Fits

However, before we get ahead of ourselves, we need to ask why we're talking about irresistible grace in the first place. In fact, even before we get to the *irresistible* part, we must concentrate initially on the *grace* part, and where it fits into the picture.

According to Calvinism, the "picture" is this. Through the gospel invitation freely extended to all mankind, there is an outward, universal call which promises salvation to each and every person who believes and repents. Yet, given man's depravity, this external outreach to the whole world would be universally rejected by all who hear the gospel were it not for a special inward call made by the Holy Spirit to the already-chosen elect.

This is where *grace* enters the picture. By God's grace, working through the Holy Spirit to open the hearts of the elect and give them a new, godly nature, conversion is made possible. Without that grace, the preaching of the gospel alone would never result in faith and repentance, nor the promised salvation which comes thereby.

On behalf of all those who are never touched by that special grace, one can only ask how the preaching of the "good news" is anything but bad news.[210] Or how, in any truly honest sense, the gospel could be described as an "invitation" to those who from eternity have been *specifically uninvited*. Or how the gospel's promise of salvation to those who believe and repent can be at all sincere when the unregenerate have no capacity to do

---

[209] It is sufficiently challenging for non-Calvinists to reconcile man's free will with God's providential master plan (as best seen in pivotal individuals like Pharaoh, Judas, and Pilate). But at least non-Calvinists don't have to explain how in non-providential cases (the norm) an individual can be both "totally free" and simultaneously acting pursuant to God's irresistible control in matters pertaining to *salvation*.

[210] It is bad enough that the Gospel is "foolishness" and a "stumbling block" to those who refuse to accept it (1 Corinthians 1:18-24), but at least it's their choice to refuse the good news. Where no such choice exists, the gospel of salvation through Christ is just about as much "good news" as a condemned man being informed of his death sentence. Indeed, in Calvin's words, "the utterly clear teaching of truth can be nothing but the stench of death unto death." [Calvin's Catechism of 1538, trans. by Ford Lewis Battle, sec. 13.]

either.[211] Or how, therefore, the "outward universal call to salvation" could possibly be anything other than a sham offer, mocking the non-elect, who are given no choice but to reject the gospel they are hearing.[212]

As if that result weren't sufficiently monstrous, the even more amazing feature of Calvinism is that the elect have no more choice than the non-elect. By Calvinist teaching, their conversion is not simply made *possible* by this grace, but *certain* and *unavoidable*. Indeed, it is both inevitable and necessary.

This "special grace," therefore, is a grace that cannot even remotely be rejected by those upon whom it is so graciously bestowed. The Spirit graciously gives the elect sinner no choice but to acquiesce. So, regardless of whether you and I might choose on our own to accept Christ, the Holy Spirit graciously causes us to believe, repent, and come "freely and willingly" to Christ. (Is it just me, or is there something wrong with this picture?)

God's special grace, then, (putting it as benignly as possible) is "efficacious"–that is, effective. It never fails to achieve its purpose. Less benignly, this special grace is "irresistible." However charitably or ruthlessly it may be put, it is this so-called "doctrine of irresistible grace" that gives us the "I" in *TULIP*.

So tell us again why God's merciful grace must act in so Draconian a fashion? Is it not because, otherwise, you and I would be left with a genuine, bona fide free will that could reject the gospel or accept it? Which

---

[211] Calvinists point to Isaiah 6:8-13 as an example of God-ordained preaching in the face of certain rejection. Are we to believe that the people of Israel had no choice over the corrupt practices for which God was bringing judgment against them? By contrast, when people have been consigned to eternal damnation before the creation of the world, the supposed "Fall," their emergence from the womb, and their own personal sin, there is not even the remotest possibility that they might "understand with their hearts, and turn and be healed." For non-elect reprobates, preaching the "good news" would be a complete sham.

[212] J. I. Packer illustrates perfectly the Calvinist blind spot regarding proclamation of the gospel to the non-elect. "Our calling as Christians," says Packer, "is not to love God's elect, and them only, but to love our neighbour, irrespective of whether he is elect or not." Sure, but the issue at hand is, How are we to love our non-elect neighbor in terms of evangelism? "If, then, our neighbour is unconverted, we are to show love to him as best we can by seeking to share with him the good news without which he must needs perish."

Packer seems oblivious to the problem that if our neighbor happens not to be among the elect, there is absolutely nothing he can do in the face of the gospel but to reject it. For all intents and purposes, our neighbor "perished" at the moment God chose whom he would regenerate and whom he would not. Since the non-elect must always remain unregenerate, how possibly could they respond to the gospel? And how, then, in any sense can the gospel be "good news" to the non-elect?

[See J. I. Packer, *Evangelism and the Sovereignty of God* (Downers Grove: InterVarsity Press, 1961), 99]

would mean, of course, that we would have something to do with our own spiritual destiny; which somehow, supposedly, puts God's sovereign grace at risk. Most threatening of all, it would single-handedly undermine the fundamental Calvinist doctrine of unconditional election.

Are we really to believe that, in order to ensure the exclusive saving power of God's grace, that very grace must force itself ever so ungraciously upon those who cannot possibly resist it? Does this make any sense at all?

The Thorny Intricacies of Regenerating Grace

To understand precisely what Calvinism teaches about irresistible (or efficacious) grace, one must begin with its primary underlying assumption: total depravity. If man is totally depraved, then he has no ability whatsoever to respond to the gospel or to come to God in faith. Spiritually speaking, fallen man is as "dead" as was Lazarus in the grave, completely and totally unable to contribute in any way to his spiritual regeneration. Hence, as with Lazarus, only God can bring a depraved soul back to life by a unilateral divine act of "operative grace." Of necessity, this exclusively divine (monergistic) action precludes any notion of man's own (synergistic) cooperation in the process.[213]

But here is where one must listen ever so closely to the Calvinist argument. It's not simply a squabble over whether man has a role to play in the process of salvation. That's a separate issue. For the moment, the issue is whether man has the ability to act out any role whatsoever.

Whereas non-Calvinists fully accept that the actual regenerative *power of spiritual transformation* rests wholly and solely in the hands of God, they are not laboring under the same difficulty which faces Calvinists. Given man's innate free will, the only question is whether a person who hears the gospel will open his heart to God's transforming power or, instead, slam

---

[213] The comparison between the raising of Lazarus and the regeneration of the unbeliever who is dead in sin is a false analogy. Whereas Lazarus, being physically dead, was beyond all sentient and physical capability, the one who is spiritually dead still has every faculty of conscience, thought, and decision-making.

the door in the face of grace. For non-Calvinists, there are no pre-conditions to having faith. No red tape. No fine print.

For Calvinists, it's not that simple. Because of Calvinism's pre-commitment to the doctrine of total depravity, one can't even get to the question of *whether* a person is going to respond to the gospel in faith without first resolving the problem of man's *inability to respond*. For that to happen, nothing short of a miracle can raise fallen man from his grave of depravity and empower him with the ability to respond to God in faith.

It is this initial, threshold regenerative act with which Calvinism's irresistible grace is associated. The theory is that, once regenerated by irresistible grace, then (and only then) a person has the ability to turn to Christ in faith. As Sproul puts it: "Monergistic regeneration has to do, not with the whole process of redemption, but strictly with the initial condition or first step of our coming to faith."[214]

But at this point Calvinism is forced to accommodate yet another doctrinal pre-commitment. That, of course, is the doctrine of election, whereby only the predestined elect are to be saved. Which means that only the predestined elect will ever come to faith. Which means that only the predestined elect will ever be regenerated so as to have the *ability* to have that faith.

Yet precisely because they are *the elect* (having been predestined and foreordained from eternity), it also means that it is absolutely impossible for them *not* to be regenerated in order to have faith; and equally impossible for them *not* to have the faith for which they are regenerated. Which in a shorthand kind of way explains why the word *irresistible* is tacked onto the word *grace*. Not only *can* the elect now respond to the gospel, they most certainly *will* respond.[215] Which is to say *shall*. Or *must*.

Here's where it all becomes a delicate juggling act. To say that the elect *will*, *shall*, and inevitably *must* respond in faith is to suggest that the elect have no free will regarding either their regeneration or their faith. Yet with all the might it can muster, Calvinism is adamant that the soul–once regenerated–is absolutely and completely free when it comes to Christ in faith. That in the process of regeneration the soul is not only freed from the

---

[214] Sproul, 185
[215] See Sproul, 184.

debilitating bondage of original sin and depravity but is so wholly transformed in nature (being made a new creation) that it freely and willingly gives itself in faith to God.

Can there be any doubt, however, that the resulting faith that is "freely offered" by the believer is a foregone conclusion, having been foreordained from eternity? To use Calvinism's own argument against what is considered to be the heretical, non-Calvinist doctrine of "free will," how could anything predestined and foreordained from eternity be "free"? If God has already determined that the elect will be saved through faith, as a gift which absolutely will not under any circumstances be refused, then what possible freedom of human will or action remains?

The obvious logical implication running between predestination and freedom of will was not lost on Martin Luther. In his *Assertio*, Luther says plainly: "*free will is really a fiction* and a label without reality, because it is in no man's power to plan any evil or good....*everything takes place by absolute necessity.*"[216]

Inconsistency Only Blind Dogmatism Can Accommodate

If only the problem of human free will in the face of divine determinism were a genuine antinomy or paradox that could be assumed to make sense in some higher framework. (As in how Christ could be both fully man and fully God. Or as in how we can have eternal life even now before we die.) But in the conflict between man's absolute free will and God's absolute sovereign will over man's will, we are well and truly faced with the impossible task of reconciling the irreconcilable.

Indeed, *isn't that Calvinism's very starting point!* Before all the back-peddling begins in an attempt to rationalize the many biblical passages which clearly imply man's free agency, doesn't Calvinism categorically insist from the word "Go" that, since man can contribute nothing to his regeneration (much less salvation), it follows that he cannot be seen to have any free will of his own?[217] What could be stranger than Calvinism's dogged insistence (in aid of the doctrines of sovereignty and election) that man has

---

[216] Martin Luther, *Assertio*, Article 36.

[217] Or, as sometimes argued in the reverse: man has no natural, inherent will capable of exercising faith, and therefore salvation must absolutely be all of God and nothing of man.

absolutely no free will whatsoever, quickly followed with equal insistence (in aid of man's not being a pre-programmed automaton) that the regenerate elect, at least, *do* have free will![218]

Both scripturally and experientially, of course, we are all too painfully aware of the inherent conflict between "my will" and "Thy will." Taking a cue from the prophet Amos, how can two walk together, unless they are agreed? (Amos 3:3). Yet, the real problem is what happens when two wills are *not* agreed? Surely, to impose one will upon another–*irresistibly*–is to rob the other of the freedom to will. Do you not agree?

Speaking of robbery, there's that threatening demand of the masked bandit: "Your money, or your life!" What kind of real choice is that? When the money is nervously handed over by the fearful victim, is that a *free* act of the will?

For similar reasons, the law recognizes that compulsion is a defense to virtually all criminal charges. Why? Because a person who is acting only under duress, necessity, or irresistible compulsion is no longer responsible as a free moral agent. His will has been overcome. Why, then, should it be any different in the realm of faith?

Recently, a friend told me the sad story about when her domineering (faithless) father said to her: "It's up to you. Either you can go to Harvard University, or to Harvard University, or to Harvard University." All along, her father knew she desperately wanted to go to a small, relatively-unknown Christian college, but Harvard University was his alma mater, and there was nothing doing but that his daughter would follow in his footsteps.

So she had a choice: either Harvard, or Harvard, or Harvard! It was her decision. She was free to choose! Or was she...? What do you think? (In case you're wondering, she went to Harvard!)

---

[218] Richard Mouw points to Covenant Theology as Reformed Calvinism's way of softening the harsh, robotic ring of predestination. "Covenants are made between *partners*," says Mouw (although acknowledging that there could certainly be no equality of partnership between God and man). [Mouw, 66-67] But to speak of "partners" in a "transaction" runs afoul of Calvinism's insistence that salvation must be monergistic, not synergistic. And how by any stretch of the imagination can a person acting in every way pursuant to sovereign control have anything like the genuine free will necessary to covenant, *or not to covenant*, as he chooses? How can one who is *wholly acted upon* volitionally agree to the conditions of any partnership? Given the obvious lack of volition, not a court in the land would uphold such a "covenant" as valid.

On an eminently grander scale, it is this very dilemma that forces Calvinism to resort to its fall-back bundle of secret eternal decrees to explain how, at one and the same time, man can be absolutely and totally powerless to resist the working of the Holy Spirit, yet still be acting voluntarily as a free creature.

By these obscure decrees, supposedly, there are two types of "free" actions. As we've mentioned before, man's free acts of a sinful nature are said to be "permissive" (yet somehow still *certain* since God retains sovereign control over all things). By contrast, we are told that, whenever man does anything good, it's merely the "efficacious" power of God at work.

In other words, we are free to be bad on our own (as long as it's consistent with the certainty demanded by God's absolute sovereignty); yet inexorably bound to be good (and entirely free to be so), if that's what God wants us to be.

I'm afraid most folks would call these tortured explanations *hedging*–or, at the least, *equivocating*. Once the grotesque mutant of "determined free will" is around the corner and out of sight, we are quickly reassured that absolutely nothing happens without the sovereign God willing it. That God is the moving force behind all things, whether "accidental," "causal," or "moral." That there is nothing–absolutely nothing–of which God is not the purposing, planning, and implementing cause. Well, not at least, until someone brings up the subject of sin and evil, and then suddenly we are whisked back once again to the secret eternal decrees which mysteriously kiss the pain of evil all better.

On this score, Robert Picirilli's particularly insightful observation is well worth sharing: "Sometimes Calvinists make a distinction between the primary and secondary causes of an event, and represent human decisions as the latter. In this case, however, human agency is reduced to being God's instrumentality. This seems no different from a 'hard determinism' that finally makes all freedom an illusion and traces all events to prior, necessitating causes."[219]

Like concrete, once determinism is allowed to harden, it's next to impossible to soften it again.

---

[219] Picirilli, 60

Hardly anything is more mystifying than watching Calvinism's logic-defying contortions. In the same breath, we are assured that God exerts such a powerful influence upon the human spirit as to make it irresistibly willing to accept Christ; but in no way is this an "overpowering" force inconsistent with man's free agency. Since God is the creator of man's will, God would never act contrary to that created will so as to make man's faith and repentance "compulsory."[220]

I'm afraid not many average reasonable jurors would be convinced. Merely consider, for example, these quite extraordinary attempts by Loraine Boettner to reconcile God's sovereign control and man's free agency: "The elect are so influenced by divine power that their coming is an act of voluntary choice"[221] Excuse me? And again: "God sends His Spirit and...sweetly constrains the person to yield...." Yet, "this change is not accomplished through any external compulsion."[222] And still again: "God so governs the inward feelings, external environment, habits, motives, etc., of men that they freely do what He proposes"![223]

R.C. Sproul provides more grist for amazement, saying: "Irresistible grace is not irresistible in the sense that sinners are incapable of resisting it." No? No, you see, "*Irresistible grace* means that the sinner's resistance to the grace of regeneration cannot thwart the Spirit's purpose. The grace of regeneration is irresistible in the sense that it is invincible."[224] Not to jump to too hasty a conclusion, I've just pulled out my Webster's and looked up the word *invincible*. As I suspected, the definition is pretty straightforward.

---

[220] Arguing conversely, Calvinists often cite Luke 14:23 (where the man in the parable sends his servants out with orders to "make" or "compel" strangers come into his banquet) as proof that God's grace irresistibly compels the elect whom God chooses to regenerate unto faith and salvation. How possibly does one justify such exegesis, given Jesus' obvious teaching point: that "not one of those men who were invited will get a taste of my banquet." If anything, this is a parable about reprobation, not election. What is more, these people will miss out on the banquet precisely because they are freely and voluntarily offering worthless excuses for not showing up. If perhaps the strangers in the highways are being *morally constrained* to fill the house, it's clear from the offending refusals that no one is being *forcibly compelled* to attend the banquet against his will.

[221] Boettner, 178

[222] Boettner, 177

[223] Boettner, 214

[224] Sproul, 189

Invincible is anything "that cannot be overcome." Isn't that awfully close to "incapable of resisting"...?[225]

And then there is the astounding language of the Westminster Confession of Faith, affirming the power of the Word and the Spirit on behalf of the elect, "...effectually drawing them to Jesus Christ: yet so, as they come *most freely*, being *made willing* by His grace."[226]

Does not all this seem to you like evasive double-talk? For myself, it looks suspiciously like, "Either you can go to Harvard, or to Harvard, or to Harvard. It's entirely up to you!"[227]

A variation on theme is the classic Calvinist illustration of the man carrying a bowl of goldfish wherever he pleases.[228] The intended point is that, wherever the fish are carried, they are still free to move unrestrained within the bowl. What can one say! Does this not, instead, brilliantly demonstrate how truly *un*free man is regarding his eternal destination? If the so-called "freedom of movement" man is permitted has nothing whatsoever to do with *where he is heading*, then he acts with no more free choice than the fish in the bowl. As it turns out, what could better illustrate Calvinism's ultimate reductionism whereby man becomes little more than a bowl-bound goldfish![229]

---

[225] Consider also Sproul's response to the argument that "for a person to come to Christ, God the Holy Spirit must first woo or entice them to come." Says Sproul, "I am persuaded that this explanation is incorrect. It does violence to the text of Scripture, particularly to the biblical meaning of the word *draw*....Linguistically and lexicographically the word means simply 'to compel'" (Sproul, 153).

[226] *The Westminster Confession of Faith*, 10.1 (with my emphasis)

[227] We are told with a straight face that the flip-side is true as well. Says Calvinist Roger Smalling, "Curiously, the reverse is true of the Universal Call, even though it is the same message. He allows the non-elect to resist His offer of mercy if they want to. They always want to." (http://www.geocities.com/JoyfullyServing/Essays/call.html)

[228] Boettner, 221

[229] Luther, too, speaks of a will which acts without compulsion, "but responsively of its own desire and inclination." Which he proceeds to illustrate (with no thought, seemingly, of the inherent inconsistency) as follows: "Thus the human will is like a beast of burden. If God rides it, it wills and goes whence God wills [citing Psalm 73:22]. If Satan rides, it wills and goes where Satan wills. Nor may it choose to which rider it will run, nor which it will seek. But the riders themselves contend who shall have and hold it." Man, no more free than a brute beast, yet acting without compulsion...? [Luther, *Bondage of the Will*, [635], 97]

Playing Games With the Secrets of God

When all the contorted attempts at reconciling the irreconcilable finally reach a futile end, what we hear from Calvinists is that it's a great, inscrutable mystery which we cannot explain in our present state of knowledge. One of the frustrating things about any discussion of Calvinism is that, when forced into any obvious cul-de-sac of illogic, invariably its proponents resort to the great mysteries of God, and specifically to Deuteronomy 29:29: "The secret things belong to the LORD our God, but the things revealed belong to us."[230] Is there something in Scripture that is embarrassingly incompatible with Calvinism? Then fall back on the secret things of God. Talk about God's ways being higher than our ways and his thoughts than our thoughts (Isaiah 55:9).[231]

No one denies that, notwithstanding God's divine revelation, "beyond all question, the mystery of godliness is great" (1 Timothy 3:16). At best, human knowledge can catch only a glimpse of the eternal. Yet, even when Paul says, "we speak of God's secret wisdom, a wisdom that has been hidden and that God destined for our glory before time began" (1 Corinthians 2:6-16), it is clear that God's "secret wisdom" has now been revealed (at least all that God has chosen to reveal). "'No eye has seen, no ear has heard, no mind has conceived what God has prepared for those who love him,'" says Paul, "but God has revealed it to us by his Spirit. The Spirit searches all things, even the deep things of God."

Never is Calvinism more disingenuous than when it talks a good line about the secret things belonging to God, yet then turns right around and insists there are secret, unrevealed decrees that somehow manage to grease the way for doctrine that has become hopelessly stuck.

Not to put too fine a point on it, what's secret is *secret*! Unless it has been revealed in the pages of Holy Writ, that which is truly "secret" is utterly and completely unknowable. Thus, for Calvinism to enlist in their support the "secret will of God" can be nothing short of brazen, pre-

---

[230] "Deuteronomy 29:29 is a much-quoted verse in the Calvinist tradition...." [Mouw, 45]

[231] Among the "secret things," for example, is the "covenant of redemption" whereby God the Father gave the number of the elect to his Son. Ever read about this "covenant" anywhere in the Bible?

sumptuous, self-serving speculation contrary to the biblical injunction: "Do not go beyond what is written" (1 Corinthians 4:6).

Calvinism's penchant for propping up its doctrines with "secret decrees" is a departure even from John Calvin's own warning: "Let us then, in the first place bear in mind, that to desire any more knowledge of Predestination than that which is unfolded in the word of God, indicates as great folly as to wish to walk through impassible roads, or to see in the dark."[232]

That Calvinism would even feel the need to resort to anything "secret" must surely set off alarm bells, warning us that Calvinism faces an otherwise insoluble problem standing up against what has been revealed. Why else go outside the Sacred Page?

For a last, summary word on the matter, we could do worse than pay heed to the arch-Calvinist, Martin Luther. His crucial distinction between *God* and *Scripture* is worth hanging onto. "Nobody doubts that in God many things are hidden of which we know nothing," says Luther (in response to his antagonist, Erasmus). "But that there are in Scriptures some things abstruse and not quite plain, was spread by the godless Sophists...."[233]

While even Luther goes on to acknowledge that the Scriptures are not always as "plain" as one might wish, what *is* plain is that the God of all mysteries has chosen to reveal himself with sufficient plainness that we cannot justly cry "Mystery" when confronted with that which is plain indeed.

A More Biblical View of Free Will

When one confines himself to the Sacred Page, one readily sees the plethora of passages to which Calvinists themselves eagerly point as proof of compatibility between God's sovereign will and man's free will. (Non-Calvinists couldn't agree more!) What one does not see is Calvinism's extremist view of an all-controlling sovereignty which could not possibly be compatible with man's genuine free will.

As for the undisputed compatibility, consider this passage from Isaiah which—directly appealing to reason (and addressing *sinners*)—comfortably

---

[232] Calvin, *Institutes*, 3.21.2
[233] Luther, *Bondage of the Will*, [606], 90

accommodates both God's sovereignty and man's genuine free will. "'Come now, let us reason together,' says the LORD. '...If you are willing and obedient, you will eat the best from the land; but if you resist and rebel, you will be devoured by the sword. For the mouth of the LORD has spoken'" (Isaiah 1:18-20).

The key word, of course, is "if." "*If* you are willing," as contrasted with "*if* you resist." Whether there will be reward or punishment depends entirely upon a contingency in the hands of man, not irresistible force emanating either directly or indirectly from the hand of God. Yet *that very contingency* (together with its potential reward or punishment) has itself issued forth from God. "For the mouth of the LORD has spoken!"

If you are a Calvinist, have you ever stopped to ask why, from cover to cover in the Bible, God repeatedly makes conditional promises, if all along it is his unconditional sovereign will that determines whether man will obey or disobey?

As a result of God's own expressly revealed sovereign decree (in contrast to the clandestinely secret decrees somehow perceived only by Calvinists), you and I have the genuine, unforced, unprompted freedom of will either to respond to God's grace or to resist it with all our might, as we so choose. *The only thing we cannot resist are the devastating eternal consequences of resisting.* "For the mouth of the LORD has spoken!"

The Potter and the Clay

The amazing thing is that the free exercise of our will even elicits a response from God's own divine will. As God put it to the people of Israel: "'Return to me,' declares the LORD Almighty, 'and I will return to you,' says the LORD Almighty" (Zechariah 1:3).

Yet at the mere hint that God might dare respond to man in this way, it wouldn't take a mind-reader to know what you're probably thinking. Surely, you must be asking: "But what about Paul's potter and clay discussion? When the mouth of the LORD has spoken, how can we possibly resist?" Interestingly, your question is the very question Paul anticipated he would trigger from his insistence that God has mercy upon whom he will have mercy.

Before we revisit this passage, let's read it again:

> *One of you will say to me: "Then why does God still blame us? For who resists his will?" But who are you, O man, to talk back to God? Shall what is formed say to him who formed it, "Why did you make me like this?" Does not the potter have the right to make out of the same lump of clay some pottery for noble purposes and some for common use? (Romans 9:19-21).*

As we noted earlier, we mustn't forget the context. Paul's extended discussion in this section of Romans is about how God has worked providentially through history to make Israel his chosen nation; and about how it is now possible (through faith rather than Jewish ethnicity and strict law-keeping) for Gentiles as well as Jews to become God's chosen people.

Paul was all too aware that many Jews would interpret Israel's loss of special status in God's eyes as a matter of personal rejection. He knows they will want to shift the issue from God's election of national Israel to God's election of themselves as individuals (precisely as Calvinists have done).

Even despite this subtle shift, however, they end up asking a particularly perceptive question: If God deals as arbitrarily with individuals in the matter of salvation as he does with nations (having mercy upon whom he will have mercy, and hardening the hearts of whomever he wills), how could God justly condemn anyone who is unable to resist his will? Apart from the inherent fallacy of the opening assumption, what a great question!

But Paul won't be drawn into a fuller discussion of that re-framed issue. Instead, he immediately brings these Jews back to what he knows is the real reason for their pouting, which is Paul's proclamation that the Gentiles are now just as eligible for "chosenness" as the Jews. Speaking to that point, Paul launches into his potter and clay analogy, verifying that–with regard to national Israel and the Gentile question–the Jews were absolutely right to understand that they were in no position to resist God's will in the matter.

When it comes to God's implementing his scheme of redemption, nothing and no one is going to stand in his way. Nothing and no one can thwart his eternal purpose. And nothing and no one can resist his sovereign will![234]

That said, whether you and I individually lack the ability to resist God's will for us to be saved is an altogether different question. Consider, for example,

---

[234] Isaiah 14:27, 46:9-11, 55:11, and Job 42:2 all speak to the unthwartable nature of God's plan. "I will bring it to pass." "My word shall accomplish what I please."

the independence of action implied by this passage from Isaiah: "'Woe to the obstinate children,' declares the LORD, 'to those who carry out plans that are not mine...'" (Isaiah 30:1). And again, "I called but you did not answer, I spoke but you did not listen" (Isaiah 65:12). And yet again, "I tried to cleanse you but you would not be cleansed from your impurity" (Ezekiel 24:13).[235]

Do those texts sound anything like Calvinism's insistence that absolutely everything happens irresistibly according to God's eternal master plan–including every thought, motive, and act of man? If it were true that God calls (elects) and then predestines, how could any person *not answer* that sovereign call?

A good test of Calvinism's basic premise is applying it, not to the elect, but to the lost. If God is not willing that any should perish (2 Peter 3:9), and yet broad is the way that leads to destruction (Matthew 7:13), what else can we conclude but that God isn't forcing his will on those who themselves choose the path to perdition?

Of course, Calvinists who reject "double predestination" might readily agree. Yet, there remains for them the problem that it was the sovereign God himself who brought the non-elect into this world, unconditionally condemned by original sin and steeped in total depravity. So, whether directly or indirectly, the eternal perdition of the non-elect would still be according to God's will–*irresistibly*–from first to last.

On the direct issue of whether we can resist the Holy Spirit, serious attention has to be given to that intriguing line from the martyr, Stephen. In the face of certain death at the hands of his frenzied fellow Jews, Stephen pulled no punches, proclaiming boldly: "You stiff-necked people, with uncircumcised hearts and ears! You are just like your fathers: You always resist the Holy Spirit!" (Acts 7:51).[236]

---

[235] Calvinists object that if man is able so easily to reject God's desire that they be saved, then God must be something of a failure. How, they ask, can the sovereign God possibly be foiled, defeated, and disappointed by sinful man? The answer is as profound as it is simple: Because God is big enough and powerful enough to *allow* it! (Not to mention that he's also big enough and powerful enough to punish all those insisting on resisting. While he may certainly be disappointed, he will never be foiled or defeated.)

By contrast, when Calvinists insist that, despite predestination and election, God would "secretly desire" all men to be saved, they face an even greater problem. How possibly can God's absolute, predestining sovereignty remain intact in the face of man's "undesired" rebellion? (Indeed, how could God have such a burning secret desire, yet not be disappointed when his desire is foiled by man's depraved rebellion?)

[236] See also Luke 7:30, where the Pharisees "rejected God's purpose for themselves."

The question is: If it is the Holy Spirit who supposedly imposes God's grace irresistibly on the hearts of the elect, how could anyone "resist the Holy Spirit," as Stephen charged his accusers? The stock Calvinist answer, of course, is that *everyone* resists the Holy Spirit, because that's what totally depraved people do. It's only the elect whose resistance is overpowered by the grace-endowing Holy Spirit.[237]

Apart from this argumentation being based upon the false assumption of man's depravity, the important question is whether there is any scriptural support for the view that God's saving grace cannot successfully be resisted? In our search for clarity, let's take a look now at some of the key Calvinist proof-texts. Can any of them overcome the clear import of Galatians 5:19, in which the warning ("Do not put out the Spirit's fire") unquestionably was directed to the regenerate elect? Are we to believe, then, that the Spirit cannot be resisted...even after it supposedly has done its work so irresistibly?

Scrutinizing the Proof-texts

To begin with, if Calvinists themselves didn't go to such an extent to highlight the unique, *implementing* work of the Holy Spirit, in contrast to the *foreordaining* work of the Father and the *atoning* work of the Son, it would hardly bear mentioning. But the fact is that most of the passages cited in favor of the doctrine of irresistible grace refer to *God the Father* as being the implementer of that grace, not the Holy Spirit.

Beyond that minor detail, all too often there is flagrant abuse of context associated with many Calvinist proof-texts.[238] For example, we are pointed to the following passage as evidence of the notion of irresistible grace:

---

[237] At the very least, God's elect nation certainly had the ability to buck God's will. Merely consider Ezekiel 24:13: "Because I tried to cleanse you but you would not be cleansed from your impurity, you will not be clean again until my wrath against you has subsided."

[238] One of the curious features of the debate over Calvinism is how often *both* sides accuse the other of abusing the context of the passages under discussion. All I can say is that I do often get the feeling that Calvinists haven't been as circumspect as they claim in this regard, often ignoring even the verse either immediately preceding or following the one in question. (See, for example, Acts 2:39 and verse 38; Romans 10:20 and verse 21; Deuteronomy 30:6 and verses 2-5; 1 John 5:1 and verses 2-5; and Exodus 10:1 and verse 9:34.)

In view of this particular problem, I have been spurred to make an even greater personal effort not to be an offender myself. Even where I have not specifically referenced the context, I have tried to double-check every referenced passage with this problem in mind.

"The LORD your God will circumcise your hearts and the hearts of your descendants, so that you may love him with all your heart and with all your soul, and live" (Deuteronomy 30:6). Apparently, this circumcision of the heart is as irresistible as ordinary circumcision is to a newborn baby boy.

But when and under what circumstances does this spiritual "circumcision" take place? Simply from reading the immediately preceding verses, it's clear that the text assumes a crucial prerequisite: "*When you and your children return to the LORD your God and obey him* with all your heart and with all your soul according to everything I command you today, *then* the LORD your God will restore your fortunes and have compassion on you...." (Deuteronomy 30:2-3). From this text, what does it look like to you? Whose court is the ball in first?

Another favorite Calvinist text is Ezekiel's classic passage about God "giving a new heart" and "putting a new spirit in you." But read it for yourself in its full context.

> "*Therefore say to the house of Israel, 'This is what the Sovereign LORD says: It is not for your sake, O house of Israel, that I am going to do these things, but for the sake of my holy name, which you have profaned among the nations where you have gone. I will show the holiness of my great name, which has been profaned among the nations, the name you have profaned among them. Then the nations will know that I am the LORD, declares the Sovereign LORD, when I show myself holy through you before their eyes.*
>
> "*For I will take you out of the nations; I will gather you from all the countries and bring you back into your own land. I will sprinkle clean water on you, and you will be clean; I will cleanse you from all your impurities and from all your idols. I will give you a new heart and put a new spirit in you; I will remove from you your heart of stone and give you a heart of flesh. And I will put my Spirit in you and move you to follow my decrees and be careful to keep my laws. You will live in the land I gave your forefathers; you will be my people, and I will be your God'*" (Ezekiel 36:22-28).[239]

---

[239] See also Ezekiel 11:18-21; 18:31.

What do you think? Is this passage telling us that the Holy Spirit imparts grace irresistibly into the hearts and spirits of individuals unconditionally elected by the Father for salvation? Or, is Ezekiel talking here about the restoration of *national Israel*, and how, through the process of captivity and renewal, God is ridding her, root and branch, of her spirit of idolatry? (If you have any lingering doubts about that, go back and begin reading from verse 16. See also Ezekiel 37:1-14–that famous vision of the dry bones coming to life.) As always, it's context, context, context.

A third standard Calvinist proof-text is John 1:12-13: "Yet to all who received him, to those who believed in his name, he gave the right to become children of God–children born not of natural descent, nor of human decision or a husband's will, but born of God."

Are we not therefore *born of God*, Calvinists ask? Well, of course we are...and all the more so in contrast to human birth. It's no mystery that, first, we are born physically, and thereafter spiritually–which is to say, not simply "of man," but "of God."[240]

Yet, where does this even begin to imply that the faith of the elect results solely from a special outpouring of God's grace, overwhelming their otherwise depraved will? To the contrary, look again at the sequence: "*To those who believed*, he gave the right to become children."

Indeed, hear it again from the King James Version: "*As many as received him*, to them gave he power to become the sons of God." The power didn't come in order to *bring* faith (much less *force* it); the power was given *because of* faith! Nor is anyone given a special, exclusive "right" to have faith; rather, one's faith results in the quite marvelous right to claim the new status of being God's child![241]

---

[240] One wonders what influence the King James Version may have had on Calvinist thinking. Its rendering of the crucial clause ("Which were born, not of blood, nor of the will of the flesh, nor of the will of man, but of God") could easily be misconstrued as suggesting that spiritual conversion is not at all the will of man, but God's will alone. The NIV's rendering clarifies that the only contrast intended is between *spiritual birth* (which is "of God") and *physical birth* (which is "of man," whether by procreation generally, or specifically by a couple's decision to bring a child into the world, or even by a husband's overbearing will).

[241] When James says, "He chose to give us birth through the word of truth..." (James 1:18), he is merely highlighting one of the many good and perfect gifts that come down from the Father of lights. And how is that birth accomplished? Not through selective regeneration leading to the hearing of the word, but to the hearing of the word which–when believed–leads to regeneration.

Yet another proof-text is 1 John 5:1 where John writes: "Everyone who believes that Jesus is the Christ is born of God, and everyone who loves the father loves his child as well." Far from taking the natural sense of the text–that a person is born of God by faith, Calvinists insist that a person has faith *because* he is born of God. Having been born of God, we are told, one is brought irresistibly to faith.

While that interpretation is not outside the realm of plausibility, the problem is that such an interpretation is nullified by the context. Even in the ending clause of that single verse we see what John is actually getting at: our need to love all who are born of God since they are our spiritual siblings. John is not directly addressing the issue of *how* we are born, whether by irresistible regeneration leading to faith, or a freely-chosen faith leading to regeneration. Yet, if you had to choose between those two scenarios based on this text alone, the latter version would win hands-down.

Just look where John puts the emphasis in verses 4 and 5: "This is the victory that has overcome the world, even our faith. Who is it that over-comes the world? Only he who believes that Jesus is the Son of God." The emphasis here is not on our being born of God, less yet our being irresistibly regenerated. The clear emphasis is on faith and its power to transform our ethical habits from hatred to love, especially for our broth-ers and sisters in Christ. You mean faith acting apart from God? Of course, not! The power of faith is that it leads to our being born of God...making us his children...making us in his likeness...thereby making us more loving than we could ever possibly have been if merely acting on our own.

And finally, we are presented with Hebrews 12:2, which typically refers to "Jesus, the author and perfecter of our faith." Seizing on the word "author," Calvinist spin would have us believe that Jesus is the origin and source of our faith, which is to say that he is not only the object of our faith but also its irresistible cause. Without reiterating the conundrum cre-ated when so-called "faith" is wholly predetermined, inevitable, and irre-sistible, suffice it to say that the word "author" may not best capture the sense of the original word in its context.

As you will recall, Hebrews 11 is that great "roll call of the faithful," which recounts, individual by individual, the faith of the ancients. (By faith Abel...by faith Noah...by faith Abraham...by faith Moses...and so forth.) As the writer reminds us, these spiritual giants were trailblazers for our own faith...and steadfast faithfulness. Their perseverance through various trials is set before us as an example of our own need to persevere.

Yet who better exemplifies steadfast faithfulness than Jesus Christ, "who for the joy set before him endured the cross"? When it comes to any roll call of the faithful, Jesus himself heads the list. He is the Prime Example among all who have endured trials because of their faith. He is the Prince of Faith, the Captain of Steadfastness, and the Chief Pioneer blazing the trail ahead for the rest of us. Hence the appropriate (and linguistically accurate) rendering given in the RSV: "...let us run with perseverance the race that is set before us, looking to Jesus the *pioneer* and perfecter of our faith...."

As an author myself, I've always felt a special affinity with the traditional translation of this passage. And given the importance of having one's late-night musings thoroughly (even brutally!) edited, I often think of Jesus not just as "the author and finisher" of my faith, but as the author and *editor*. It is Jesus the Author who has written the story-line of faith on my heart, and Jesus the Editor who calls me to perfection. But it simply begs belief that anyone would attempt to use this passage in support of the doctrine of irresistible grace. Such a strained interpretation could only result from one's own surreptitious editing of what the Author of Life himself has revealed.

It's the Same Old Story

Unless we are to believe that God's way of implementing his grace radically changed with the coming of Christ, wouldn't we expect to find evidence of the Holy Spirit irresistibly opening the hearts of the righteous in the Old Testament as well as in the New? Whatever you believe about God's hardening of Pharaoh's heart, at most the "Pharaoh factor" could only support Calvinism's reprobation of the wicked. It's the irrepressible regeneration of the *righteous* we need to think about here.

What evidence is there, for example, that God himself tipped, hedged, fudged, or forced the choice between "life" and "death" when Moses set that well-known, decisive option before the Israelites?

> *"This day I call heaven and earth as witnesses against you that I have set before you life and death, blessings and curses. Now choose life, so that you and your children may live and that you may love the LORD your God, listen to his voice, and hold fast to him." (Deuteronomy 30:19-20)*

Is there anything in this passage (directed to *individuals* within God's elect nation) leading us to believe that the Holy Spirit directly or indirectly influenced their *individual* choices? YES? NO? (That most of those "elect" children of Israel chose "death" instead of "life" must surely speak volumes about whether the Holy Spirit was working irresistibly in their lives.)

And what instrumental role, if any, does it appear the Holy Spirit played in thrusting God's grace irresistibly upon individual wills when the Israelites were challenged by Joshua to choose between the false gods of both the Egyptians and the Amorites and the one true God of heaven?

> *"Choose for yourselves this day whom you will serve, whether the gods your forefathers served beyond the River, or the gods of the Amorites, in whose land you are living. But as for me and my household, we will serve the LORD." (Joshua 24:15)*

Is there any suggestion here that Joshua and his family had been prompted irresistibly by the Holy Spirit to serve the Lord? YES? NO? Indeed, why challenge the rest of the Israelites to choose *for themselves*, if–when all is said and done–it would be God's choice, not theirs?

Abortion advocates unquestionably have given the term a bad name, but in the debate regarding free will versus determinism, God is fanatically pro-choice. If there is anything that's irresistible, it is our having been created (irresistibly) with the unfettered free agency (and irresistible responsibility) to make moral and spiritual choices affecting our eternal destiny.

The problem is, it always has to be either our choice or God's. Not unlike abortion itself, if it is not the mother's free choice to abort her unborn baby, then the only alternative is that God himself is responsible for the abortion. Yet because that would never set well, Calvinists play God's sovereignty both ways, depending on which is more advantageous to the issue at hand. God is said to be the cause of every act, event, thought, and motive until it comes to anything that would be inconsistent with his holiness. Then, suddenly, it is the mother who alone is responsible for the death of her unborn child. It's a convenient explanation, but not a consistent one.

Nor is it consistent to say that God has predetermined the eternal destiny of each soul, but that we nevertheless retain free moral agency. Nor that God's grace works "effectually" or "irresistibly" through the Holy Spirit to bring us to faith, yet somehow that faith is freely ours, either to have or not have. These self-contradictory arguments are as self-serving as those presented by the pro-abortion forces–that if the mother *wants it to be a baby* then it *is a baby*, but if she *doesn't want it to be a baby* then *it's not a baby*. Whether in morals or in theology, you can't play it both ways just to suit the desired result.

Lessons From a Strong-Willed Prophet

If anyone could tell us about the interaction between divine determinism and human free will, it would be the reluctant prophet, Jonah. Lying there in the belly of the great fish, Jonah was learning more than he wanted to know about personal choices, free will, and God's grace. Of all people, Jonah knew what it meant to be pursued relentlessly by the Hound of Heaven.[242] Try as Jonah might to escape his mission, God had a pre-determined plan to save the idolatrous people of Nineveh–a plan in which Jonah was to play a crucial, providential role.

As we know, the story of Jonah doesn't end in the fish's belly, but in the grace imparted to the repentant Ninevites. That's *imparted*, not *imposed*. How could it be otherwise? "When God saw what they did and how they

---

[242] From Francis Thompson's poem by that name.

turned from their evil ways, he had compassion and did not bring upon them the destruction he had threatened" (Jonah 3:10). What do you think? Are *compassion* and *compulsion* natural soul mates?

Though it was God who had moved heaven and earth, a great fish, and one petulant prophet to give the Ninevites their opportunity to repent, the marvelous result is that the Great Mover himself was greatly moved! Not by anything he had done to force the issue, but by what he saw in one freely penitent heart after another.

Yet, the story could well have had a different ending. Not unlike us, the people of Nineveh had a choice. Along with us, they just as easily could have blown it. How do we know that? While still in the belly of the great fish, Jonah (through the inspiration of the Spirit) revealed the great truth that "those who cling to worthless idols *forfeit the grace that could be theirs*" (Jonah 2:8).

So is Calvinism right about "irresistible grace"? Not if you or I could have forfeited so easily the grace that otherwise would have been ours.

Determinism and Providence

From the account of Jonah and the Ninevites we also learn that there are crucial distinctions to be made between the two ideas of *determinism* and *providence*. Whereas free will and hard determinism are mutually contradictory notions, free will and divine providence are scripturally compatible....usually!

In the life of Jonah, interestingly, we have an unusual case of *incompatibility*. As we've seen, God takes this stubborn-as-a-mule prophet, very much with a mind of his own, and uses him as a reluctant instrument in reaching out to a city full of idolaters. Not unlike my friend and her "choice" of schools, God told Jonah he could go to Nineveh, or to Nineveh, or to Nineveh! Free will in this instance? Not exactly.

In the case of Pharaoh, there is yet more to consider. When God "hardened Pharaoh's heart" in order to set Israel free from Egyptian bondage, some might say that God's overarching, providential determinism may have necessitated a partial or temporary loss of Pharaoh's free will. Is that really so?

We're familiar, of course, with Exodus 10:1, which tells us: "Then the LORD said to Moses, 'Go to Pharaoh, for *I have hardened his heart* and the hearts of his officials....'"[243] But in the immediately preceding verse (9:34), we read: "When Pharaoh saw that the rain and hail and thunder had stopped, *he sinned again: He and his officials hardened their hearts.*"

Are we to believe that God directly caused Pharaoh *to sin?* Or might there be some way of explaining how God providentially "hardened Pharaoh's heart" while Pharaoh had independently (and sinfully) hardened his own heart?[244] Don't simply take my word for it. Surprise of surprises is this commentary by none other than our resident Calvinist, Loraine Boettner:

> *The hearts of the wicked are, of course, never hardened by the direct influence of God—He simply permits some men to follow out the evil impulses which are already in their hearts, so that, as a result of their own choices, they become more and more calloused and obstinate. And while it is said, for instance, that God hardened the heart of Pharaoh, it is also said that Pharaoh hardened his own heart (Ex. 8:15; 8:32; 9:34). One description is given from the divine view-point, the other is given from the human view-point....The inspired writer in graphic language simply says that God does it; but never are we to understand that God is the immediate and efficient cause.*[245]

Refreshingly candid, this Calvinist commentary is precisely what non-Calvinists have been saying all along about that whole collection of passages which talk about God's hardening and opening of hearts; or putting evil into hearts; or being a stumbling stone; or directing the wicked to God's own ends; or sending delusions; or hiding the truth; or blinding eyes and closing ears.[246]

---

[243] Which obviously is the basis for Paul's reference to Pharaoh in Romans 9.

[244] Compare 2 Thessalonians 2:9-14. God sends a powerful delusion so that men will believe the lies to which they have made themselves vulnerable because they have set their course to reject truth. Note also that, from the beginning, it was always God's plan to save the lost "through the sanctifying work of the Spirit and through belief in the truth." If that sounds vaguely Calvinistic, it couldn't be further from salvation by unconditional election. The text could hardly be clearer: "They perish because they refused to love the truth *and so be saved.*

[245] Boettner, 112

[246] John 12:39-40; Acts 16:14; Revelation 17:17; 1 Peter 2:8; Proverbs 16:4; 2 Thessalonians 2:11; Matthew 11:25; Isaiah 6:9-10; Matthew 13:10-15; Mark 4:12; Luke 8:10; John 12:40; Acts 28:26-27; Romans 11:7-10.

Just when we think God is the bad guy, it turns out that *we ourselves* are the bad guys. Stop too soon in Romans, and all we read is: "Since they did not think it worthwhile to retain the knowledge of God, he gave them over to a depraved mind, to do what ought not to be done" (Romans 1:21-28). Keep reading and we see it even more clearly: "But because of your stubbornness and your unrepentant heart, you are storing up wrath against yourself for the day of God's wrath, when his righteous judgment will be revealed" (Romans 2:5).

The Wonder of God's Providential Working

Throughout the Scriptures, man's defiant intentions and God's providential intentions often walk hand in hand. One instance in particular is a classic example (cited even by Calvinists in aid of their belief that free will is compatible with unconditional election). Remember when Jacob died and Joseph's brothers cowered in fear before him, thinking Joseph would finally take revenge for their having sold him into bondage? Joseph must surely have surprised them when he said, "You intended to harm me, but God intended it for good to accomplish what is now being done, the saving of many lives" (Genesis 50:20).[247]

Do you not find it fascinating that Jesus could have spoken those very words to Judas, as well as to Pilate, Annas and Caiaphas, and the entire Jewish mob demanding Jesus' crucifixion? In fact, those very players figure into the words of Peter and John, who prayed: "Indeed Herod and Pontius Pilate met together with the Gentiles and the people of Israel in this city to conspire against your holy servant Jesus, whom you anointed. They did what your power and will had decided beforehand should happen" (Acts 4:27-28). Their wicked conspiracy had played perfectly into God's own divine conspiracy.[248]

We see the same mix of divine providence and individual free will when Jesus says of Judas: "The Son of Man will go as it has been decreed, but woe to that man who betrays him" (Luke 22:22). Referencing this very

---

[247] See also 1 Samuel 2:25; 2 Samuel 17:14; 1 Kings 12:11,15; Ezra 6:22; 7:6; Proverbs 16:9; 19:21; Isaiah 10:5-15; 44:28.

[248] Compare also Acts 2:23.

verse, even J. I. Packer acknowledges: "God's sovereignty and man's responsibility are taught us side by side in the same Bible; sometimes, indeed, in the same text."[249]

However it happens, the unmistakable message of these intriguing passages is that God need not overpower the will of those whom he uses providentially to advance his own eternal purposes. Even where their intent is to do great evil, God has a way of using that intent in the furtherance of his own will.[250]

Providence is all about God making lemonade out of lemons. Sometimes he does the squeezing. Most of the time, the "lemons" do it themselves.

That God is able to honor man's free moral agency while simultaneously insuring a predicted—indeed *promised*—outcome is the entrancing story of God's providence.[251] The way in which God directs fallible actors on stage to perform an infallible script of his own writing is wonderfully witnessed in the lives of all who have been blessed to be God's instruments down through the centuries.

By stark contrast with God's behind-the-scenes providence, however, when God pursues lost souls for salvation (as with the people of Nineveh), the most we see him doing is wielding the proverbial carrot and stick. Though, to be sure, there are threats of punishment for disobedience as well as promises of reward for obedience, what God asks of us is hardly in the same category as the masked bandit we spoke of earlier. God's demands are neither harsh, unfair, nor unattainable.

When you think about it, a system of rewards and punishments is precisely what loving parents employ in the moral formation of a wilful child. And as any parent can tell you, the child still has a mind of his own...which is the very problem!

By contrast, Calvinism's "irresistible grace" is a giant leap from carrot and stick. For the non-elect, it's only and always the stick. For the elect (at

---

[249] J. I. Packer, 22. (Illustrating this same point, see also Genesis 20:6.)

[250] See, for example: Judges 9:23; 1 Samuel 16:14; 2 Samuel 12:11; 1 Kings 12:15; 22:20-23; 2 Kings 22:20; 1 Chronicles 5:22; Isaiah 45:7; Amos 3:6.

[251] When Calvinists make a similar argument in trying to reconcile free will with predestination, there is the inherent contradiction of God's controlling will versus man's own will. By contrast, providence works *alongside* man's inherent free will, not irresistibly or even efficaciously *against* it.

least ultimately), it's only and always the carrot. Which in each instance is determinism. Hard, unrelenting, involuntary, unchangeable, irresistible, determinism. Determinism of a type which leaves no room whatsoever for anything approaching "freedom of will" or "free moral agency."

No one understood this unrelenting dichotomy more clearly than Martin Luther who insisted that "God knows nothing contingently, but that he foresees, purposes, and does all things according to His immutable, eternal and infallible will. *This thunderbolt throws free will flat and utterly dashes it to pieces.*"[252]

What, possibly, are his fellow Calvinists thinking to suggest, on one hand, that there is a compatibility between the hard determinism of sovereign election and genuine freedom of will whereby a person has both free choice and commensurate responsibility regarding his own eternal destiny? Or to insist just the opposite (that any seeming freedom of will which man might possess is always and inevitably overpowered by God's own sovereign will)—when the argument demands it?[253]

---

[252] Luther, *Bondage of the Will*, [615], 92

[253] Contrary to his own logic, above, Luther himself hedges in at least two important aspects, conceding first of all that, "though I should grant that free will by its endeavors can advance in some direction, namely, unto good works, or unto the righteousness of the civil or moral law, it does yet not advance towards God's righteousness...." [Luther, *Bondage of the Will*, [767], 117] While it is true that man's will on its own could not begin to approach God's righteousness (the fundamental error of Pelagianism), nevertheless the undifferentiated entity of the will itself cannot be so easily bisected, as if free in one area yet not free in another. To play on a familiar phrase, free will is *one notion*, indivisible, with liberty for all.

Second, Luther confuses the nature and functioning of the human will with the ultimate results which man's will might or might not achieve. We all agree that human will is not free to override divine will, but that does not preclude the obvious (as Luther is forced to acknowledge): that man freely exercises human will in more temporal matters. Says Luther, "we may still use [the term] in good faith denoting free will in respect not of what is above him, but of what is below him. This is to say, man should know in regard to his goods and possessions the right to use them, to do or to leave undone, according to his free will." [Luther, *Bondage of the Will*, [638], 98]

Even this limited view of free will becomes problematic, as best seen in the rich young ruler (Matthew 19:16-22) who, with regard to selling his goods and giving them to the poor, exercised his free will in rebellion against divine will. Because how one exercises the will regarding the temporal often has eternal consequences, it cannot be said that we have free will in one arena, but not in another.

What Would Jesus Say About Irresistible Grace?

Have you ever wondered what Jesus might say about Calvinism's doctrine of irresistible grace? I suggest we get a pretty good idea simply from paying careful attention to one of his most well-known parables: that of the sower. Unlike most other parables, Jesus' explanation of this particular parable is recorded for us:

> *Listen then to what the parable of the sower means: When anyone hears the message about the kingdom and does not understand it, the evil one comes and snatches away what was sown in his heart. This is the seed sown along the path. The one who received the seed that fell on rocky places is the man who hears the word and at once receives it with joy. But since he has no root, he lasts only a short time. When trouble or persecution comes because of the word, he quickly falls away. The one who received the seed that fell among the thorns is the man who hears the word, but the worries of this life and the deceitfulness of wealth choke it, making it unfruitful. But the one who received the seed that fell on good soil is the man who hears the word and understands it. He produces a crop, yielding a hundred, sixty or thirty times what was sown" (Matthew 13:18-23).*

Is there in this passage any hint, mention, suggestion, or inference about irresistible grace? YES? NO? Given such a perfect "teachable moment," surely an omission of this magnitude is like Sherlock Holmes' dog that didn't bark. What better time for Jesus to have mentioned the role of the Holy Spirit in irresistibly regenerating the will of "the one who received the seed that fell on good soil"? Yet, there's not a whisper of such a notion.

Instead, what we see is that each of the four types of hearers identified in the parable has two simple choices: 1) whether to listen closely enough to understand, and 2) whether or not to accept the good news. In each instance, it's entirely up to them.[254]

As for the listening part, here we have yet another super opportunity for Jesus to instruct us about irresistible grace. But does he? Again, no.

---

[254] Actually, there are three choices to be made, the third and last being whether to remain faithful to the Kingdom or to fall away after having "received it with joy." Of course, that too runs counter to Calvinism and its doctrine of perseverance, as we shall see in the next chapter.

Instead, he points to the fulfillment of Isaiah's prophecy about those who will hear the gospel without bothering to really listen:

> *In them is fulfilled the prophecy of Isaiah:*
>   *"You will be ever hearing but never understanding;*
>   *you will be ever seeing but never perceiving.*
> *For this people's heart has become calloused;*
>   *they hardly hear with their ears,*
>   *and they have closed their eyes.*
> *Otherwise they might see with their eyes,*
>   *hear with their ears,*
>   *understand with their hearts*
> *and turn, and I would heal them." (Matthew 13:14-15)*[255]

Note, crucially, that God is not the cause of their calloused (hardened) hearts and closed eyes.[256] It is *they* who have closed their ears and eyes.[257] Why? For starters, what Jesus was teaching them didn't mesh with (as it were) what their parents and Sunday School teachers had taught them, or what they were told by their preacher or their college professor. Sometimes it's just plain hard to listen when something runs so counter to what we've always believed....

For many who had closed their eyes and ears, it was a problem of worldly seduction. As Paul puts it: "The god of this age has blinded the minds of unbelievers, so that they cannot see the light of the gospel...." (2

---

[255] Calvinists would point us to the lead-in to this passage (Matthew 13:10-12): "The disciples came to him and asked, 'Why do you speak to the people in parables?' He replied, 'The knowledge of the secrets of the kingdom of heaven has been given to you, but not to them. Whoever has will be given more, and he will have an abundance. Whoever does not have, even what he has will be taken from him. This is why I speak to them in parables." Is there anything in this passage to suggest that it was the elect generally, rather than the apostles specifically, to whom secret knowledge of the kingdom of heaven had been given? Do the elect today have *secret* knowledge that reprobates don't have equal access to through the Scriptures?

[256] Compare what Jesus "quoted" from Isaiah with the words actually found in Isaiah 6:9–"*Make* the heart of this people calloused; *make* their ears dull and close their eyes." This, of course, was with reference to national Israel, who would reject Isaiah's warnings. The beauty of Christ is that, both literally and spiritually, Jesus opened the eyes of the blind and the ears of the deaf. Anyone who remains spiritually blind and deaf in the presence of the good news of Jesus, has only himself to blame.

[257] In Psalm 95:7-10 and Proverbs 28:14, note the assumption that we can harden our own hearts.

Corinthians 4:4). The "god of this age" is the same Satanic, worldly philosophy of every age that has hardened man's heart to truth, purity, and virtue. This world's standards (or the lack of them) has hardened us and seared our consciences.

We see a good example of this hardening in an unlikely passage (Matthew 19:7-8). "Why then," they asked, 'did Moses command that a man give his wife a certificate of divorce and send her away?" Jesus replied, "Moses permitted you to divorce your wives because *your hearts were hard*. But it was not this way from the beginning."

Nor from the beginning has it been God's way to selectively harden the hearts of some while softening the hearts of others. As Origen first suggested, the same heat from the sun that melts wax also hardens mud.[258] Whereas an unwilling heart bakes hard like clay at the preaching of the gospel, the willing heart is like melting wax in the presence of God's truth. For those with an open heart and mind, nothing more is needed apart from the radiating warmth of the Son.

"But," you ask, "doesn't this beg the question of whether the Holy Spirit has regenerated the heart and the mind so as to make them willing?" If only Jesus had said that. Or even implied it. Instead, all we hear from his lips are the words of Isaiah: "Were their hearts not so hard, they would turn and I would heal them." It's certainly a far cry from what he might have said: "Since I was the one to irresistibly harden their hearts in the first place, it is left to me to irresistibly soften the ones I choose." Or even: "Since their hearts were hardened from their fallen state of depravity, it takes a divine act of regeneration so as to free their hearts to believe."[259]

Listening to Jesus, one searches in vain to find even the tiniest mention of irresistible grace. To the contrary, what we find is this:

---

[258] Origen, *On First Things*.

[259] See Mark 6:51-52 where Jesus' own disciples "had not understood about the loaves," because "their hearts were hardened." Are we to believe that this "hardening" of those who were already regenerate would require a *second* regeneration? Perhaps through this verse more than any other we can see how the phrase "hardened hearts" need not have any connotation of total depravity or moral inability. In fact, it need have nothing to do at all with that which is sinful. As here, it can simply refer to one's lack of full appreciation for what might yet come to be understood with progressive teaching.

"I tell you, whoever acknowledges me before men, the Son of Man will also acknowledge him before the angels of God. But he who disowns me before men will be disowned before the angels of God." (Luke 12:8-9)

It's a choice. A free choice.

"Come to me, all you who are weary and burdened, and I will give you rest. Take my yoke upon you and learn from me, for I am gentle and humble in heart, and you will find rest for your souls." (Matthew 11:28-29)

It's a free choice given to all.

"For my Father's will is that everyone who looks to the Son and believes in him shall have eternal life...." (John 6:40)

It's a free choice consistent with God's own will.

The Sublime Beauty of Laying Down One's Own Will

Far from Scripture teaching that your will and mine are irresistibly overridden by the Holy Spirit, at least two of the most familiar passages in all of Scripture implore us to lay down our wills voluntarily.

In the familiar "Lord's prayer," we find the timeless entreaty of humble believers down through the centuries: "Our Father in heaven, hallowed be your name, your kingdom come, *your will be done* on earth as it is in heaven" (Matthew 6:9-10). In one sense, obviously, God's will is going to be done "on earth as in heaven" whether or not we invoke that result in our prayers. Even so, our fervent petitions toward that end acknowledge both to God and to ourselves that we are freely and voluntarily submitting our will to his.[260]

For Jesus himself, certainly, laying down his will was no academic exercise. In the agony of the garden, our incarnate Savior humbly and freely

---

[260] This passage, along with the many others presented in this chapter, provides the basis for my response to the objection that "free will" is a philosophical notion, not a biblical term. While it may not be a biblical term, strictly speaking (apart from "freewill offering"), it is certainly a biblical concept.

submitted his own will to the will of his Father, with those familiar words: "not as I will, but as you will" (Matthew 26:39).

It is, then, in the laying down of our wills to God that we come to share in the mind of Christ. Whereas "irresistible grace" is an oxymoron of the highest order, "petitioned Lordship" reflects a degree of humility and dependence of the highest order. Given our usual obstinance and slowness of heart, could there possibly be anything more glorifying to God than the extraordinarily courageous act of yielding our own proud will to our Creator's infinitely higher will?

And so we sing with aspiration:

> *My stubborn will at last hath yielded;*
> *I would be Thine and Thine alone;*
> *And this the prayer my lips are bringing,*
> *"Lord, let in me Thy will be done.*
>
> *Sweet will of God, still fold me closer,*
> *Till I am wholly lost in thee.*[261]

"Wholly lost in thee"? Suddenly, I'm beginning to wonder if maybe I need to re-think whether free will and determinism can co-exist simultaneously in the human soul.

While I couldn't disagree more with the New Age psychobabble vainly seeking to harmonize "me-generation" self-will with the hard determinism of karmic fate, maybe New Agers are onto something after all about reincarnating souls eventually returning to the Oneness of all there is.

No, no, not that we become God, as New Agers believe! But just think. What does it mean that I should give my will so completely over to God's that I am "wholly lost in thee"? In the resulting marriage of wills, do not "the two become one"?

And talk about a reincarnation! "It is no longer I that live, but Christ living in me"![262] In a way New Agers could never hope to dream, God's

---

[261] "Sweet Will Of God," Mrs. C. H. Morris
[262] Galatians 2:20, ASV

divine determinism makes itself at home as an invited guest in the free will of a humble heart.

As for Calvinism's Herculean attempt to reconcile "irresistible grace" and man's free will, I remain unconvinced. In fact, had "irresistible grace" not been an obvious and necessary implication of unconditional election, it's unlikely anyone ever would have thought it up. Certainly, no amount of hopeful proof-texting gives any credibility to the notion that the Holy Spirit forces himself upon the unwilling. In the Scriptures, only consensual touching is allowed.

But still...I have to confess that I'm more and more irresistibly drawn to the whole idea of "irresistible grace." Should anyone be amazed that John Newton's "Amazing Grace" is one of the most beloved hymns ever written? When I stare aghast at my tarnished, sin-stained soul, together with Newton I can only stand amazed at how God could forgive "a wretch like me."

Try if you can to wrap your mind around it! Grace that calls. Grace that saves. Grace that justifies. Grace that blesses. Grace that builds up.[263] How can all that grace be anything but genuinely and truly, marvelously and wonderfully, *irresistible!*

What, short of actual compulsion, could be more compelling? What, short of being overpowered irresistibly, is more irresistibly overpowering?

As a Calvinist oxymoron, "irresistible grace" has no place in the doctrine of salvation. As a biblical paradox, "irresistible grace" is the very heart of salvation.

"...like slaves of Christ, doing the will of God from your heart."

Ephesians 6:6

---

[263] 2 Timothy 1:9; Acts 15:11; Eph 2:7-8; Titus 2:11; Romans 3:24; Titus 3:7; John 1:16; Acts 20:32.

Chapter Summary

- When comparing Calvinism with Hinduism and Buddhism, one of the surprising parallels is between karma and irresistible grace, both of which result in a hard determinism that is both irreversible and unalterable.

- Yet one of the ironies is that each of these belief systems calls for lives of personal responsibility, as if each person has the ability to alter one's predetermined fate.

- It is impossible to reconcile hard determinism and genuine free will. Either God's sovereign will must be truly and totally irresistible, or man must of necessity have some degree of responsibility regarding his eternal destiny.

- What *can* be reconciled is God's immutable, eternal plan of salvation which permits each person to freely choose or reject the gospel.

- If the opening or closing of hearts by the Holy Spirit were necessary to enable the elect to respond in faith to the preaching of the gospel, it is strange indeed that Jesus' parable of the sower makes no mention of it whatsoever.

- While Calvinism's version of irresistible grace could not be more unbiblical, the very thought of God's woefully-undeserved and magnanimous grace is truly irresistible!

Reality Check: If the elect were arbitrarily chosen for salvation before time began, then God's grace is not so much irresistible as immaterial. "Saving grace" has little meaning when one is never really and truly lost to begin with.

Chapter 10

Preservation and Perseverance: Two Sides, Same Coin

I will be an infidel at once when I can believe
that a saint of God can ever fall finally.
If God hath loved me once, then He will love me forever.

–Charles H. Spurgeon

The visual images and emotions of September 11, 2001, are forever etched in our memories. We'll never forget where we were, nor the nightmarish sequence of those surreal events. From the moment American Airlines Flight 11 out of Boston crashed into the north tower of the World Trade Center at 8:45 a.m., we sat transfixed, witnessing the carnage. At 9:03 we watched in horror as United Airlines Flight 175 from Boston unexpectedly came screaming into view and crashed into the south tower.

Then came the unimaginable collapse, first of the south tower, at 10:05, and then the north tower at 10:28. In the meantime, at 9:43, American Airlines Flight 77 had crashed into the Pentagon, leading to a partial collapse at 10:10. At that same minute, United Airlines Flight 93 crashed in Somerset County, Pennsylvania, despite the never-to-be-forgotten heroism of its brave passengers who bequeathed to the rest of us the courageous challenge: "Let's roll."

With the smoke still rising over Manhattan, America was forced to come to grips with a new reality. Our world as we knew it had changed forever. In all of America's wars combined, nothing approached what a handful of terrorists achieved in only two horrific hours: robbing America of its deep-seated sense of national security.

In the immediate aftermath of 9-11, the White House rushed to establish a new office of Homeland Security, given the responsibility to restore our emotional sense of security, both nationally and personally. Soon, we were caught up in a psychological "push-pull." Even while "heightened vigilance" and "extreme caution" became the intoned watchwords on the six o'clock news, we were being urged to "get on with life as normal."

The trouble was, life *wasn't* normal. With great prescience, the terrorists had chosen to target the World Trade Center, an icon of America's economic, financial, and monetary success. I suspect even the terrorists themselves scarcely could have imagined what a broad-sweeping impact their dastardly mission would have upon the lives of millions of ordinary citizens whose financial security suddenly collapsed alongside the fallen Twin Towers. Whole lifetimes of savings and pension schemes shrank overnight, leaving retirement plans in tatters. Financial security? Not anymore.

For passengers on airlines, the nerve-wracking process of checking in and boarding became, not just frustrating, but unsettling. Could you trust the system to prevent hijackers getting on board? And could that sinister-looking guy seated across the aisle possibly be a terrorist? If you, yourself, walked up toward the front of the plane would it attract the nervous attention of fellow passengers...or, worse yet, some undercover, trigger-happy sky marshal? From 9-11 onwards, any thoughts of personal security had to be tempered by unfamiliar paranoia.

If there is anything everybody wants, it's a sense of security. National security. Financial security. Home security. Personal security. That the cataclysmic events of September 11th have served to highlight this need for Americans at the beginning of the 21st century begs little proof. Yet the primal human need for security is as fundamental as breathing. It begins in the womb, continues in the crib, demands a security blanket for the two-year-old, and extends to marriages, families, jobs, and retirement.

Of all the securities important to the human race, of course, none is more crucial than eternal security. No generation has been unconcerned about it; and, no matter how misguidedly, every generation has sought in some way to assure it. If you could bottle it, you could sell it. If you could guarantee it, you'd have no end of takers.

Little wonder that, in the wake of September 11th, Bibles were flying off the shelf and church attendance skyrocketed. When, all around you, one assumed safety net after another has been torn to shreds, where do you turn for true and lasting security?

It's hardly surprising, then, that the final petal in Calvinism's *TULIP* has always been so reassuring. You can call it "perseverance of the saints" if you wish, or "preservation of the saints," or even "once saved, always saved." At base and at core, what it's all about is eternal security, *guaranteed*!

No Question About the Guarantee

If there is anything on which we all can agree, it is the sense of security God's people can have in their salvation. Founded on the assurances of the One who cannot lie, the Christian's personal assurance need not be shaken by doubt. May I share with you just a few of the great passages which proclaim God's faithful promises to his saints?

> *Who shall separate us from the love of Christ? Shall trouble or hardship or persecution or famine or nakedness or danger or sword? As it is written: "For your sake we face death all day long; we are considered as sheep to be slaughtered." No, in all these things we are more than conquerors through him who loved us. For I am convinced that neither death nor life, neither angels nor demons, neither the present nor the future, nor any powers, neither height nor depth, nor anything else in all creation, will be able to separate us from the love of God that is in Christ Jesus our Lord. (Romans 8:35-39)*

May God himself, the God of peace, sanctify you through and through. May your whole spirit, soul and body be kept blameless at the coming of our Lord Jesus Christ. The one who calls you is faithful and he will do it. (1 Thessalonians 5:23-24)

And you also were included in Christ when you heard the word of truth, the gospel of your salvation. Having believed, you were marked in him with a seal, the promised Holy Spirit, who is a deposit guaranteeing our inheritance until the redemption of those who are God's possession—to the praise of his glory. (Ephesians 1:13-14)[264]

For no matter how many promises God has made, they are "Yes" in Christ. Now it is God who makes both us and you stand firm in Christ. He anointed us, set his seal of ownership on us, and put his Spirit in our hearts as a deposit, guaranteeing what is to come. (2 Corinthians 1:20-22)

Praise be to the God and Father of our Lord Jesus Christ! In his great mercy he has given us new birth into a living hope through the resurrection of Jesus Christ from the dead, and into an inheritance that can never perish, spoil or fade—kept in heaven for you, who through faith are shielded by God's power until the coming of the salvation that is ready to be revealed in the last time. (1 Peter 1:3-5)

I know whom I have believed, and am convinced that he is able to guard what I have entrusted to him for that day. (2 Timothy 1:12)

Can anyone doubt that, not unlike a trustworthy banker, God keeps our eternal salvation in the safety of a locked-tight security deposit box? But don't forget who holds the second key....

Our Part of the Covenant

Perhaps you've seen the bumper sticker: "Feeling distant from God? Who moved?" As the passages above assure us, God himself is faithful.

---

[264] To the same effect, see Ephesians 4:30.

Calvinists believe that; Arminians believe that; and all the rest of us believe that. The only question is, Are *we* faithful?

Even regarding that question, there seems to be agreement on all fronts that we are *not* faithful–at least not completely. Where we divide is over the separate question of whether a saint can ever be so unfaithful to God as to lose his promised salvation. (Or, the Calvinist question-within-a-question: Was such a person ever really a saint to begin with?)

By now, you'll not be surprised when I tell you I believe the Bible teaches that those who once were saved by grace can so renounce that very grace as to relinquish it. No, I'm not talking about living moment-by-moment in the fear that committing even a single sin will forfeit our eternal inheritance. Though I do know people who seem to be haunted by such insecurity, I have to say I don't know many non-Calvinists who feel any less secure about their salvation than Calvinists.

We, too, sing:

> My hope is built on nothing less
> than Jesus' blood and righteousness.[265]

And:

> We have an anchor that keeps the soul
> Steadfast and sure while the billows roll;
> Fastened to the rock that cannot move,
> Grounded firm and deep in the Savior's love.[266]

Despite those assurances, no one doubts that steadfast perseverance is a mandatory requirement imposed upon Christ's disciples. It's the flip-side of God's faithful preservation of the saints through his irrevocable promises. Scripture could not be clearer: It is possible for those who have tasted of salvation, having been justified and sanctified through obedient faith, to turn their backs on God so completely as to lose their promised inheritance.

I'm speaking here of "prodigal sons" who never come home to the happy ending we read about in the familiar story. Of "sows" who return

---

[265] Edward Mote, "My Hope Is Built On Nothing Less"
[266] Priscilla J. Owens, "We Have An Anchor"

permanently to the muck and mire of a life of sin from which they once were washed. Of believers (even teachers) who once communed with us as brothers, but have denied their Christ and now preach a godless message. Of those whose hearts "received the Word with joy" (as in the parable of the sower), but then became hardened and choked by the thorns of this world's vain charms.[267]

Support From Surprising Quarters

If you pretty much expected to hear me say all of that, take a careful look at the following three paragraphs, after which I want to ask you a question.

Whereas we previously emphasized the *preservation* of the saints, we must also emphasize the *perseverance* of the saints in faith and holiness. Too many people have been led to think that if they have ever made a profession of faith, or ever prayed a "sinner's prayer," or were baptized and joined a church, they can rely on their having been "once saved and always saved." Insufficient emphasis is given to God's requirement that *we must persevere to the end* in a life that seeks after holiness.

I am convinced that there will be many who think that heaven is certain, but will realize too late that their sense of security in Christ was actually a false hope. While they acknowledged Christ as their Savior, their lives did not reflect a genuine relationship with him, and consequently they were still dead in their sins. There was no perseverance, no running of the race to the end, only a mere profession made in a moment but quickly forgotten.

God preserves us, beyond any doubt. Yet we have a responsibility to persevere in the faith to the end (striving after holiness), and if we do not hold out, we have no basis for assurance that God is preserving us.

What do you think? Do you agree? YES/NO

I wonder if you might be surprised by who *does* agree? As it happens, the words in the preceding three paragraphs (including "striving after holiness") are taken directly (with the exception of one "I am" instead of "we are") from the classic Calvinist defense manual: *The Five Points of Calvinism,*

---

[267] 2 Peter 2:22; Jude 8-13; 2 Peter 2:1-22; Matthew 13:3-9

2nd Edition, by David Steele, Curtis Thomas, and Lance Quinn, with a Foreword by Roger Nicole and an Afterword by John MacArthur Jr.[268]

In fact, the authors go even further to suggest that "One could almost speak of the six points of Calvinism, the *fifth* point being the *preservation* of the saints and the *sixth* point being the *perseverance* of the saints. The Bible repeatedly emphasizes both sides of this wonderful doctrine."[269]

What can I say but amen! This concession by staunch Calvinists is as refreshing as it is remarkable. In fairness, the authors do maintain the traditional Calvinist position that those who fall from grace were never in grace to begin with. But that classic argument doesn't sit at all comfortably with this more personally-responsible face of Calvinism–not to mention the very scriptures they cite in support of their newfound concern. (And that's literally *pages* of Scripture–including, uncharacteristically for Calvinists, much of Hebrews.)

A Truth Beyond Paradox

As part of their attempt to present a proper balance between *perseverance* and *preservation*, the "Five Points" authors place these two concepts in a category which they describe as "antinomy." Listen in for a moment on their discussion:

This is one of those doctrines that we classify as an *antinomy* (containing two teachings which appear contradictory to the human mind, but which in God's mind are not in tension). Other examples of antinomies are God's sovereignty in salvation and yet man's responsibility to respond in faith; the fact that God is three, yet one; and the truth that Christ was fully God, but also fully human. Our minds are limited, and to us these truths are irreconcilable, but to God there is no problem. Both are true, though we cannot fathom how that can be.[270]

---

[268] Steele, Thomas, and Quinn, *The Five Points of Calvinism*, 2d Edition (Phillipsburg, NJ, P & R Publishing, 2004), 148-149

[269] Ibid.

[270] Ibid., at 149

In passing, I cannot help but note how far Calvinists have come even to talk in terms of "man's responsibility to respond in faith." Though the language of human responsibility can be found among Calvinists (and even argued to be true), man's having anything at all to do with his own salvation certainly isn't in line with Calvinism's fundamental assumptions to the contrary. (Whatever happened to all the castigation of synergism and insistence on monergism?)

Yet I suggest that neither God's sovereignty versus man's responsibility nor God's *preservation* versus man's *perseverance* fits neatly in the category of either antinomy or paradox. Unlike the mind-boggling nature of the divine "Word made flesh," and the inexplicable nature of the Godhead, there is nothing all that mysterious or difficult about a sovereign God deciding to create man with the responsibility of freely choosing or rejecting faith. (Cannot God do *as he pleases*? Is he limited to only one model of creation?[271]) Perceived difficulty arises only when Calvinism insists on a view of God's sovereignty that automatically excludes any genuinely free decision regarding faith.

Nor is there any truly insoluble conflict between God's *preservation* and man's *perseverance* which might require our resort to antinomy or paradox for lack of a clearer explanation. The resolution is as clear and simple as everyday life.

Suppose, for example, you decide to splash out and buy a ticket to the best seat in the house for a popular Broadway production. There, in bold letters on your ticket, are the words: "Admit One to the Royal Box."

What do you think is going to happen when you show up at the theater and present your ticket? Do you think the usher is going to show you to the cheap seats in the nose-bleed section up top; or perhaps deny you admission altogether? No way! Follow where she leads, and you'll soon be the envy of everyone in the theater. Why? Because your ticket is a good-as-gold, solid-as-a-rock promise from the theater. Unlike a lottery ticket conditioned on having the winning number, this ticket absolutely guarantees you a seat. A reserved seat. The *best* reserved seat in town.

---

[271] As Boettner reminds us (Ibid., p 32), "He could Himself work marvelously on the heart of every person so that no one would be lost." So if universalism was as much an option as salvation by unconditional election, why not the third option of salvation by faith freely chosen? Whatever happened to God's absolute sovereignty?

Suppose, however, that on your way to the theater you suddenly decide you don't want to see the play after all. It seems that a movie marquee has caught your eye. Quick as a flash, you've parked your car, bought a ticket for the seven o'clock showing, and within minutes you're munching on popcorn while watching the previews of coming attractions. You never get to the Broadway production. In fact, as you're waiting for the main feature to appear on the screen, you fumble in your pocket, pull out the ticket to the play, and idly rip it to shreds.

Now, what do you think? Will you still get to sit in the royal box that night? Of course, not. Why? Because the theater reneged? Not a chance. From their standpoint, you had a reserved (*preserved*) seat. Let's face it, it was you who blew it.

So why talk about a paradox here...or an "antinomy"? That one side is unalterably committed to a covenant which the other side fails to honor is not a huge mystery. It happens every day. Spiritually speaking, as long as one remains true to Christ, then all the benefits which attach to being in Christ–including one's eternal security–are good-as-gold and solid-as-a rock. (Merely consider the present promise of eternal life found repeatedly in passages such as John 4:14; 5:24; 6:47, 51; Philippians 1:6; 1 John 5:11, 13.) The one and only condition is that we not whimsically, angrily, or intellectually tear to shreds the present relationship we have in Christ.

Indeed, God has already gifted us with every possible means of holding on to our preserved place in heaven. Just in case we find ourselves being attracted by the world's seductive marquees, God provides us with the direct avenue of prayer, with scriptural warnings and inspiration, with the fellowship of other believers, and even with the discipline of the church, if necessary, to save our spirits for the day of the Lord.[272]

More amazing still, he has made us the temples in which his Holy Spirit dwells.[273] Was this not the gift promised by Peter and the apostles on the day of Pentecost to those who were willing to repent and be immersed?[274] Was this not the same "Holy Spirit, whom God has given to those who

---

[272] 1 Corinthians 5:1-5
[273] 1 Corinthians 6:19
[274] Acts 2:38

obey him" (Acts 5:32)? Why is the Holy Spirit within us, if not to nudge, warn, and renew?

But this merely brings us back to the crucial, ongoing question of whether God through his Holy Spirit ultimately overpowers our own will so irresistibly as to absolutely prevent us from falling away. Arguing that God would be a horrible Father if he allowed any of his children to perish, Calvinists insist that he overrides our free will, if necessary, to keep us from fully and finally falling away.

Yet, what kind of a loving Father gives with one hand, only to take back with another? Has no one noticed all the flip-flopping going on? By Calvinist teaching, you and I have no free will unless and until we are selectively regenerated pursuant to God's unconditional election. At that point (flip-flop), we then have the "free will" to place our faith in Christ and be saved. But just when we are getting used to our new-found freedom of will (flip-flop), suddenly it is whisked away in order to insure our unfailing perseverance to the end.

If none of us were bound by God's revealed will, it would hardly matter that a system of doctrine contains such head-spinning flip-flops. Yet, as Calvinists fully agree, the only real question can be: What saith the Lord?[275]

Not Even a Close Call in the Text

Space doesn't permit more than a taste of the many passages which speak to the possibility of apostasy on the part of God's saints. In the brief sample that follows, note carefully the frequency of the word "if," indicating the contingency attached to our receiving the promised inheritance.

> I am the vine; you are the branches. If a man remains in me and I in him, he will bear much fruit; apart from me you can do nothing. If anyone does not remain in me, he is like a branch that is thrown away and withers... Now

---

[275] Even when, prior to the final fall of Jerusalem, God promised to restore Israel and thereafter make an everlasting covenant so that they would never again turn away from him (Jeremiah 32:36-44), the fact remains that Israel *did* turn away from him following the return from Exile. If this passage has overtones speaking also of God's new covenant people, the church, the most that can be said is that the church, as corporate body of God's people, would never turn away from him. That saved *individuals* within the church fell away is well documented.

remain in my love. If you obey my commands, you will remain in my love...."
(John 15:5-6; 9-10)[276]

Because of the increase of wickedness, the love of most will grow cold, but he who stands firm to the end will be saved. (Matthew 24:12-13) Then if any one says to you, 'Lo, here is the Christ!' or 'There he is!' do not believe it. For false Christs and false prophets will arise and show great signs and wonders, so as to lead astray, if possible, even the elect. (Matthew 24:23-24 RSV)

Let us not become weary in doing good, for at the proper time we will reap a harvest if we do not give up. (Galatians 6:9)

But now he has reconciled you by Christ's physical body through death to present you holy in his sight, without blemish and free from accusation–if you continue in your faith, established and firm, not moved from the hope held out in the gospel. (Colossians 1:22-23)

Therefore, dear friends...be on your guard so that you may not be carried away by the error of lawless men and fall from your secure position. (2 Peter 3:17)

If we deliberately keep on sinning after we have received the knowledge of the truth, no sacrifice for sins is left, but only a fearful expectation of judgment and of raging fire that will consume the enemies of God. (Hebrews 10:26-27)

You need to persevere so that when you have done the will of God, you will receive what he has promised. (Hebrews 10:36)

Nowhere in any of these passages is it said that the saved inevitably will persevere; rather, that those who persevere inevitably will be saved.

At this point, Calvinists likely will protest that Calvinism has always taught both preservation and perseverance in equal measure. As with

---

[276] It begs belief that Calvinists not only miss the warning against regenerate apostasy oozing out from this text, but actually turn the text around to argue the necessity of unilateral regeneration before depraved man can come to faith. "Apart from me, you can do nothing" is not about regeneration but the futility of those who are already in Christ detaching themselves from their only source of life.

other Calvinist doctrines, however, the problem has always been a lack of internal consistency. It bears repeating that according to classical Calvinism, man's salvation must not be dependent in any way on what man does. So, to say that man must persevere to be saved is to suggest a contingency that could never exist.

Add to this the obvious conflict between the absolute, unconditional predestination of the elect and any notion that the elect could in any way put their predetermined eternal destiny in jeopardy. Given Calvinism's bedrock assumption of predestination, saying that the elect *must* persevere can only mean that the elect *will* persevere. Since falling away is simply not a possibility for the elect, why the charade about a perseverance that is inevitable?

The Calvinist answer, of course, is that the plethora of biblical warnings about apostasy serve the purpose of motivating the elect to the eternal destiny already pre-determined for them. In effect, the warnings are God's *means* of achieving his sovereignly-chosen *end*. What Calvinists fail to appreciate is that they nullify those very warnings when they turn right around and reassure their audience that failing to persevere isn't possible after all!

But What About Those *Other* Passages?

In fact, when the velvet glove of beneficent warnings is finally removed, what we see is a clenched fist of defiance against any possibility of apostasy. At this point, the need for perseverance is but a fleeting image in the rear-view mirror, while any number of texts are argued as irrefutable proof that the child of God cannot under any circumstances forfeit his inheritance.

As we take a closer look at these standard proof-texts, what I suggest you'll see is that God protects us from anything and everything that might threaten our salvation *except our own open rebellion.*

There is John 10:27-28, for example, where Jesus says: "My sheep listen to my voice; I know them, and they follow me. I give them eternal life, and they shall never perish; no one can snatch them out of my hand." True, nothing and no one can interpose between us and our loving

Shepherd so as to snatch us out of his hand, but Jesus here does not rule out our leaving the fold on our own volition.[277]

To say that God loves me forever is to miss the point. The point is that my falling away is never his choice. It's mine. Or as God himself puts it: "Through your own fault you will lose the inheritance I gave you" (Jeremiah 17:4).

We see this very dynamic at work in Judas' betrayal of Jesus. Remember Jesus' prayer for the safekeeping of his apostles (John 17:12)? "While I was with them, I protected them and kept them safe by that name you gave me. None has been lost except the one doomed to destruction so that Scripture would be fulfilled."[278] But we must remember that Judas was no less "in Christ" and specially chosen than the other eleven.[279] Yet–to his eternal destruction–he threw it all away.

There is also Jude 24: "To him who is able to keep you from falling and to present you before his glorious presence without fault and with great joy...." But this verse, too, has to be seen in conjunction with Jude's immediately preceding caution: "Keep yourselves in God's love as you wait for the mercy of our Lord Jesus Christ to bring you to eternal life." If there is no possibility of falling away, why the warning to remain in God's love? Or why the warning in Revelation 3:11: "I am coming soon. Hold on to what you have, so that no one will take your crown"?

In Hebrews 10:14, we are told that "By one sacrifice he has made perfect forever those who are being made holy." But check the context, and you'll see that nothing more is intended than a contrast between the continual sacrifices of the priests under the law and Christ's once-and-for-all sacrifice. (And while we're checking contexts, is it not the case that

---

[277] The same reasoning applies to John 6: 39-40 and 2 Timothy 4:18. God will protect us from any and everything but our own wilful renunciation of faith. (What Jesus says in Matthew 18:12-14 and Luke 15:1-7 about the shepherd and lost sheep is not relevant to a discussion of eternal security. As we see from Luke 15:1-2, the question Jesus is addressing concerns *unsaved* sinners, and the rejoicing in heaven is over those "sinners" who repent unto salvation.)

[278] Calvinists might argue that the words, "the one doomed to destruction," indicates that Judas, if certainly among "the chosen," was never counted among the elect. Indeed, the same argument could also be made from John 6:70: "Have I not chosen you, the Twelve? Yet one of you is a devil!" However, it must not be forgotten that, as one of the Twelve, Judas had preached the gospel to the lost, healed the sick, and cast out demons. That one of the *chosen* would later turn away from being among the *chosen*, doesn't mean he wasn't among the *chosen* to begin with. [For a fuller discussion of Judas' case, see David Pawson, *Once Saved, Always Saved?* (London: Hodder & Stoughton, 1996), 164-168.]

[279] See Acts 1:17

Romans 11:29–"God's gifts and his call are irrevocable"–is speaking only of Israel's not losing out on the hope of salvation simply because the Gentiles were also being called and gifted?)

When the so-called "golden chain" of Romans 8:29-30 gets to the last link–"glorified"–Calvinists insist that none who were foreknown, predestined, called, and justified could possibly miss out on the glory of heaven. They are right, of course, to the extent that God simultaneously sees the whole of eternity from beginning to end. Where Calvinists go wrong, however, is to insist that foreknowledge is the same as foreordination.[280]

We come, then, to those passages about the names which are written (or not written) in the book of life. Calvinists would certainly want us to consider Luke 10:20, where Jesus tells "the seventy-two" to "rejoice that your names are written in heaven." And there is also Revelation 17:8, which speaks of "the inhabitants of the earth whose names have not been written in the book of life from the creation of the world [who] will be astonished when they see the beast...."

Yet these passages only take us back to our earlier discussion about whether God actually foreordained what he foresaw. That is, did God write (or not write) individual names in the book of life pursuant to an unconditional predestining of both the saved and the lost; or simply record the roll call of mankind according to what he foresaw by his divine omniscience?

Revelation 3:5 provides an important clue. "Yet you have a few people in Sardis who have not soiled their clothes," says the Lord. "They will walk with me, dressed in white, for they are worthy. *He who overcomes* will, like them, be dressed in white. *I will never blot out his name from the book of life*, but will acknowledge his name before my Father and his angels."

Time now for a couple of fill-in-the-blank questions about that passage from Revelation:

1)   The name of the one who overcomes will not be

          _____.

---

[280] Calvinists ask: If the saved in heaven are still free yet cannot be lost, why is it illogical for the saved to be free on earth and yet never lose their salvation? Surely Jesus' piercing rebuff to the Sadducees is the most appropriate response possible: "Are you not in error because you do not know the Scriptures or the power of God?" (Mark 12:24). If there is no marriage in heaven, nor dying, tears, or suffering, we are put on notice that heaven will be a radically different reality from that which we experience on earth.

2)   But if one does *not* overcome, then his name will be

_____.

Given those answers, are we to believe that, because of God's own pre-destining election, the book of life was written in indelible ink? Is it not abundantly clear, instead, that even those names which have been written in the book of life can, for good cause, be blotted out as if they had never been included? Would it not be exceedingly odd to speak of a "blotting out" if in fact it could never happen?

While Calvinists reject the idea that the saved could ever lose their *salvation*, some propose that the saved could lose their *rewards*. Their argument derives from 1 Corinthians 3:10-15 where Paul says:

> *By the grace God has given me, I laid a foundation as an expert builder, and someone else is building on it. But each one should be careful how he builds. For no one can lay any foundation other than the one already laid, which is Jesus Christ. If any man builds on this foundation using gold, silver, costly stones, wood, hay or straw, his work will be shown for what it is, because the Day will bring it to light. It will be revealed with fire, and the fire will test the quality of each man's work. If what he has built survives, he will receive his reward. If it is burned up, he will suffer loss; he himself will be saved, but only as one escaping through the flames.*

Are we to believe that someone could be saved and glorified, yet not enjoy the rewards of heaven? Or even that a person could be in a saved state on earth, yet be stripped of the blessings which automatically attach to being a child of God, including especially the gift of the Holy Spirit? What "lost rewards" are we conceivably talking about?

If we go back and re-read the first four chapters of Paul's letter, we will see that Paul is addressing the problem of division over those who have preached the gospel to the Corinthians. Having made the point that some evangelists lay foundations upon which other evangelists build, Paul then reminds the Corinthians that no human preacher is the foundation for faith, but only Christ himself. And further that, if one fails to build upon that divine bedrock, then–even if they themselves are not spiritually lost–the results of their evangelism (as shall be made manifest in the testing fires of Judgment) will be a complete loss.

Despite superficial appearances of plausibility, not a single passage presented by Calvinists can withstand careful, contextual scrutiny. The plain fact is that those who are in Christ have it within themselves to throw away the salvation that otherwise would be theirs.

So who or what can possibly separate us from the love of Christ? No one and nothing...but ourselves!

But Were They Ever Truly Saved?

Faced with overwhelming scriptural evidence, virtually all that Calvinists can do is to insist that anyone who falls away was never really and truly in Christ, never really saved. In aid of that proposition, we are pointed especially to 1 John 2:19. Speaking there of the antichrists (those who denied Jesus was the Messiah), John says: "They went out from us, but they did not really belong to us. For if they had belonged to us, they would have remained with us; but their going showed that none of them belonged to us."[281]

Even assuming for the moment that these antichrists were never saved, that can't possibly be said of those to whom John's letter is addressed. Writing to "my dear children," John follows up verse 19 with this admonition in verses 24 and 25: "See that what you have heard from the beginning remains in you. If it does, you also will remain in the Son and in the Father. And this is what he promised us–even eternal life."

Once again, along with the certainty of God's own personal promise, the contingent word "*if*" tells the tale from our side.

Of all the passages which directly refute the "never really saved" argument, perhaps no scripture is more graphic than this one from Peter:

---

[281] Making virtually the same argument in the reverse, Calvinists cite 1 John 3:9 for the proposition that *true* believers will always continue in the faith, so how could they ever be lost?

"No one who is born of God will continue to sin," says John, "because God's seed remains in him; he cannot go on sinning, because he has been born of God." Are we to believe that a person who is born of God *cannot* sin? What could be more obvious than that those who are born of God both *can* and *do* continue to sin–which is the very problem John is addressing! John is not saying born-again believers are somehow so protected from sin that they can never fall, but rather that a life of sin is so inconsistent with life in Christ, that Christians cannot sin without doing serious violence to their newborn nature. Which is to say, we *must* not sin.

If they have escaped the corruption of the world by knowing our Lord and Savior Jesus Christ and are again entangled in it and overcome, they are worse off at the end than they were at the beginning. It would have been better for them not to have known the way of righteousness, than to have known it and then to turn their backs on the sacred command that was passed on to them. Of them the proverbs are true: "A dog returns to its vomit," and, "A sow that is washed goes back to her wallowing in the mud." (2 Peter 2:20-22)[282]

Nor is the point any less obvious when the Hebrew writer warns:

See to it, brothers, that none of you has a sinful, unbelieving heart that turns away from the living God. But encourage one another daily, as long as it is called Today, so that none of you may be hardened by sin's deceitfulness. We have come to share in Christ if we hold firmly till the end the confidence we had at first. (Hebrews 3:12-14)

What happens to passages such as these in Calvinist argumentation is simply astounding. By a barely-noticeable sleight of hand, the biblical *stipulation* (*if* you endure, you will inherit as one of the elect) is magically transformed into the Calvinist *conclusion* (*because* you've endured you must be among the elect). But let no one be fooled by the subtlety. When a conditional promise becomes a promise of the condition, it's obvious that something has gone terribly awry.

What do you think? Can there be any doubt in the following passage that we're talking about those who "once were saved"?

It is impossible for those who have once been enlightened, who have tasted the heavenly gift, who have shared in the Holy Spirit, who have tasted the goodness of the word of God and the powers of the coming age, if they fall away, to be brought

---

[282] When Calvinists insist that, despite being washed, a sow remains a sow, they miss the whole point of the washing, which as a theme-line throughout the whole of Scripture always infers a spiritual cleansing and change in relationship. One might just as well say that a sinner, despite being washed in Jesus' cleansing blood, is no different from the sinner he once was.

If there is a lesson for God's people to learn from the Exodus generation, it is that what God has solemnly promised to his chosen people can be withdrawn from them when they repudiate the very covenant relationship whereby the promise was given.

back to repentance, because to their loss they are crucifying the Son of God all over again and subjecting him to public disgrace. (Hebrews 6:4-6)[283]

Before resorting to an excruciating argument attempting to explain away this passage as nothing more than a rejoinder to the law-centered theology of the Judaizer heresy within the early church, R.C. Sproul acknowledges the obvious. "This reference to repentance convinces me that the author is describing regenerate Christians."[284] How, indeed, could anyone honestly conclude otherwise? (In the book cited, curiously, Sproul does not even attempt to engage the other passages in Hebrews which teach so explicitly about the possibility of apostasy on the part of these same regenerate Christians.)

The fact that a once-saved person can not only fall from grace but do so with potentially no way back ought to be a sobering thought indeed.[285] Too bad Demas didn't weigh his options more carefully. As Paul lamented to Timothy, "Demas, because he loved this world, has deserted me and

---

[283] Some argue that the warning passages in Hebrews are not directly addressed to individuals, but rather to the New Covenant community *corporately*, as the anti-type of the Old Covenant community (the Exodus generation), whose wilful rebellion resulted in their being barred from the Promised Land. There are five significant difficulties with this proposition: 1) Several of the warning passages are directly addressed to individuals, including Hebrews 3:12 and 4:1 ("none of you"); 6:11 ("each of you"); and 10:28-29 ("a man deserves to be punished"). 2) Whereas the election of individual Jews was through the corporate election of Israel, corporate election in Christ comes through individual election. Indeed, even in Elect Israel, salvation itself was never corporate, but individual. 3) How, practically speaking, could the New Covenant community wilfully sin *as a community*, either universally from its first-century establishment until now, or even in one generation? 4) What conceivable danger is there that the entire, universal New Covenant community, of any or all generations, might be denied entry into the Promised Rest of heaven's glory? Why warn against an eventuality that from every aspect is outside the realm of possibility? 5) The "corporate warnings" hypothesis gains nothing on behalf of any doctrine of eternal security, for if the corporate community can so apostatize as to be forever lost, it only means that the same is true of every individual within the corporate community.

If there is a lesson for God's people to learn from the Exodus generation, it is that what God has solemnly promised to his chosen people can be withdrawn from them when they repudiate the very covenant relationship whereby the promise was given.

[284] Sproul, 213-216. Geisler agrees, saying (at p. 130), "...some of the phrases are very difficult to take any other way than that the person was saved.

[285] This is not to say, of course, that one who has turned his back on God even once (or for a lifetime) can never reclaim the promise of eternal life–only that such repentance and restoration is not possible as long as he remains in denial about the only thing that can save him: Christ crucified.

has gone to Thessalonica" (2 Timothy 4:10). Demas hadn't deserted just Paul, of course, but more crucially his Lord.

If ever we wanted a crystal clear example of someone who was undoubtedly elect but still facing the possibility of falling away, we could hardly do better than the apostle Paul. Remember that passage we cited earlier? "I beat my body and make it my slave," says Paul, "so that after I have preached to others, I myself will not be disqualified for the prize" (1 Corinthians 9:27). Surely, you're kidding! The *Apostle Paul* even remotely subject to being disqualified for the prize?[286]

Needless to say, if even that quintessential man of God was careful not to forfeit his prize, we should be no less careful. As Paul himself warns us: "So, if you think you are standing firm, be careful that you don't fall!" (1 Corinthians 10:12).

Calvin on Perseverance

Yet at the mention of Paul you may ask, What about Romans 8:1? If the truly saved can somehow become unsaved, what was Paul talking about when he wrote: "There is now no condemnation for those who are in Christ Jesus..."? Surely he must have meant once saved, never again condemned....

May I bring in a guest commentator on this one? Many Calvinists will be surprised to learn what John Calvin himself had to say about this verse. Of Paul's discussion, Calvin says [with my added emphasis]: "There he teaches that those whom the Lord has once received into grace, engrafts into the communion of his Christ, and adopts into the society of the church through baptism—*so long as they persevere in faith in Christ* (even though they are beseiged by sin and still carry sin about in themselves)—are absolved of guilt and condemnation."[287]

Here Calvin recognizes three important features which seem to have gotten lost in the conversation about eternal security. First, is the implicit

---

[286] Actually, there may indeed be a better example. In arguing for election even among the angels, Boettner (p. 92) insists that angels were "created in a state of holiness," yet that nevertheless "the evil angels voluntarily forfeited their estate by sinning." Whether or not there was election of the angels, Boettner has described perfectly how those who are created holy can voluntarily forfeit their inheritance.

[287] Calvin, *Institutes*, 4.15.12

contingency of the believer's own perseverance as compared with the non-contingency of what Christ himself has done to secure our salvation.

Second, is the astute observation that our ongoing sin is not what disqualifies us for the prize, else who possibly could be saved? For Calvin, as with Scripture, there is a huge gulf between the believer who continues to sin, yet begs God's forgiveness, and the outright, premeditated, total rejection of God's grace by one who would renounce his faith in the Savior.

Third–and of most immediate importance–Calvin is speaking here of one who unquestionably is engrafted into communion with Christ–not of one who has never been saved.

Yet (as with his earlier commentary that Christ's atonement was not limited to the elect) Calvin seems not to have fully appreciated how incongruous his thinking is in various instances with his overall systematic theology. That Calvin feels obliged in this text to insert the qualifier–"so long as they persevere in faith"–indicates his awareness that even a person who has been engrafted into Christ would be a branch cut off from the vine should he fail to persevere in faith. Yet he seems not to have taken this crucial qualifier into account when asserting his view that no true believer can possibly fall away so as to be lost.[288]

If only Calvin had merged both views into one consistent position affirming the fact that no one can possibly fall away *as long as he remains a steadfast and true believer*. Which, of course, begs the question of whether the one who *has been* a true believer *continues* to be a true believer. Whereas Calvin seems to recognize this crucial distinction in his commentary on Romans 8:1, he appears to ignore it when his pre-commitment to predestination would dictate that no one who is unconditionally elect could ever reject the faith he once had.

Judgment of the Elect

Reading through Calvinist literature, one is struck by the lack of any genuine, substantive "judgment" of individual saints at the Judgment. (In his

---

[288] See Calvin, *Institutes*, 3.24.6-11. Even in this discussion, Calvin notes that "Paul himself also dissuades us from overassurance: 'Let him,' he says, 'who stands well, take heed lest he fall' [1 Cor. 10:12]."

Institutes, Calvin typically transposes all references to God's future, final, eternal Judgment into present, temporal chastisement or exhortation.) That's hardly surprising, given the fact that judgment of any kind introduces an element of contingency into the picture. Logically, the idea of a "Final Judgment" is awkwardly out of sync with the teaching that, from the very beginning, each and every soul has been irreversibly predestined, either for salvation or damnation. For Calvinists, the "First Judgment" (unconditional election and predestination) is all that really counts.

Of course, even non-Calvinists often wonder aloud what Judgment is all about, since God surely already knows the outcome for each soul. Is it to be more like a judicial sentencing; or perhaps something of a "show trial" for our benefit, not God's? Yet the non-Calvinist can also appreciate in a way that Calvinists can't the very real possibility that we could throw away our eternal inheritance by renouncing the very faith by which we were saved. (To be *saved by faith* is to be *lost without it.*) Having to face God's judgment keeps us honest as believers. It disabuses us of any notion that we can wilfully tread on God's grace and get away with it.

The connection between judgment and our present discussion is highlighted in Hebrews 10:26-30.

> *If we deliberately keep on sinning after we have received the knowledge of the truth, no sacrifice for sins is left, but only a fearful expectation of judgment and of raging fire that will consume the enemies of God. Anyone who rejected the law of Moses died without mercy on the testimony of two or three witnesses. How much more severely do you think a man deserves to be punished who has trampled the Son of God under foot, who has treated as an unholy thing the blood of the covenant that sanctified him, and who has insulted the Spirit of grace? For we know him who said, "It is mine to avenge; I will repay," and again, "The Lord will judge his people." It is a dreadful thing to fall into the hands of the living God."*

It should not escape notice that God's elect will be treated the same as God's enemies if, having once known his saving grace, they trample it under foot. That single, jarring clause–"the Lord will judge his people"–packs a mighty wallop. That we are told they are "his people" leaves us in no doubt that the writer is talking about those who are the elect. And the fact that the Lord is going to *judge* them suggests a personal accountability light-years removed from election, predestination, and the impossibility of apostasy.

If, as we all agree, the Day of Judgment is for the wicked and the reprobate, even so it is also the Day of Judgment for the elect of God, who will be first in line.

> *For it is time for judgment to begin with the family of God; and if it begins with us, what will the outcome be for those who do not obey the gospel of God? And, "If it is hard for the righteous to be saved, what will become of the ungodly and the sinner?" (1 Peter 4:17-18).*

All of us, whether Calvinists or non-Calvinists, tend to forget that the Bible speaks more about God's judgment of those who unquestionably are in Christ than it does about those who unquestionably are lost. (Condemnation of the lost seems to be so obvious as to be assumed.) Merely consider Paul's warning to *the saints* in Corinth: "For we must all appear before the judgment seat of Christ, that each one may receive what is due him for the things done while in the body, whether good or bad" (2 Corinthians 5:10).

And it was to "all in Rome who are loved by God and *called to be saints*" that Paul addressed the words we wrongly tend to associate only with the wicked. Look first at Chapter 2, where Paul warns these saints about judging others when they themselves are in spiritual jeopardy:

> *Because of your stubbornness and your unrepentant heart, you are storing up wrath against yourself for the day of God's wrath, when his righteous judgment will be revealed. God 'will give to each person according to what he has done.' (Romans 2:5-6)[289]*

Paul repeats virtually the same theme in Chapter 14:

> *You, then, why do you judge your brother? Or why do you look down on your brother? For we will all stand before God's judgment seat. It is written:*

---

[289] See also Psalm 62:12 and Proverbs 24:12.

"As surely as I live,' says the Lord,
'every knee will bow before me;
every tongue will confess to God.'"
So then, each of us will give an account of himself to God. (Romans 14:10-12)

How can one meaningfully "give an account of himself" when he has no effective say regarding his eternal destiny? And to whom but Jesus' own disciples came the following stark warning? (Well, *us*, actually!)

Do not be afraid of those who kill the body but cannot kill the soul.
Rather, be afraid of the One who can destroy both soul and body in hell.
(Matthew 10:28)

How, possibly, could Jesus' own disciples be in jeopardy of hell, if they were specially chosen for duty by our Lord? Perhaps we should ask Judas. Of all people, he would know. Even while Judas was scheming the greatest betrayal in history, Jesus was warning the remaining eleven: "If anyone does not remain in me, he is like a branch that is thrown away and withers; such branches are picked up, thrown into the fire and burned" (John 15:6). We mustn't overlook the details. The "destroyed branches" Jesus is talking about here were once an integral part of the vine–which is to say, they were "in Christ."

Watchfulness Undergirded By Assurance

In view of Judgment, then, we who are saved must maintain a critical, tight-rope balance between, on the one hand, never doubting our salvation, and, on the other, never blithely taking it for granted.

Peter speaks of that very balance, saying: "Therefore, my brothers, be all the more eager to make your calling and election sure. For if you do these things, you will never fall, and you will receive a rich welcome into the eternal kingdom of our Lord and Savior Jesus Christ" (2 Peter 1:10-11).

We see that balance again in Hebrews 4:1, where the writer warns: "Since the *promise* of entering his rest still stands, let us be careful that none of you be found to have *fallen short* of it." And once again from the same writer: "We want each of you to *show this same diligence to the very end*, in order to *make your hope sure*. We do not want you to become lazy, but to imitate those who through faith and patience inherit what has been *promised*" (Hebrews 6:11-12).

Promise linked with watchfulness. Watchfulness linked with promise.

In verse after verse, our eternal security is all about two sides of the same coin. In his second letter to Timothy, Paul flips that coin in the air, making it turn over and over so as to show both sides. But he lets it fall, finally, where it rightly belongs—in the hands of a faithful God. Faithful to reward those who finish the course and keep the faith. Faithful to withhold the prize from those who obstinately and resolutely choose not to cross the finish line.

> *Therefore I endure everything for the sake of the elect, that they too may obtain the salvation that is in Christ Jesus, with eternal glory.*
> *Here is a trustworthy saying:*
>> *If we died with him,*
>>   *we will also live with him;*
>> *if we endure,*
>>   *we will also reign with him.*
>> *If we disown him,*
>>   *he will also disown us;*
>> *if we are faithless,*
>>   *he will remain faithful,*
>>   *for he cannot disown himself.*
>>   *(2 Timothy 2:10-13)*

If ever we needed a modern image to replace "sows returning to the mire" and "dogs returning to their vomit," perhaps there is yet something good to be salvaged from the horrible nightmare of September 11th. It could easily have been said of the Twin Towers, "once standing, always standing." Who ever would have guessed how terribly vulnerable they were? Who could have imagined how unexpectedly and quickly they would fall...and with them a whole nation's sense of security?

Yet if any structure deserves to come crashing down, it is a doctrinal system that permits a false sense of spiritual security never intended by the One who made us, loves us, and one day will judge us. If eternal security is what you're looking for, you'll find it only through steadfast trust in that invincible Tower of Strength who himself can never fall, and who will never let us down.

———————————

Let us hold unswervingly to the hope we profess, for he who promised is faithful.

Hebrews 10:23

———————————

Chapter Summary

- For his part, God can be trusted to keep our salvation safe and secure. The problem is our own lack of faithfulness to God.

- The Scriptures are replete with warnings against the believer falling away and forfeiting his inheritance.

- A close inspection of the biblical texts reveals that Calvinism is wrong to insist that if anyone finally and fatally "falls away" he was never saved in the first place.

- "Falling away" requires more than the sin with which all of us are so easily beset. It requires a deliberate, once-and-for-all rejection of the saving grace of Christ's blood.

- The believer has every reason to be confident of his salvation, but no reason simply to take it for granted.

Reality Check: If the eternal destiny of every soul was locked in before any soul ever sinned, then "once saved, always saved" must surely be a comforting thought for the elect, who have done absolutely nothing to merit their salvation and perseverance. Yet the obvious corollary–"once condemned, always condemned"–must apply with equal force to the non-elect, who at the time of God's election could not possibly have done anything whatsoever to merit their eternal damnation.

Chapter 11

It's a Package Deal

The five points, though separately stated, are really inseparable.
They hang together; you annot reject one without rejecting them all.

–J.I. Packer

In our earlier chapter on the evolution of Calvinism, we observed (as most Calvinists would agree) that the so-called "five points of Calvinism" form a tightly woven, interlaced belief system in which each individual doctrine is logically integral to the whole. Taken together, the five core doctrines are as symbiotic as horse and carriage, love and marriage.

Surely by now it should be crystal clear that Calvinism is a package deal. Its core doctrines stand or fall together. All for one, and one for all. Do you know of any belief system that has tighter logic and cohesion? But for Calvinists that is simultaneously good news and bad. The good news is that the internal logic of the system provides a superficial patina of plausibility, and each doctrine conveniently serves to reinforce every other doctrine. The bad news, of course, is that if ever you knock the props out from under one or more of the premises which together comprise the bundle of doctrines collectively known as Calvinism, the whole bundle falls.[290]

Earlier, we saw how the entire *TULIP* quickly wilted when we snipped the stem down at its base. Once the underlying premise was shown to be false (that man cannot possibly participate in his own salvation without somehow nullifying God's sovereignty and grace), there was nothing left to sustain viability.

But the Calvinism package is at equal risk even if you work, instead, from the top down. The fact is that Calvinism's exceptionally high degree of interdependence creates an equally high degree of mutual vulnerability. By tragic analogy, Calvinism's vaunted cohesion suffers from the World Trade Center syndrome we touched on in the previous chapter. Not unlike the seemingly invincible Twin Towers, Calvinism is a vulnerable five-story structure which collapses in on itself when the top floor fails to hold.

If on Floor 5 there is no automatic perseverance of the saints, but rather the possibility that we can reject the salvation that we might otherwise have had, then it means that Floor 4 also collapses, since God's grace obviously *can* be resisted. Which also means, then, that Floor 3 no longer holds, because Christ's atonement would not be limited to those who are unable to resist it; that Floor 2 is the next to go, since election could no longer be unconditional, but contingent upon one's faith; and that, finally, Floor 1 gives way, since no one is so totally depraved that they lack the free will to choose faith and salvation. No one can escape the inevitable. Once the top floor of irreversible eternal security buckles under the weight of biblical teaching, all the supporting propositions collapse as well, leaving nothing but rubble at ground zero.

As we have just seen, the doctrine of perseverance ("once saved, always saved") simply cannot withstand close biblical scrutiny. Along with Floor 3 (the utterly sacrilegious notion of limited atonement), the structural defect in Floor 5 is one of the most readily apparent of all the "floors" in Calvinism's ostensibly impregnable edifice. With its inglorious demise, the remaining floors in our Trade Center analogy begin to collapse. "One, two, three, we all fall down!"

---

[290] Boettner agrees (Ibid., 59). "Prove any one of them true and all the others will follow as logical and necessary parts of the system. Prove any one of them false and the whole system must be abandoned."

When the Middle Collapses

In traditional wars, there is little concern about top-to-bottom collapses of towering structures, but great concern about the middle of a strategic line giving way. Without the middle standing firm, no other part of the line can be assured of holding on. As it happens, this very vulnerability is found in the soft center of Calvinism's defensive line.

In Chapter 8, we spoke at length about the special perniciousness of Calvinism's fiercely defended doctrine of limited atonement (all for the sole purpose of preserving the internal logic of the Calvinist system!). But just why is there such a fierce defense of the vaunted "L" strategically located in the middle of *TULIP*? Precisely because Calvinists understand what's ultimately at risk. The "L" is not just the serendipitous centerpiece of a colorful acronym. Without the "L," the entire *TU_IP* collapses in a heap.[291]

Of far greater consequence, Calvinists intuitively sense that they are uniquely exposed on that particular point of doctrine.[292] Far and away, limited atonement is the most demonstrably unbiblical tenet of the entire system. And because its patent weakness can be penetrated so easily, the whole of Calvinism is put in full retreat.[293]

Want to know if Calvinism is biblical? All you need do is answer this single, simple question: Did Christ shed his blood for *all* lost souls, or for only a preselect number? If Christ died for *all* (genuinely, honestly, and sincerely giving hope of salvation to *all*), then Calvinism, with its core doctrine of limited, special election is a theology gone tragically wrong.

Next time you sing "The First Noel" in celebration of the Savior's birth, don't overlook the carol's last line, which points to the *real* reason

---

[291] Considering the J. I. Packer quotation at the head of this chapter, it is interesting, to say the least, that Packer hedges on the notion of "limited atonement" in his chapter, "The Love of God: Universal and Particular," in *Still Sovereign,* Schreiner and Ware eds. (Grand Rapids: Baker, 2000), 287-288. To say that Christ's atonement is not limited, only definite for those who accept Christ, comes close to collapsing the centerpiece of the *TULIP.*

[292] "The doctrine of limited atonement has been the most debated of the TULIP teachings *within* the Calvinist camp, and there are more than a few Calvinists who...simply reject it outright." [Mouw, 40]

[293] When "Calvinists" such as Millard Erickson acknowledge the obvious (that Christ's atonement was not limited, but universal) they are forced into all sorts of logical incongruities, best witnessed in the strained argumentation of sublapsarianism, as previous noted. That such "Calvinists" are forced to admit their view is "a modification of Calvinism" merely serves to underscore how indispensable limited atonement is to classical Calvinism. To "modify" Calvinism on this key point is not just a matter of tactical retreat, but total capitulation.

for the season. "And with his blood," insists the song, "*mankind* hath bought." If, as those lyrics attest, Christ's blood was truly shed for *all mankind*, then Calvinism's doctrine of limited atonement cannot stand. And once limited atonement falls in the face of overwhelming scriptural assault, so too must the doctrine of unconditional election. And if unconditional election, then so too irresistible grace, and perseverance of the saints, and total depravity. The lot!

That's the problem with a doctrinal system whose theological centerpiece, though scripturally untenable, is made necessary as a matter of logic. In the end, Scripture triumphs over logic. What that means in this case is that there can be no "L" in *TULIP*; and without that missing middle letter, nothing of Calvinism's vaunted *TULIP* can possibly survive.

If that's bad news for Calvinism, think of the good news it would be for the countless masses of humanity eternally barred by the misguided doctrine of election from ever having access to Christ's atoning blood.[294] One can imagine the joyous carol they might sing in response to the *TU_IP*'s great demise:

> No "L", no "L",
> No "L", no "L".
> *Gone is the bane of Ishmael.*

Say You're a Two, Three, or Four-Point Calvinist?

I confess I have a certain respect for those Calvinists who might be labeled "strict Calvinists" or "hyper-Calvinists," and for those who staunchly maintain allegiance to all five points of Calvinism. At least there is a fundamental consistency about those positions that can't always be

---

[294] It is often claimed by Calvinists that not one more soul will be saved whether Christ's atonement was limited or unlimited. The saved are the saved are the saved—and all through Christ's atonement! But this argument does nothing more than assume the conclusion to be reached. To say that not one more student will graduate than those who finally graduate ignores altogether the possibility that far fewer would have graduated had there been no master teacher to take a special interest in them, or that far more would have graduated had there been such a teacher. Master Teacher or no Master Teacher, Calvinism would limit in advance the number of those who can graduate even before they matriculate!

claimed by others. How many times have you heard someone say, for instance, "I'm a two-point Calvinist," or "I'm a three-point Calvinist"? What in the world are they thinking? Isn't that something akin to saying, "I'm a two-point Christian"? Or, "I'm a three-point Mormon?"

Are these folks saying that they buy off on unconditional election (predestination), but not irresistible grace? Or accept limited atonement, but not unconditional election? Or profess unconditional election while denouncing total depravity?

It's possible, of course, to affirm both some form of innate depravity as well as "eternal security" yet deny unconditional election, as do a significant number of Southern Baptists.[295] (Yet that wouldn't be Calvinism.) Or to strongly disagree with all points of Calvinism except total depravity, as do classical Arminians. (But, in that case, especially, it's not likely any Arminians are going to claim to be even one-point Calvinists!)

In a rear-guard skirmish with Dispensationalists, R.C. Sproul challenges their claim to be "four-point Calvinists" (since they reject the doctrine of limited atonement). Observing that at least some Dispensationalists also reject the correlative doctrine of irresistible grace, Sproul argues correctly that this slippery slope eventually brings them dangerously close to rejecting total depravity.[296]

Ironically, of course, John Calvin himself was only a four-point "Calvinist"–eschewing the notion of limited atonement, and (at least arguably) not accepting perseverance of the saints to the same degree, or at least for the same reasons, as today's classical Calvinists. (So maybe we should call it 3.5!) Calvin's glaring inconsistencies can partly be explained by the fact that, in formulating so broad-sweeping a theology, he had not fully considered all of the interlacing implications of his fundamental premises. Given the highly-developed, systematized Calvinism which has evolved from Calvin's seminal ideas, there is little room for any similar excuse today.

---

[295] With his idiosyncratic view of conditional "unconditional election," Norman Geisler also comes to mind. [See Geisler,68-75.] It should be noted that Southern Baptists are currently debating what degree of credence should be given to Calvinism.

[296] Sproul, 194-195

In England, there's a popular expression: "In for a penny, in for a pound." Others say: "If you buy the premise, you buy the bit." The idea in both maxims is that commitment to the lesser is commitment to the greater. Given Calvinism's tightly packed bundle of doctrines, if you take one, you pretty much have to take them all. What use would any one of them alone be in any event?

It reminds one of a tepee with five poles lashed together near the top. You might just get away with having only four poles, or possibly three. But can you imagine having a two-point tepee? At the slightest breeze, you'd undoubtedly have a *no-point* tepee! And that's even more true of Calvinism. Take away a point or two and suddenly you'd have no-point Calvinism. What *would* be the point? Why bother at all?[297]

Going In Circles

There is also this to consider: Were it not for being lashed together, it would be difficult for any of the five "poles" of Calvinism's "tepee" to stand alone. The proof comes in virtually any discussion of the issues one

---

[297] I realize there are those who claim to be Calvinists despite espousing man's independent free will and personal responsibility for his final destiny. I've already alluded a number of times (mostly in the footnotes) to Norman Geisler's peculiar doctrinal configuration in this regard. There is also Neal Punt's equally problematic "biblical universalism," which is virtually the flip-side of Geisler's theory of conditional "unconditional election." Punt's view is that "*all* persons are elect in Christ *except* those who ultimately reject or remain indifferent to whatever revelation God has given of himself to them whether in nature/conscience or in gospel presentation" [See www.biblicaluniversalism.com.]

Not only is this position so fundamentally inconsistent with Calvinism's core doctrine of special election as not to merit the label "Calvinism," but, given its assumed exceptions to universal salvation, it could hardly be considered "universalism." Far more important, the view is so contrary to biblical teaching as not to merit the label "*biblical* universalism." That the Bible typically couches salvation in terms of conditional *acceptance*, not conditional *rejection*, tells us that universal *election* would not likely be the divine starting point.

Given the enormity of the paradigm shift from God's unilaterally determining one's salvation to God's thrusting that decision into man's own heart and mind, it's hard to think in terms of two-, three-, or four-point Calvinism. (Not even these "Calvinist" proponents characterize themselves in this way.) Radically nuancing each of Calvinism's central tenets to the extent done by Geisler, Punt, and others is like saying the Bomb *nuanced* Hiroshima. Whatever remains of classical Calvinism's "five points" is reduced to such incoherence that "Calvinism"is scarcely worth mention. (While this book does not directly address these pale imitations of Calvinism, I would let the overall discussion stand as my response.)

might have with Calvinists. The minute you challenge any single pole, other poles are immediately drafted in for support of the first.

Consider this exchange, for example:

Q: Just how can we be sure that God's grace is irresistible?

A: Because it is the sovereign God of Creation who has predestined the elect.

Q: But how could God contravene man's own free will?

A: Man has no free will in the matter of regeneration.

Q: And why?

A: Because God's grace to save the elect is irresistible!

And here's another:

Q: Doesn't God's arbitrary election of the saved reek of partiality and injustice?

A: Absolutely not. Every one of us has already forfeited God's blessings.

Q: But how did we forfeit them?

A: By sinning.

Q: And why do we sin?

A: Because we are totally depraved.

Q: And why are we totally depraved?

A: Because God imposed that penalty on mankind in the wake of Adam's sin.

Q: So is there no hope for man?

A: Certainly. There is hope for the elect.

B: But if only for the elect, doesn't that reek of injustice and partiality?

A: No, not at all. You see, every one of us has forfeited God's blessings....

With each pole necessarily relying on all the other poles, Calvinism's reasoning ends up being as circular as the bottom of a tcpcc!

Where the Package Falls Apart

There is no greater irony associated with Calvinism than the cold hard fact that Calvinists aren't really all that Calvinistic after all–at least, not in the way they live out their faith life. When it comes to what Calvinists believe *in reality* as compared to what they believe *in theory*, there is nothing even remotely approaching a "package deal." In fact, call it deep-seated schizophrenia; or perhaps cognitive dissonance. Not to be confused with hypocrisy, what we're talking about here is the dualistic way in which Calvinists think and operate.

The phenomenon I'm describing here is not unlike the reply Richard Mouw received when he challenged a Mormon friend regarding some of Mormonism's more daunting doctrines. "Well," said his friend, "I like to think of some of those uniquely Mormon beliefs as my shelf-doctrines. They are part of my belief system, but they don't function in my life on a day-to-day basis." (Mouw goes on to say of his own, Calvinist beliefs: "Most of us who subscribe to a complex theological system have shelf-doctrines. I know I do. Indeed, at least one of the TULIP doctrines functions as a shelf-doctrine for me: the **L** [limited atonement]."[298])

Do you recall our discussion about how Calvinism is presented to us on two distinct (and often competing) levels, especially regarding the issue of free will? On the surface, Calvinism insists that man has the free agency either to live in rebellion to God (and thus deserves condemnation and punishment), or to obey God's call (and is thus to be rewarded). Yet, beneath the surface, assumptions are made that simply would not allow for such free will. As we have seen, Calvinism teaches that God's eternal, immutable will has already determined the eternal destiny of each soul, and further that God is the primary moving cause of every thought, act, and event.

The truth of the matter is that absolute free will and absolute determinism are absolutely irreconcilable. Not even Calvinism's mysterious "secret decrees" can overcome the inherent inconsistency of man's complete freedom and God's complete control over man's freedom.

---

[298] Mouw, 40

In the same way that Calvinist doctrine is inconsistently two-tiered, I suggest that Calvinists themselves are inconsistently two-tiered. On the upper tier are the theoretical and doctrinal thought processes which espouse and vigorously defend the teachings of Calvinism. On the lower tier are the practical and operational thought processes which cause Calvinists to act altogether differently from what they espouse and defend.

Simply consider the issue of free will itself. By Calvinist teaching, only the regenerate elect have the free agency to respond in faith to God's call and escape the total depravity which otherwise deprives them of free moral agency. Yet day in and day out Calvinists operate on the assumption that all men and women are imbued with free moral agency. Hour by hour and moment by moment, judgments are made about how that free agency is exercised even by the unregenerate. In fact, Calvinists who sit on juries, or on the bench as judges, regularly impose punishments upon those who have exercised their free will in violation of society's moral expectations.

Just like everybody else, Calvinists take it for granted that all men and women have free moral agency for which they are personally accountable. Yet that assumption hardly matches pure Calvinist theory, by which man is a pre-programmed being from start to finish.

As for God's sovereign control over every thought, act, and event, you can be sure that Calvinists don't read history books, nor yet their morning newspapers, with that thought in mind. Was God the primary (or even secondary) cause of all the robberies, rapes, and murders that took place overnight? Is he to be blamed for the deaths of millions who are dying even now because of famine, AIDS, abortion, and war? Is God responsible for the genocide of six millions Jews in the Holocaust, or for the countless thousands of deaths from the Indian Ocean tsunami?

Even if we all acknowledge the very real possibility that, for his own purposes, God might well be the moving cause behind any given event no matter how seemingly tragic, Calvinists, no less than non-Calvinists, rarely if ever blame God for this world's evil. Together with the rest of us, Calvinists may blame an endless stream of wicked perpetrators out there–from Hitler to the local gang member–but not the all-predestining, all-planning, all-controlling sovereignty of God, about which (at least on one level) Calvinism is so adamant.

In this regard, have you ever stopped to consider why Calvinists pray? It sounds good when Benjamin Warfield argues that even non-Calvinists are Calvinists when they pray, because they speak "as if they were dependent on God's mercy alone."[299] (And certainly non-Calvinists *do* pray with that very understanding.) But for a people who believe that God is the controller of every thought, act, and event–*from before the beginning of time*–prayers of petition cannot help but be a meaningless exercise.

To begin with, God himself, not the believer, would be the moving force behind every prayer. In effect, God would be scripting prayers to himself. That aside, any petition that God's divine power might be brought to bear to change a given circumstance, or to heal, or to forgive would make no sense in light of the predetermined course of events fixed in divine concrete before the dawn of Creation.

Why pray that your loved one's life be extended, if the moment of his or her death was decided before time began? Why pray that your child be healed, when the outcome has been eternally decided? Why pray that your sins be forgiven, or that souls be saved, when in each instance forgiveness or damnation has been foreordained intractably one way or the other? At the bottom line, if you don't believe that prayer can bring about real change, why pray?

Since everyone knows that invoking God's power to bring change is the very object of the exercise, there's a curious physiological phenomenon you may never before have considered–that Calvinists are remarkably transformed into non-Calvinists at the mere bending of the knee.

Going in a completely different direction altogether, consider for a minute that wondrous moment when a precious little newborn emerges from the womb. One simply has to believe that the last thing any Calvinist parent has on his or her mind is the possibility that their darling little bundle of joy is even theoretically depraved, innately sinful, and eternally damned.

Perhaps it's a strange question, but are Calvinists ever troubled by the thought that their children might not be among the elect, but instead are among the countless "misshapen vessels" which the sovereign, predestining "Potter" has already chosen not to save from eternal perdition? (The

[299] Benjamin B. Warfield, "What Is Calvinism?" in *Benjamin B. Warfield: Selected Shorter Writings*, vol. 1, ed. John E. Meeter (Phillipsburg, NJ: Presbyterian and Reformed Publishing, 1970), 390

non-elect have to be *somebody's* children! Does Calvinism teach that all the children of the elect will themselves be elect, and that the children of the non-elect are also non-elect?)

The point is that, just like non-Calvinists, Calvinist parents raise their children as best they know how, teach them right from wrong, discipline them when they are wilful, and pray for their soul's salvation—all, I suspect, without a moment's thought about whether or not their children are among the elect.

As reflected in how they train, nurture, and discipline their kids, it's obvious that Calvinist parents proceed on the assumption that their children are free moral agents, individually responsible for their own moral choices. (Indeed, it might be surprising how many Calvinist parents make a conscious connection between those choices and their child's ultimate eternal destiny.) Through it all, one is probably safe to suggest that all this conscientious parenting happens without the slightest concern about the child's innate depravity, or about the unconditionally selective process of regeneration which—given the odds—just might exclude their child.

From these and any number of other questions which might be asked, one suspects that, for most Calvinists, the theoretical flight of fancy regarding total depravity and original sin rarely touches down on the runway of reality.

What About the Other Petals of the *TULIP*?

There is not a single petal in Calvinism's *TULIP* that doesn't end up being betrayed by one's faith walk. For example, Calvinists can talk all day long about "unconditional election," but there's not a chance in the world that Calvinists really and truly believe they have absolutely no role to play in their relationship with God. Show me a Calvinist who doesn't affirm he has to believe in order to be saved—or to repent, or maybe even to be baptized. While a Calvinist is always going to say that his faith was made possible only through the predestined regeneration of the Holy Spirit, that abstract creedal affirmation relates to little more than the *mode* of faith.

The fact remains that no Calvinist is going to deny that "without faith it is impossible to please God." Even if it is thought that God makes possible the conditions leading to one's faith, Calvinists would be the first to tell you that no one can just sit back, let God do his predestining thing, and rest comfortably in the fact that he is saved. When it comes to theoretical musings about predestination, Calvinists may not believe in free will; but neither do they believe in free passes. Forgetting everything else one might believe about divine cause and effect, the Calvinist and non-Calvinist meet at the bottom line: No personal faith and repentance, no salvation.[300]

When it comes to the doctrine of "limited atonement," it is somewhat more difficult to identify a gap between one's doctrine and one's operational reality. The reason is that the doctrine of limited atonement is a highly theoretical tenet of Calvinism made necessary sheerly by the internal logic of the larger system.[301] As we saw earlier, if predestination of the elect and reprobation of the non-elect were true, it would stand to reason that Christ's atoning blood has meaning only for the elect. (By the same token, if Christ's atoning blood in fact holds out the hope of redemption for any and all who would believe in Jesus, then it stands to reason that predestination of the elect is *not* true.)

Gap or no gap, the doctrine of limited atonement must surely be a source of embarrassment to thoughtful Calvinists. It certainly doesn't appear to be the most compelling "altar call" or gospel invitation in any evangelistic effort to save the lost–which itself may suggest where the operational inconsistency occurs with this particular petal of the *TULIP*. Motivated by the belief that God calls his elect through the preaching of the gospel (and amen to that, properly understood), evangelistically-minded Calvinists proclaim Christ's blood shed for sinners, just as do non-Calvinists. What other hope can be held out to the lost?

---

[300] In his debate with the hyper-Calvinists, Spurgeon made this very point, saying: "I hold as firmly as any man living, that repentance and conversion are the work of the Holy Spirit, but I would sooner lose this hand, and both, than I would give up preaching that it is the duty of men to repent and believe and that it is the duty of Christian ministers to say to them, "Repent and be converted, that your sins may be blotted out." [*Metropolitan Tabernacle Pulpit*, vol. 14, 196]

[301] Mouw acknowledges at least this much, saying: "The doctrine of the limited atonement gains much of its force as a matter of logic." [Mouw, 41] Perhaps this partially explains his saying: "I don't hold to it [limited atonement] with the passion I have for the other Calvinist basics. It is there for me, but for the most part it just sits on my theological shelf." [Mouw, 40]

The pesky problem for Calvinists, of course, is that there are no truly "lost" among the elect, and no elect among the truly lost. So if, regarding evangelism, one believes that the object of the exercise is not being "fishers of men" but simply trolling for the elect who haven't yet been hauled safely on board, any talk of Christ's blood being shed for *all* sinners would make no sense whatsoever.

Yet, listen to any on-fire evangelist who happens also to be a Calvinist, and you'd never suspect that Christ's blood was shed only for some and not for others; or that salvation is a limited offer extended only to a select number of sinners in the audience. I dare say there's not a Calvinist evangelist out there (Charles Spurgeon[302] and Jonathan Edwards[303] having been notable examples) who doesn't preach as if Christ's atoning blood was shed universally for all sinners. But that central, undeniable feature of the gospel simply doesn't square with the doctrine of limited atonement, nor the notion of unconditional election which makes limited atonement logically necessary. When it comes to evangelism, Calvinists are operating at the highest possible level of cognitive dissonance.

With the doctrine of "irresistible grace," we have yet another theoretically-necessary corollary to unconditional election and predestination. If God in his sovereign power has eternally decreed you and me to be his elect, then we are powerless to refuse our salvation. Given the underlying assumption, the conclusion is inescapable. Even so, Calvinists don't talk or act as if they are pre-programmed robots responding to some irresistible spiritual force.

Instead, just as with those of us who are non-Calvinists, the talk is all about having given one's heart freely to God in response to his love. And about the free gift of God's grace. Know any Calvinists who don't believe deep down in their soul that they made a conscious, willing choice to accept Jesus as their Savior wholly apart from some gracious, effective

---

[302] Rebuffing hyper-Calvinists, Spurgeon declared: "Brethren, the command to believe in Christ must be the sinner's warrant, if you consider the nature of our commission. How runs it? 'Go into all the world, and preach the gospel to every creature.' It ought to read, according to the other plan [hyper-Calvinism], 'preach the gospel to every regenerate person, to every convinced sinner, to every sensible sinner.' But it is not so; it is to 'every creature.'" [*Metropolitan Tabernacle Pulpit*, vol. 7, 148-149.]

[303] See, especially, Edwards' most famous sermon: "Sinners in the Hands of an Angry God."

force of the Spirit that enabled them to choose Jesus against every depraved instinct in their body?[304]

Perhaps the more intriguing question is why Calvinists are so defensive when the words *robot* and *puppet* are tossed their way. If man were as predestined, programmed, and divinely manipulated as Calvinism teaches at the most fundamental level, there would be little difference between robots, puppets, and ourselves. But no less than the rest of us, Calvinists intuitively know that we are *not* robots and puppets, nor merely passive instrumentalities in the hands of an all-controlling God. As logically necessary as "irresistible grace" may be to the Calvinist system, Calvinists are not fooled in the least by what they believe in theory. No wonder they bristle when we use words more fit for what they believe in theory than for what they really and truly believe in reality.

As for "perseverance of the saints," I have yet to meet a Calvinist who doesn't believe that the saints themselves must persevere steadfastly in faith to the dying end. Never is this more clear than when Calvinists insist that anyone turning to a reprobate life after claiming to be a Christian was never truly a Christian in the first place. As biblically untenable as that explanation is, the element of truth it contains about the imperative of Christian steadfastness is as crystal clear to Calvinists as it is to non-Calvinists.

And that's precisely how conscientious Calvinists live their lives before God. I suppose there could be Calvinist believers who, having turned away from following God, maintain some false sense of eternal security. But you can be dead sure that Calvinists on the whole would reject as noxious and unworthy any thought that, once they are saved, they can tread on God's grace by living unrighteously.

---

[304] Addressing the reverse side of personal choice and responsibility, hear again the words of Spurgeon: "Oh, my hearers, Will any man choose for himself to be lost? Will he count himself unworthy of eternal life, and put it from him? If you will be damned you must do it yourselves. Your blood be on your own heads. Go down to the pit if you deliberately choose to do so; but this know, that Christ was preached to you, and you would not have him; you were invited to come to him, but you turned your backs on him; you chose for your selves your own eternal destruction! God grant that you may repent of such a choice, for Christ's sake. Amen." [*Metropolitan Tabernacle Pulpit*, vol. 33, 333.]

At the level of practical Christian living, "once saved, always saved" is a moot issue for conscientious Calvinists. And why not? As with other tenets of Calvinism, the doctrine of perseverance of the saints is nothing more than a logical corollary of the doctrine of predestination. So if that abstract corollary suddenly disappeared in a puff of smoke, Calvinists could care less. What they see in the written Word is the same thing that non-Calvinists see: the unmistakable call to steadfastness, faithfulness, and unceasing perseverance. It doesn't take a non-Calvinist to understand the serious, compelling import of the admonition: "Take heed lest you fall."

For that matter, it doesn't take a Calvinist to understand that God, for his part, could never renege on his promises regarding eternal security, so our salvation is not the least bit in jeopardy from his side. But that is not the crucial issue addressed by "perseverence of the saints." What God has promised is inviolable. It's what we ourselves have promised that is cause for serious concern, as both Calvinists and non-Calvinists are all too painfully aware. Though Calvinists might contend to the death that one who is truly elect could never fall, when all is said and done they live and act as if they actually could.

In the end, the single crucial aspect of Calvinism that doesn't somehow get rectified in practice is the inevitable, irreversible damnation of those who were arbitrarily passed over in the process of election. Because this feature of Calvinism was never anything more than a logical corollary to the arbitrary predestination of the elect, it was always highly suspect. Can such an immeasurably monstrous result really and truly be an indispensable, non-negotiable doctrine that Calvinists couldn't live without? Indeed, is it a doctrine with which one can conscientiously live?

Spurgeon was right to observe that "A man cannot have an erroneous belief without by-and-by having an erroneous life."[305] But he did not distinguish carefully enough between what one believes in theory and what one believes in reality. That Calvinists generally exhibit upright and exemplary lives is confirmation, not of the truth of their doctrinal beliefs, but of the truth of what they intuitively believe to the contrary.

---

[305] From *C.H. Spurgeon, Autobiography*, Vol. 1, *The Early Years: 1834-1859* (Edinburgh: Banner of Truth, 1962), 163-75

Though speaking graciously of faith-filled non-Calvinists, Spurgeon better captures the cognitive dissonance we're speaking about here regarding Calvinists when he said, "We do hope that the hearts of many are a great deal better than their heads. We do not set their fallacies down to any wilful opposition to the truth as it is in Jesus, but simply to an error in their judgments, which we pray God to correct."[306]

So it is that, no matter which petal of the *TULIP* we pick, what Calvinists believe in their hearts is a far cry from what Calvinists intellectually affirm. Mimicking the two-tiered Calvinist system itself, Calvinists may find assurance in doctrinal theory on one level, but day in and day out they function confidently to the contrary on quite another level.

So when is a Calvinist *not* a Calvinist? The surprising answer is: Most of the time.

Unexpected Similarities Among Non-Calvinists

Adding irony to irony, if Calvinists are intellectually schizophrenic, non-Calvinists are no less so. Take, for example, the issue of total depravity and original sin. I watch with amazement as parents who would vehemently deny the practice of infant baptism spawned by those twin doctrines turn right around and encourage their young children to be baptized at earlier and earlier ages. Why do they do that if not for fear that, were their seven- or eight-year-old to die unbaptized, the child's soul would be in eternal jeopardy?

Early youth baptisms reveal a deep-seated troubling concern that youngsters are spiritually at risk. (Just how far removed is this from Calvinist teaching that infants are innately condemned in the womb?) Without even recognizing the inconsistency, what the non-Calvinist believes doctrinally on one level suddenly gets nudged out by what he fears on yet another level.

A similar disparity happens regarding "unconditional election." Even among those who would soundly reject predestination and particular salvation, the idea of things in life being pre-programmed is very much alive and well. Just listen to how folks talk. How many times have you heard someone say: "It was meant to be," or "It wasn't meant to be"? Especially regarding love and marriage, there are those well-worn lines: "They were meant for each other," or (in case of a failed romance) "They just weren't meant for each other." And when there's a death, of course, you can expect to hear someone (not necessarily a Calvinist) observe: "It was just his time to die, that's all."

Probably no less than Calvinists, predestination-denying believers speak of God having "a plan" for their life. (I myself pray daily for God to reveal any plan he may have for me.) Even recognizing the huge difference between predestined salvation and God's providential hand moving in one's life, it's interesting how doggedly deterministic we free-will folks can be in the way we think and speak.

We mentioned earlier the inconsistency in Calvinists between what they believe doctrinally about "limited atonement" and the universal atonement they preach so powerfully when evangelizing the lost. By contrast, after espousing a high view of Christ's universal atonement for the sins of all mankind, we non-Calvinists too often fail to fully appreciate the serious implications of what we insist to be true. For if Christ's blood really and truly was shed for all mankind, it means that, unless and until they are saved by that atoning blood, all mankind is really and truly *lost*. Eternally lost and hell-bound!

Quite unbelievably, non-Calvinists can engage their Calvinist friends in vociferous arguments about the extent of Christ's atoning sacrifice, and yet be unable to remember the last time they themselves confronted any lost soul about his or her eternal destiny. It's not at all uncommon for non-Calvinists to cite every proof-text in the Bible showing that Christ died for the whole world, yet take precious little interest in personal evangelism. Typically, they can content themselves with being part of a church that has a "vibrant missionary outreach" to the lost souls of darkest Africa while never mentioning a word about Jesus to their own next-door neighbors.

If forced to choose between winning the debate over the doctrine of limited atonement, or having a genuine, passionate zeal to reach the lost for Christ, there would be no contest. For non-Calvinists (as for

Calvinists), the issue ought not to be whether the *argument* is won, but whether *souls* are won.

Even when it comes to Calvinism's basically-artificial doctrine of irresistible grace, non-Calvinists are not far behind Calvinists in believing that, without the gift of God's grace in our lives, our feeble efforts to live righteously would be woefully lacking. Of this you can be certain: "Amazing Grace" is not alone a Calvinist anthem.

Most non-Calvinists sense the same dependency on God's grace for their salvation as do Calvinists. We too acknowledge that "there but for the grace of God go I." What can that sentiment possibly imply but that the Spirit of God is working at the most fundamental level to overcome what you and I could never achieve on our own?

And what does that further imply but that the Spirit is in some way constantly moving us from point A to point B? Even if it doesn't happen in such a way as to irresistibly overpower one's free will, as Calvinists insist, for non-Calvinists (no less than for the Calvinist hymn writer John Newton) the wonderful fact remains: "'Twas grace that taught my heart to fear; and grace my fears relieved." How else explain the well-worn line: "I once was blind, but now I see!"

With the fifth petal in Calvinism's *TULIP*, we come to the point at which non-Calvinists are most vulnerable to thinking Calvinistically. "Once saved, always saved" is as enticing and comforting a thought to non-Calvinists as it is to Calvinists. As we noted earlier, it is altogether possible for Calvinists to firmly believe (on an intellectual level) the doctrine itself, yet (on a practical level) act entirely as if they didn't believe it. In like fashion, it is equally possible for non-Calvinists to soundly reject the theory (on an intellectual level), yet (on a practical level) act entirely as if they believed it.

I dare say that, over the centuries, millions of "Christian" adherents who never once heard of Calvinism have rested their eternal security on the basis of little more than a single act whereby they became identified in their own mind as Christians. Whether it's having been sprinkled as an infant, or immersed as an adult, or having said the "sinner's prayer" in front of the television–the perceived result is guaranteed entrance through the pearly gates. The "baptized, but unconverted" can always convince themselves that heaven is a sure bet, and that ongoing sanctification and perseverance is of little value. Pretty much no matter what they do, they're still saved...or so they believe.

So whether or not "perseverance of the saints" is one's official doctrine, there's no question but that it is the unofficial doctrine of countless believers. "Once saved, always saved" is not protected by a Calvinist copyright.

Is this as strange to you as it is to me? When you leave the doctrinal level and begin to observe the actual faith walk of adherents on both sides of the debate, five-point Calvinists turn out not to be real Calvinists after all, while even rabid non-Calvinists can end up being five-point Calvinists!

Potentially Pernicious Packaging

As a non-Calvinist, I am more reticent to discuss what Calvinists themselves are able to talk about freely among themselves regarding some of the potential pitfalls facing Calvinists. But in full candor, it simply has to be said. While the actual faith walk of Calvinists is not always cohesive with Calvinist doctrine itself, Calvinism does seem to come pre-packaged with the potential for certain built-in dangers. According to Reformed author Curt Daniel, for example, these include inordinate pride, excessive intellectualism, the reluctance to evangelize, obsessive antiemotionalism, and chronic introspection.[307]

At the top of this list is the particular problem of Calvinist pride. And what irony! For a belief system whose most fundamental reason for existence is preventing man from having any pride in his own salvation, Calvinism–perhaps more than any other religious system–bears within itself the very seeds of human pride.

To begin with, there is often an unseemly hubris about the vaunted doctrinal system itself, never more evident than in the following statement by Charles Spurgeon. "I have my own private opinion," says Spurgeon, "that there is no such thing as preaching Christ and him crucified, unless we

---

[307] See Curt Daniel, *The History and Theology of Calvinism* (Dallas: Scholarly reprints, 1993), 465-70. Copies may be obtained from the author at Reformed Bible Church, 4850 Old Jacksonville Road, Springfield, IL 62707.

preach what nowadays is called Calvinism. It is a nickname to call it Calvinism; Calvinism is the gospel, and nothing else."[308] What can one say?

Sadly, Spurgeon isn't alone among Calvinists in arrogating the gospel to their own private reserve. In fact, Loraine Boettner is so bold as to lay claim to the apostle Paul as the original Calvinist! Out of all the Calvinist missionaries, says Boettner, the greatest and most influential was "St. Paul, whom the more liberal opponents of Calvinism admit to have been responsible for the Calvinistic cast of the theological thought of the Church."[309]

And then there is, quite incredibly, Boettner's brash, grand conclusion: "We close with the statement that this great system of religious thought which bears Calvin's name is **nothing more or less than the hope of the world**."[310] Actually, one might have thought that the hope of the world is Jesus Christ.... (As for "this great system of religious thought which bears Calvin's name," of course, it gives hope only for *the elect*, not for the world–which is precisely the heresy of "this great system"!)

On a more personal basis, the "chosenness factor" remains perpetually troublesome in the pride department. If we were to ask the people of ancient Israel, at least the honest ones would tell us that pride was a perennial problem. Were they not God's elect nation? Had not God chosen to love them above all people? Did not the heathen Gentiles deserve their divine rejection?

As we have already seen, there simply could not have been a more difficult hurdle for the apostle Paul than convincing the Jews that they were no longer to be God's exclusive chosen ones. And just how ironic is it that Calvinism would draw so heavily for its rationale on the very passages in Paul's letter to the Romans where he was addressing the pride problem arising out of Israel's special election?

Even though thoughtful Calvinists would be the first to denounce such pride, it's more than a little difficult to escape either of two thoughts. One is that a person must have been chosen because he or she is somehow special (and thus a worthy of object of having been eternally foreloved). Or there is the flip-side: that, despite being wholly unworthy, one is now spe-

---

[308] Spurgeon, *Autobiography*, 163-75
[309] Boettner, 427
[310] Boettner, 431

cial *because* he or she has been eternally chosen. Either way, being "special" can become a source of pernicious pride unbefitting a child of God.

I wonder, for example, if something of this unbefitting pride doesn't underlie the following statement by Charles Spurgeon:

> *Sometimes, when I see some of the worst characters in the street, I feel as if my heart must burst forth in tears of gratitude that God has never let me act as they have done! I have thought, if God had left me alone, and had not touched me by His grace, what a great sinner I should have been![311]*

As one who is unquestionably a "great sinner" myself, I doubt if it's really a good thing to compare ourselves with "the worst characters in the street." Even relative righteousness pales when comparing our own abject sinfulness to God's holiness. In fairness, Spurgeon does go on to say, "Looking back on my past life...there was a natural hatred in my soul of everything holy and good." But his inference that God's special election had somehow elevated him above the mire of "great" moral failure has more than a whiff of self-righteous conceit.

Just how far removed is Spurgeon's exclamation of gratitude from the Pharisee's proud prayer: "God, I thank you that I am not like other men—robbers, evildoers, adulterers...." (Luke 18:10-12)? Besides, how did Spurgeon know for certain that those "worst characters" weren't also God's elect, only not yet regenerated? By his own Calvinist teaching, he himself was once such an unregenerate reprobate.

Perhaps I could give Spurgeon more benefit of the doubt had he not followed up his first statement with this second one:

> *Did not God Himself appoint our parents, native place, and friends? Could He not have caused me to be...brought forth by a filthy mother who would nurse me...and teach me to bow down to pagan gods, quite as easily as to have given me a pious mother, who would each morning and night bend her knee in prayer on my behalf?[312]*

---

[311] Spurgeon, *Autobiography*, 163-175
[312] Ibid.

Laying aside Spurgeon's injudicious reference to the "filthy pagan mother," what strikes me is not just the ongoing nauseous scent of pride hovering over the doctrine of special election, but larger and more fundamental questions.

Beyond the Problem of Pride

How, for instance, do Calvinists explain the seemingly-sporadic historical and geographical distribution of God's grace in special election? With the coming of Christ and the universal call of the gospel, one might reasonably assume that God's grace would be evenly distributed throughout the world in every time and culture. But there seem to be protracted periods of spiritual darkness where the light of faith has barely flickered; and entire cultures where any Christian witness has been all but non-existent.[313]

So what about those pagan nations which over the centuries have far outnumbered the people of God living in "Christian nations"? Are Spurgeon's "filthy pagans" not just the great unwashed, but also the great un-elect? If you and I had been born in a Hindu, Buddhist, Muslim, atheistic, or animistic culture, what are the odds we could expect to be counted among the elect?[314]

Again, Spurgeon's comments put the spotlight squarely on this issue:

> *Why is the gospel preached to us today, to us Englishmen? ...Why no grace for the Japanese? Why no gospel preached to the inhabitants of Central Africa? ...Assuredly, divine sovereignty passing by many races of men, has been pleased to pitch upon the Anglo-Saxon family, that they may be as the Jews were aforetime, the custodians of divine truth, and the favorites of mighty grace."*[315]

---

[313] This is a sufficiently challenging question for non-Calvinists as well, but at least without the additional complication of God's sovereign, special election to consider.

[314] This, too, is a disturbing question for non-Calvinists, which ought to spur evangelistic fervor all the more. But for Calvinists the *only* answer can be that God in his sovereignty has chosen purposely not to save huge swathes of nations and cultures.

[315] Spurgeon, *Metropolitan Tabernacle Pulpit*, Sermon (No. 553) delivered February 7th, 1864, at the Metropolitan Tabernacle, Newington. [http//www.spurgeon.org/sermons/0553.htm]

Thanking God that we were born of Christian parents in a Christian culture raises more than just thorny questions about unseemly pride and national chauvinism. It ought also to raise any number of red flags about the doctrine of special election and particular salvation.

Merely consider the case for election prior to Christ, for example. Surely, we aren't being asked to believe that all Israel was saved simply because they were God's elect nation. More interesting still is the eternal destiny of the millions of Gentiles who lived alongside the Jews throughout those early centuries. Are we to presume that none of them could possibly have been saved simply because they were not among God's elect nation?

Indeed (as with Israel herself), how are we to know who, among professing Christians, are really the elect? Would the elect include every believer in Christ of every doctrinal stripe? Every genuine believer, whether nominal or fervent? Every conscientious believer, whether Calvinist or non-Calvinist? Every believer, baptized or not baptized? Every truly committed believer, no matter their particular moral and spiritual failings?

Heading in a slightly different direction, is it possible to firmly believe with all your heart that you are a faith-filled follower of Christ, and yet be self-deluded, not realizing that you are *not* among the elect? Surely, among the billions of predestined reprobates there must be some who truly and genuinely believe they are in Christ. (Were they not born into a Christian family, in a Christian nation? Do they not periodically participate in some kind of Christian worship?)

A Hugely Troubling Question For Calvinists

All of which leads to one of the most crucial questions yet to be raised in this book: *By what clear light is the believer ever to really and truly know, one way or the other, whether he is among the elect?*

If you, yourself, are a Calvinist, what assurance can you possibly have of your election? Is it enough that you have faith in Christ? (James reminds us that even the demons believe and tremble!) But you say you also do good works in the name of Christ and exhibit the fruits, or perhaps gifts, of the spirit? Yet, if none of the above–including having faith in Christ–can possibly be the *basis* for unconditional election, how can they be *proof* of election?

Apparently unfazed by his conclusion, Boettner freely admits that one of the features of Calvinism is "turning the baptism of the non-elect into an empty form."[316] What does this imply but that even baptism is of no effect if someone is so unfortunate as to be among the non-elect!

And Sproul gives cold comfort to his fellow Calvinists when he asserts that "we may think that we have faith when in fact we have no faith."[317]

Have you ever stopped to question what Calvinists really mean when they say: "All *true Christians* may know that they are among the elect"? Or "The *truly saved* know that the love of God has been shed in their hearts"? From these criteria, one gets the feeling that Calvinists are not including among the elect many who might call themselves Christians, or regard themselves as having been saved. And, of course, that is consistent with Scripture, which warns against the emptiness of what we today might call nominal Christianity. But where, exactly, does one draw the line between "nominal" and "genuine" Christian faith?

Some see that line being drawn in Romans 8:16, where Paul says: The Spirit himself testifies with our spirit that we are God's children." Although this passage and others like it (such as 1 John 5:13 and 1 Thessalonians 1:4-5) are certainly a comfort to all who believe, one has to admit that in the end our assurance is far more subjective than any of us would like. How many times have we seen people who seem utterly self-assured that the Spirit is working in them, when everything in their life is screaming out, "I don't think so!" Subjectivity can be deceiving.

Under Calvinism, the fact remains that, apart from a heart warmly stirred, there is no objective means of verifying one's *unconditional* election. A person might as easily be eternally damned as eternally saved, all depending upon how, before time began, the Potter chose to dispose of

---

[316] Boettner, 145. (While clearly the immersion of a person without faith, whether infant or adult, can have no redemptive meaning, Boettner's automatic exclusion of the non-elect from the redemptive waters of baptism says more about Calvinism than about biblical baptism, which, through the Great Commission, is offered freely to all.)

[317] R.C. Sproul, *Chosen By God*, (Wheaton, Ill: Tyndale House Publishers, 1986), 165-66

the vessels he would make. And that simply can't be known with any present assurance.

Are you one of the chosen? Are you sure...? How *can* you be sure?

Little wonder that Curt Daniel lists chronic introspection among the potential hidden dangers lurking within the package of Calvinism. For those who place a premium on the secret will of God as well as his revealed will, and who place exclusive importance on the sovereignty of God without also factoring in man's own free response, there will always be the risk of having to worry about not being among the elect.[318]

To be sure, it is also possible for non-Calvinists to obsess about whether they are lost or saved, especially given their rejection of Calvinism's doctrine of "once saved, always saved." But at least if non-Calvinists have any legitimate reason to be concerned, it is within their own hands to do something about it. (To reiterate God's assurance to Cain: "If you do what is right, will you not be accepted?") Calvinists, by contrast, are still left with the uncertainty of knowing *objectively* whether they are among the elect. Should it be, in fact, that they are not, there is absolutely nothing they could possibly do to change the outcome.

What could be more soul-wrenching than having to constantly play the spiritual mind game: He loves me; he loves me not? Why not rather follow the path of full assurance, trusting God to save each and every soul who freely turns to him in obedient faith and repentance? Why not take at face value the divine promise inherent within the apostolic commission: "Go into all the world and preach the good news to all creation. Whoever believes and is baptized will be saved, but whoever does not believe will be condemned" (Mark 16:15-16)?

Praise God, the immersed believer need not worry about special election. Or, worse yet, non-election. What bride walks up the aisle at the end of a wedding ceremony nervously worrying whether or not she is really

---

[318] There is great irony that this feature of Calvinism is sufficiently prevalent that it is identified by Curt Daniel as a "pitfall peculiar to Calvinists." For it is John Hesselink's thesis that one of two pastoral concerns most directly prompting John Calvin's belief in particular election was the need for "assurance that our salvation is grounded in God's free mercy and grace." Yet, Hesselink notes that Calvin's aim backfired almost immediately. "Apparently in Calvin's time some people were troubling themselves with the question as to whether they were elect or not. (This problem became more acute in some Calvinistic groups in later centuries.)" [Hesselink, 94, 97]

married? Neither should the bride of Christ–the called out ones, the elect of God who, individually and collectively, have experienced an objective, verifiable "wedding ceremony" in the soul-cleansing waters of full submission. By the grace of God and through the blood of Christ, we have been washed, purified, and sanctified.

Through the power of the Holy Spirit we have been saved for eternal life. No secret decrees to worry about. No hidden, unknowable selections or rejections. No already-stacked decks. No impenetrable predestined barriers. No arbitrary pre-programming. No doubts, and–most importantly–no fears.

Nor is there any reason for human pride, because all who are under the condemnation of sin have exactly the same opportunity for salvation, obeying the same divine commands in precisely the same prescribed way. If there is anything special about our salvation, it is that God has a special love for all those who would willingly and freely respond to his universal offer of grace. And why wouldn't he!

So if you're in the market for a great package deal, make sure it won't fall apart with the slightest shaking. Or induce an unwelcome schizophrenia between what you believe in theory and how you live your faith life. Or leave you ultimately with no objective, verifiable way of knowing whether or not you are chosen.

With so much at stake, there ought to be warning tags. When it come to package deals, Calvinism, sadly, is all package and no deal.

I tell you this so that no one may deceive you by fine-sounding arguments.

Colossians 2:4

Chapter Summary

- Calvinism's tight system of interdependent premises is particularly vulnerable. If one premise fails, they all come crashing down together.

- The principle arguments of Calvinism must be propped up artificially with circular reasoning.

- What Calvinists believe in reality does not match up with what they believe doctrinally. In their faith walk, even five-point Calvinists seem not to be Calvinists at all.

- Ironically, believers who would adamantly reject Calvinism in theory often live their lives as if they were five-point Calvinists.

- By its very nature, Calvinism bears within itself an unusually high potential for unseemly pride, tempered only by uncertain introspection.

- The most troubling question for any Calvinist must surely be how he can ever know with any objective assurance whether he is among the elect or the lost.

Reality Check: If your eternal destiny was unalterably fixed before you were ever born, nothing you say or do can change that destiny at this point. Regardless of either your professed doctrine or actual faith walk, whether you will end up in heaven or in hell can be no better than a fifty-fifty proposition.

Chapter 12

In the Bigger Picture

The world now, as well as in the beginning,
is the theater for the mighty works of God,
and humanity remains a creation of His hand.

—Abraham Kuyper

Just as packages come in all sizes, so too "package deals." Somewhere along the way, we invariably move to the point where the most comprehensive "package deals" of all constitute nothing less than "big picture items." They involve the grand scheme of things, including one's entire worldview...and, in the end, the very nature of God and man.

As we approach the close of our discussion, I want to share one of the more positive—indeed, exciting—aspects of Calvinism which has stirred my intellectual passion over the past several years. In my opening Preface, I noted my growing appreciation for the Reformed worldview, particularly regarding the integration of faith and learning in higher education. (To speak of a "Reformed worldview" is not to imply that Reformed Calvinists have any exclusive claim to this worldview. Even though

Reformed Calvinists have often led the way, many non-Calvinists have eloquently espoused the same grand concept.)

As one who has been an educator in both graduate and undergraduate Christian institutions, I dream of the day when Christian education far exceeds merely having the usual five touchstones of a Christian college or university: Christian faculty; Christian students; required Bible courses; mandatory chapel; and stricter than normal dorm rules.

To be truly "Christian" is to *think Christianly* about math, science, history, music, business and law. That we teach such subjects virtually the same as the secular schools around us is not just a damning indictment of our faith claims, but a tragic loss to both faculty and students.

To think Christianly is to see our world in the widest, least compartmentalized frame possible. It is to paint liberal arts, especially, on the broadest possible canvas—indeed, to catch a glimpse of the eternal canvas upon which God himself has painted.

Affirming that God is sovereign over every nook and cranny of his universe, the Reformed worldview rightly understands that nothing in all creation was brought about by blind physical forces or the will of man. Moreover, there is nothing, and no part of life, over which God is not sovereign. As put so brilliantly in the familiar refrain, "He's got the whole world in his hands."

And so it follows that there is an inherent rationality and cohesion both to our everyday world and the vast cosmos which was created so wondrously around us. No single facet is unrelated to any other facet. It all fits. Indeed, each diverse aspect is an integral part of a complex, interwoven tapestry which reveals the intelligence, power, and beauty of our Creator. God is at once the master designer, builder, artist, musician, and physician.

As all things are unified in him, so they are unified with each other. To divorce music from math is to start off on the wrong note. To miss the connection between the golden rule and the golden mean of architecture is to remain uneducated. (Divine proportion is both physical and spiritual.) To understand the sweep of history is to see God working through it. Sadly, even at the highest levels of the academy, we have so narrowed our worldview through segregated disciplines and departments that we fail to fully grasp—and thus to fully honor—the comprehensive glory of God.

Who more than Calvinists have so resolutely insisted that the lordship of Christ encompasses more than simply salvation and the hereafter? Christ's lordship is as much about lifestyle as eternal life. It is both future and present. Both sacred and secular. Indeed, the "secular" is so wholly subsumed within the sacred that it disappears altogether. (Merely consider how the undifferentiated ceremonial and civil laws of Moses seamlessly touched on every aspect of life.)

How, therefore, Christians live their lives and contribute to society is part and parcel of the widest possible picture. The "Reformed" worldview (or more appropriately the *Christ- centered* worldview) encompasses the full and complete integration of life and faith...or at least it ought to. Without doubt, nothing could be more antithetical to a Christ-centered worldview than its opposite: the godless worldview of the unbeliever, and now increasingly of believers themselves.

In the Reformed worldview, man's functional role as the appointed steward of God's handiwork stems from the command of Genesis 1:28 to "fill the earth and subdue it." Drawing from Ephesians 2:10, we understand that our calling is to do the good works that have been prepared for us to do, even from before Creation. That's not just doing charitable good works for the hungry, poor, and oppressed, as some might think. It includes all that we do to the glory of God, including the labor of our hands, how we function together as families, how we govern ourselves as a society, and so on.

Yet, for Calvinists, the Reformed worldview quickly becomes problematic, for stewardship involves both *responsibility* and *accountability*. It is no accident that the key to understanding each of those words lies in the implicit idea of *ability*. The same goes for *trusteeship*, the heart of which is the idea of *trust*. As stewards, then, we must have the unfettered ability to perform the tasks to which we have been called, and then be trusted to perform them capably.

The question is: If, as Calvinism argues, God's sovereignty is the sole cause of all good, and he himself is the prime moving force behind every act and event no matter how small, of what possible significance is human *ability*? And what could possibly remain of the concept of *trust*? Can there be any such thing as "trust" when each individual does exactly and precisely what God has predestined him to do, moment by moment, for a lifetime?

Too encompassing a view of God's sovereignty leaves little room for man's own responsibility and accountability. If perhaps such a high view seems fitting for man's salvation, what of man's artistic and entrepreneurial enterprises? Are we to believe that these activities (for which even Calvin made elbow-room), are direct acts of God? Is it God, and not the iron-worker, who builds the skyscraper? He, and not the accountant, who balances the books? He, and not the mother, whose hand is on the cradle? Being made in the image of God means sharing in his creativity, productivity, and freedom of expression. He the poet. He the painter. He the humble carpenter of Nazareth.

What Calvinists seem to overlook is that free enterprise (whether economic, artistic, or educational) goes hand-in-hand with free moral agency. To have one is to have the other. As before, it's a package deal. Does the freedom to think, decide, and choose—all of which are necessary to free enterprise—come to a screeching halt at the door of faith? Are we to believe that man has freedom and responsibility in every arena of life but the spiritual?

The Reformed worldview would reject as absurd any notion that each artistic masterpiece and inspiring orchestral score is the result of some irresistible grace. Or that the company budget and employee pension scheme were predestined by God himself long before Creation. Yet somehow all the human freedom which that implies is suddenly out the window when it comes to salvation. In a worldview stressing divine congruity, is there any room for this all-too-human incongruity?

For Calvinists, the problems only multiply. What, for example, accounts for the creative genius, or even ordinary industry, of the unregenerate? Is it simply a matter of motives—that the godly do all things to the glory of God, while the unregenerate do all things for their own glory? As we know, even the unregenerate can act for good without the slightest selfish motive.

Or *can* they actually act for good...? If we take Calvinism seriously, the unregenerate remain under the absolute sway of total depravity, unable to do any good of any kind whatsoever. Yet, how are we to explain their many courageous, humanitarian, and selfless acts which, if done by one who is regenerate, unquestionably would be declared "good"?

The usual (though by no means unanimous) Calvinist answer is that, while predestined salvation is a matter of special and particular grace, God has extended to all mankind a common and general grace that allows "good" to be accomplished even by those who are unregenerate for the ongoing functioning of society. That's certainly a convenient answer, but the real question is whether there is biblical support for such bifurcated grace.

Can we, in fact, tease out a doctrine of common grace from the fact that God "causes his sun to rise on the evil and the good, and sends rain on the righteous and the unrighteous"?[319] Or that God employed the talents and skills of the non-elect when building the magnificent temple for his chosen elect? Or that Jesus was as willing to heal the daughter of a pagan benefactor of the local synagogue as he was Peter's Jewish mother-in-law?

Well, actually, we can! The gracious gifts of God's creation do indeed fall like rain upon every one of his creatures, believer and non-believer alike. (I love that great line from Calvin: "As if God's generosity did not extend even to pigs and dogs!"[320])

For non-Calvinists, there is no problem accepting a common grace for all mankind, and even a special grace for those who are in Christ. But this biblical distinction is not to be confused with the artificial two-tiered grace system devised to accommodate both the predestination theology of Calvinism and the implicitly non-predestinarian assumptions of the Reformed worldview.

As we have seen, Calvin himself acknowledged what others have described as "common grace," but it is equally clear that he did not build his grand worldview around it. Nor is this specialized use of "common grace" readily apparent within the various Reformed creeds, which speak only of particular, predestined grace for the elect. Perhaps there is a reason why "common grace" is more of a footnote than a headline. Does it make any sense that the elect, chosen by particular grace, would then be called to honor God in their lives on the basis of a "common grace" shared with the unregenerate? How possibly does that match the Bible's call to "come out and be separate"?[321]

---

[319] Matthew 5:45

[320] Calvin, *Institutes*, 3.14.17

[321] For an informative discussion of the issues from at least one Reformed viewpoint, see the series of four editorials by Prof. David J. Engelsma published in *The Standard Bearer* (A Reformed semi-monthly magazine) from May 15 to September 15, 1998.

An Uncomfortable Common Grace

Lest anyone think I am drawing unfair conclusions about the strained linkage between Calvinism and the Reformed worldview, I need merely call attention to the teaching of Dutch theologian and politician Abraham Kuyper. It is Kuyper's theory of common grace (best known through his famous lectures at Princeton in 1898) that is most widely accepted today in Reformed circles as the basis for the Reformed worldview.

In his opening Princeton lecture ("Calvinism a Life-System"), Kuyper dared to suggest that common grace serves to inhibit and diminish total depravity.

> *[Calvinism] has at once placed to the front the great principle that there is a particular grace which works Salvation, and also a common grace by which God, maintaining the life of the world, relaxes the curse which rests upon it, arrests its process of corruption, and thus allows the untrammelled development of our life in which to glorify Himself as Creator.*[322]

"Relaxed curse"? "Arrested corruption"? What else could he say, really, without running headlong into the problem of human freedom we have already posed? Total depravity and the personal freedom assumed within the Reformed worldview are as disparate as chalk and cheese. In the end, a worldview that has become the darling offspring of Calvinism winds up devouring the very doctrine that gave it life.

So was Kuyper wrong? At the very least, I believe Kuyper was waging an uphill battle to say "Peace, peace" when there is so little logical peace possible between his "common grace" worldview and his underlying predestinarian doctrine.

In the 20/20 hindsight of a century now past, he undoubtedly was also overly optimistic in believing that his unique notion of common grace would not end up being a cultural boomerang. As witnessed in the arts and sciences, and in economics, politics, and law, the godless values of the Evil One have been imported into the cultures of both the Netherlands and

---

[322] Kuyper, *Lectures on Calvinism* (Grand Rapids: Eerdmans, 1953), 30

America with far more success than the lordship of Christ has been exported to a sinful world.

Yet what Kuyper contributed so masterfully to the conversation was his passion for allowing God's sovereignty to permeate every pore of human existence, while urging believers to capture a sense of doing all that we do—hour by hour, task by task—to the glory of God. Without specifically or perhaps even consciously setting out to do so, Kuyper championed faith-learning integration long before it became a popular mantra in the Christian academy, and planted the seeds for a whole new cultural movement based upon a Christ-centered worldview.

Had Kuyper taken his passion for a Christ-centered worldview to its ultimate and obvious conclusion, however, he would have been forced to acknowledge even further its implications regarding free will and salvation. The natural logic of the Reformed worldview points not to salvation by unconditional divine fiat as Calvinism teaches, but—as it ever must be—salvation by faith (Romans 1:17).

God, Man, and Eternity

Surely it goes without saying that to fully honor God's sovereignty is to honor *his* worldview, not one marked by inconsistency and contradiction. Equally important is that we honor God's sovereignty to do as he pleases, even if that means allowing him the unfettered, divine right to create man with complete moral freedom hinged with responsibility and accountability. To insist otherwise seems to do precisely what Calvinism is intended to prevent: to elevate man's understanding over God's.

To put it bluntly, Dare we presume that God's sovereignty can include absolutely anything and everything *except* creating us with free choice over our own eternal destiny?

That, in a nutshell, is the most important issue in this book. What's at stake in the Calvinism controversy is nothing less than the nature of God and, more particularly, the nature of man. No picture gets any bigger; no issues loom larger.

As for the nature of God, Calvinism is quite right to exalt the sovereignty of God, but quite wrong to think that a God who condemns to hell creatures whom he has arbitrarily chosen for that destiny can be a truly just and loving God. (And this, not simply from a human point of view, but by the standards of God's own self-revealed character.)

Calvinism is equally wrong to assign absolute sovereign control to the sovereign God. From Scripture itself, nothing could be clearer than that God's absolute sovereignty is not always exercised absolutely. For proof, we need only catch a glimpse of a rainbow on a stormy day. At its end is not the proverbial pot of gold but a promise for all eternity that God will never again destroy the whole earth by a flood.

Could God once again destroy the earth by a flood? Of course, he could! Does he have both the power and the right to once again destroy the earth by a flood? Of course, he does! But when the sovereign God himself sets limits on his absolute power and right, who are we to say he cannot do so without compromising his absolute sovereignty?

So it is that when God sovereignly chose to make man's salvation contingent upon faith and obedience to his divine commands, his absolute control over your eternal destiny and mine may have been self-limited, but his sovereignty was not threatened in the least. And when in love he extended his offer of salvation to all who would turn to him in faith and obedience, that too was within his sovereign power to decide.

When it comes to honoring God's sovereignty, Calvinism commendably sets a high bar for the rest of us to follow. Yet ironically it ends up dislodging that self-same high standard by attempting far too great a leap.

As for the nature of man, there is but one conclusion: To take Calvinism at face value is to strip man of any and all personal responsibility for his life, both temporal and eternal. Period. As should be clear by now, far from our having been stripped of any responsibility whatsoever for our eternal destiny, God himself has put that moral and spiritual hot potato squarely in our laps. In an ascending order of importance, God has endowed us, first, with ability; then responsibility; and, finally, accountability.

That Calvinism gets all of this so terribly wrong is not simply a matter of ordinary doctrinal disagreement. In what just happens to be the most important "big picture item" of all–God's eternal plan–Calvinism has distorted to the extreme man's role in the entire scheme. Calvinism thus constitutes the most grievous of errors, propagating a fundamentally unbiblical view of man.

When all is said and done, it comes down to this: Either Calvinism is true or false. If it's true, then no matter what you think, believe, or do, by God's choice you were either lost or saved eternally long before you were ever born–indeed, before the heavens and the earth were created.

But if Calvinism is false, then you yourself must either freely choose eternal life through Christ or insist on your eternal destruction in hell. The choice is yours, completely. God will neither dictate that choice nor tip the scales in either direction beyond showering us with what ought to be a truly irresistible love and grace.

By his omniscient power, of course, God already knows what choice you will make. But it remains your choice, not his. What's more, he has done everything necessary–including providing the perfect atonement for your sins and gifting the power of his Holy Spirit–to make eternal life with him possible. There is nothing he hasn't already done for you, and won't yet do for you...except force you to love him.

So what will it be? How shall you choose? What is to be your eternal destiny?

Now all has been heard;
  here is the conclusion of the matter:
Fear God and keep his commandments,
  for this is the whole [duty] of man.
For God will bring every deed into judgment,
  including every hidden thing,
  whether it is good or evil.

Ecclesiastes 12:13-14

Chapter Summary

- The Reformed worldview (more properly the *Christian* worldview) has much to commend itself in pointing to the pervasive sovereignty of God over every aspect of one's life whether sacred or secular (as if there were even a clear distinction between the two).

- Christian education, in particular, would benefit greatly from more wide-ranging integration of distinct disciplines.

- But the emphasis of such a worldview on the freedom and responsibility of individual enterprise implicitly undermines the fundamental predestinarian, non-free-will assumptions of Calvinism.

- Calvinism is certainly right to exalt God's sublime sovereignty and unthwartable purposes, but greatly errs in presumptuously denying to the sovereign God the right and power to create man with a genuine free will for which he is held accountable.

- Calvinism's view of man is an affront to the biblical teaching that man is created in the image of God, and for that reason alone is unworthy.

- Unlike other doctrinal issues, the error in this misguided belief system regarding the nature of God and the nature of man is of the highest order.

> **Reality Check:** If God did *not* in fact determine our eternal destiny from before Creation, but instead has charged all of mankind with the responsibility to seek him in faith and obedience, then you and I and the whole world are personally accountable to God for whether or not we accept his gracious, universal offer of salvation through the atoning blood of Christ.

Afterword

If you have considered yourself a Calvinist, but at this point are even "almost persuaded" that Calvinism is biblically flawed, where does that leave you? How do you reconstruct a belief system to take its place?

The good news is that you would be giving up very little in reality, especially in your current faith walk. As an alternative to Calvinism, consider the following propositions:

God is still just as sovereign as you have always believed him to be. His eternal plan for his Creation, and particularly his plan of salvation for mankind, cannot be thwarted in any way. The end has been known from the beginning, and none but God is in charge.

Calvinism's admirable emphasis on God's sovereignty is not misplaced in the least.

We are neither innately evil nor innately good, but we are certainly saturated with sin. The sin which you and I have committed in our rebellion against God pervades our mind, body, and spirit, leaving us wholly unworthy of God's goodness. While we have no one but ourselves to blame for our sinfulness, neither have we any reason for pride in whatever goodness we may possess.

Although Calvinism might explain the various intricacies differently, there is no disputing the fundamental problem of human sin.

Man's free will is not a threat to God's sovereignty. That a God with complete sovereign power would forego his right to pull all the strings and, instead, risk endowing us with the ability either to accept or to reject him merely reflects the extent of God's love for us. The fact that free will comes packaged with responsibility and accountability further testifies that God remains forever sovereign.

Since Calvinism teaches that, once regenerated, you and I have the free will to respond to God in faith and repentance, there can be nothing shocking or objectionable about the notion itself of free will.

God's predestined plan for his elect people serves the same ultimate purpose as before. Even though God's people are included among the elect on the basis of their own freely chosen faith (rather than by God's arbitrary selection), it remains that we are still predestined from eternity to bring glory to God through lives of holiness and good works.

Since the purpose and task of God's called-out ones remains exactly the same as if the elect had been arbitrarily predestined, departing significantly from Calvinism's doctrine of unconditional election loses nothing in its practical outcome.

Nothing you and I might do could ever merit or assure our salvation. Reaching out to accept God's gift of grace contributes nothing in the slightest to our salvation. And whatever work we accomplish for good is done only as willing slaves to Christ. Not even our faith is a deserved claim on God's grace, but rather a loving response to it.

As this premise is entirely in line with Calvinism's very starting point, nothing in the least is lost here.

We need have no hesitation to proclaim that Christ's atoning blood was shed for all who will receive it. (Why would we ever have wanted to think otherwise?) And because the gospel invitation is genuinely and truly open to every lost soul on the face of the globe, we are compelled all the more to proclaim the good news of salvation in Christ.

Since everyone acknowledges that the ultimate effect of Christ's atonement will be appreciated only by those who turn to him in faith, the wonderful fact remains unchallenged that Christ's atonement was entirely sufficient for those who believe.

Although it is possible for us to forfeit our inheritance, God's own promises remain steadfast and sure. Once saved, we are always saved...unless we intentionally walk out on a faithful God and throw it all away. God will protect us from every enemy but our own wilful desertion.

As long as we keep our eyes on the cross (as everyone agrees we must), then nothing whatsoever is lost in terms of our eternal security.

It is said that John 3:16 is the most memorized verse in the Bible.

If you have known this verse perhaps from childhood, what does it say to your heart?

Scripture References

Index